D1267563

AFRICA
SQUADRON

Also by Donald L. Canney

Lincoln's Navy:
The Ships, Men, and Organization, 1861–1865

The Old Steam Navy, Vol. 1:
Frigates, Sloops, and Gunboats, 1815–1885

The Old Steam Navy, Vol. 2:
The Ironclads, 1842–1885

Sailing Warships of the U.S. Navy

U. S. Coast Guard and Revenue Cutters, 1790–1935

AFRICA
SQUADRON

THE U.S. NAVY
AND THE
SLAVE TRADE,
1842–1861

DONALD L. CANNEY

Potomac Books, Inc.
Washington, D.C.

Library of Congress Cataloging-in-Publication Data

Canney, Donald L., 1947-
  Africa Squadron : the U.S. Navy and the slave trade, 1842-1861 / Donald L. Canney.— 1st ed.
     p. cm.
  Includes bibliographical references and index.
  ISBN 1-57488-606-1 (alk. paper)
  1. United States. Navy. Africa Squadron. 2. Slave-trade—United States—History—19th century. 3. Slave-trade—Africa, West—History—19th century. 4. Antislavery movements—United States—History—19th century. 5. United States. Navy. Africa Squadron—Biography. I. Title.
  E449.C225 2006
  382'.44097309034—dc22

                                    2006002788

ISBN 10:1-57488-606-1
ISBN 13:978-1-57488-606-1

(alk. paper)

Printed in the United States of America on acid-free paper that meets the American National Standards Institute Z39-48 Standard.

Potomac Books, Inc.
22841 Quicksilver Drive
Dulles, Virginia 20166

First Edition

10 9 8 7 6 5 4 3 2 1

CONTENTS

ILLUSTRATIONS

ACKNOWLEDGMENTS

In the process of researching the Navy's Africa Squadron, I have accumulated a list of those individuals and institutions that have been of material assistance in my efforts. The majority of the sources have been, of course, naval records at the National Archives, and I thank the staff at the Old Army and Navy Records office at Archives I in Washington, D.C., particularly Rick Peuser and Becky Livingston. The second largest group of sources was at the Naval Historical Center at the Washington Navy Yard. Dr. Michael Crawford, in Early History and Robert Cressman in the Ship's History Branches were of great assistance. Thanks also to Chuck Haberlein at the photo branch for his encouragement and knowledge, and to the staff at the Navy library. Finally, thanks to the staff at the Library of Congress manuscript division.

Thanks to the many other institutions that I visited in my search for original documents. These include libraries and collections at: East Carolina University, University of North Carolina, Duke University, University of Maryland, Maryland State Archives, Mariners Museum, Mystic Seaport Library, North Carolina State Archives, William and Mary University, Virginia Historical Society, Historical Society of Pennsylvania, Nimitz Library at the Naval Academy, and others.

From a personal standpoint, I appreciate the support and advice of Dr. Robert Browning, Coast Guard Historian; Kevin Foster of the maritime program of the National Park Service; and my coworker at the Coast Guard museum program, Gail Fuller, Coast Guard Curator. Finally, thanks for the encouragement and prayerful support of many at our church, Grace Baptist of Bowie, MD.

Not the least on my list are, of course, my wife Janice and son Brendan—the latter for allowing me computer time when needed.

DON CANNEY
FEBRUARY 2005.

INTRODUCTION

The institution of human slavery reaches back into the mists of history, along with the trade of shackled lives. It is witness of the amazing depravity of man that the practice did not begin to subside until the early nineteenth century, accompanied by the necessary ban on the traffic itself. Still more astonishing are the lengths men continued to go to not only circumvent the laws enacted to ensure human emancipation, but to justify and profit from their efforts.

In the United States, the story of the end of the legal traffic in slaves began with the U.S. Constitution, which called for the prohibition of the importation of slaves in 1808. This ban was not, however, given a formal enforcement mechanism until 1842, with the establishment of a naval squadron stationed off the west coast of Africa. That squadron, and its history, is the subject of this volume.

Before launching into the subject, I should emphasize what this book is *not* about. Though the Atlantic slave trade had been illegal for three decades prior to the Africa Squadron's institution, any study of the Navy's anti–slave trade activities in that period would be pointless. And though there were occasional captures of slavers by naval vessels, legally the enforcement of foreign trade regulations was the provenance of the Revenue Cutter Service of the Treasury Department. My treatment of this period is presented with an eye toward providing historical context only, rather than detailing the Navy's individual captures of that era.

During the roughly two decades of the existence of the Africa Squadron, the Navy captured slave traders elsewhere, notably off the coasts of Brazil and Cuba. Furthermore, federal authorities—the Revenue Cutter Service and federal marshals—were active, though with varying rates of success, in suppressing the trade as it occurred on the American coast and in its harbors. All these activities added to the sum of the American efforts to end the trade, but, again, they are of marginal value in evaluating the Navy's Africa Squadron. Again, I will present these aspects of the story for informational purposes only.

Another factor of the anti–slave trade effort is the legal issues that were involved: the frequent parsing of the federal anti-slavery statutes by the district courts and judges before which the captured (alleged) slave traders were haled. I will follow these often prolix and inexplicable aspects only as far as they bear directly on the Navy, its officers, and their efforts on the high seas. In any event, previous authors have thoroughly presented these legal aspects, which many times hampered, rather than facilitated, the Navy's enforcement efforts.

Finally, there was the diplomatic front involving statesmen, treaty obligations, local consular officials, and, most immediately, the officers of various national navies on the scene on the west coast of Africa. Most important was the American relationship with the British Africa Squadron in light of the Anglo-American Webster Ashburton Treaty of 1842, the terms of which resulted in the formation of the American anti–slave trade squadron off Africa. As far as possible I will make the ultimately practical connections between the actions of the diplomatic community and their impact on the men and vessels of the American squadron. However, this is not to be a diplomatic history as such.

On the positive side, this work *is* intended to detail the squadron and attempt to answer some very basic questions that have long plagued the reputation of that unit. In fact, the most damaging allegation has long been that the squadron was a failure. This idea can be traced nearly to the inception of the unit, and it was contained in American resentment at what was perceived by some as kowtowing to British pressure to "reign in" American vessels involved in the trade, in return for an implicit agreement by the British not to stop and search suspicious American flagged vessels. A second factor in the low repute of the unit was the onerous conditions on the station: lengthy cruises in torrid equatorial temperatures without the relief of shore liberty, accompanied by the very real threat of the Africa "fever"—malaria. The Africa Squadron was not a popular assignment, to men or officers. There was little support evinced, officially or otherwise, for the unit, and the federal courts regularly threw out cases against alleged slavers, putting them, in modern parlance, "back on the street" to again ply their trade. As will be seen, even the Navy Department itself did little for the squadron . . . despite pleadings by the flag officers for more ships, steam vessels, and better logistic arrangements. This negative atmosphere reigned during the twenty or so years of the squadron's existence, and it was exacerbated by the squadron's poor showing in actual numbers of captured slavers and freed slaves.

The negative view of the squadron was only further emphasized when prominent critics took to publishing their opinions. First was W. E. B. Du Bois, who, from the black perspective, excoriated the squadron in his book on the suppression of the slave trade, *The Suppression of the Atlantic Slave Trade*, published in 1896. Others have reiterated this negativism. Among the charges leveled against the Navy's effort were: (1) that Southern-borne or sympathizing officers deliberately avoided capturing slavers, (2) that the department only assigned the Navy's worst vessels to the squadron, (3) that steam vessels were not added to the squadron, despite their availability, (4) that totally inadequate arrangements were made for provisioning the unit, and (5) that the squadron's purpose was reinterpreted by the various secretaries of the Navy (many of whom were Southerners) to emphasize protection of American commerce (subtext: against British interference) rather than suppressing the slave trade.

Unfortunately, the number of slavers captured by the squadron, as well as the wide variation in the number of vessels arrested annually, makes it difficult to deem the squadron a success. The squadron captured only thirty-six vessels off Africa in twenty years . . . and in some years there were no captures at all. Therefore my goal is to determine if indeed this number is as inadequate as it appears, and what factors prevented the squadron from bringing in larger numbers of prizes on the high seas.

My methodology is simple, though it has not heretofore been applied in any book-length study. After examining the background—the decades between the abolition of the trade and the formation of the squadron, including the impact of the settlement of Liberia in the 1820s—I will study the squadron chronologically, from squadron commander to squadron commander. I will study the various approaches used to suppress the trade, the effect of logistics, the climate and health issues, the quality and type of vessels used, and the impact of various distractions such as support for the fledgling government of Liberia, as well as relations with the British Africa Squadron. Furthermore, I will outline the kinds and quality of support given by the Navy Department to the squadron, and I will study the impact of the federal courts and their rulings on the work of the unit.

In this book, I will make extensive use of the ships' deck logs to gain some idea of the day-to-day operations of the squadron. In particular, the logs will show the actual time spent by each vessel patrolling the coast, as opposed to traveling to and from the squadron supply depot and elsewhere. The logs will, no doubt, also reflect the hardships on the station: the days and weeks in torrid climes, with crews confined to hot, poorly ventilated wooden ships. Other major sources will be the communications between the squadron commanders and the secretary of the Navy, as well as the various journals and descriptions written by officers and bluejackets on the station.

Before this, there has not been a book-length history of the Africa Squadron, written strictly from the Navy perspective. For good or ill, I hope my attempt to fill this gap will at least provide a baseline for further study of this significant part of the history of the United States Navy.

1

THE SLAVE TRADE OUTLAWED, 1808–1821

The prohibition of the importation of slaves into the United States can be traced to the writing of the Constitution in 1787. Previously, under the Articles of Confederation, the national government had only approached the matter in its reference to fugitive slaves. This ordinance provided that if the capture were made at sea below the high-water mark, and the slave was unclaimed, he should be freed.[1]

At the Constitutional Convention there was no question that slavery itself was nearly sacrosanct in the Southern states, though, in this era before the invention of the cotton gin, there was wide agreement that the "necessary evil" would gradually disappear due to economic pressures. Given that premise, slave-holding representatives were loath to object too loudly to Northern moves to insert a specific date for the abolition of the trade itself. Eventually a compromise was reached whereby 1808 was set for the end of the legal importation of "such persons as any of the States now existing shall think proper to admit," (Article I, Section 9). It is noteworthy that all the states south to, and including, Virginia had banned the trade by 1788.[2] It is also worth noting that this was the world's first anti–slave trade legislation, and its effective date fell one year after Parliament banned the slave trade in all British dominions.

During the constitutionally declared interval, the slave trade continued, including illegal importation into some states that had their own legislative bans on the trade. This illicit activity, combined with the consternation caused by the Haitian slave revolt, engendered increased agitation for more legislation against various aspects of slavery. Prominent voices in this chorus were the Quakers and Benjamin Franklin. The result was a slave-trade law in 1794, which provided for heavy financial penalties as well as forfeiture of vessels involved in the slave trade to any foreign country. Americans and foreigners fitting out or preparing vessels for such trade and taking on board or transporting individuals "for the purpose of selling them as slaves" were in violation of this statute. The manifest shortcoming of this legislation was the absence of any enforcement mechanism, beyond that of individuals willing to bring charges.[3]

Congress passed legislation to remedy this in 1800, with a law that added imprisonment to monetary penalties and authorized naval vessels to seize the ships as prizes. Additionally, those who had any interest "direct or indirect" in the slaving voyage were liable to prosecution. The statute, however, neglected to address disposition of slaves freed during enforcement of the law.[4]

The Quasi-War with France provided the first venue for the U.S. Navy's role in enforcing anti–slave trade legislation. Early on, before enactment of the 1800 statute giving the Navy authority to seize vessels, the Navy had served to funnel information to the Treasury Department on vessels suspected of participating in the trade. The Treasury Department, which was responsible for prevention of smuggling, was, by default, the primary agency for suppression of the slave trade into the United States via the harbors and coasts. This was the stock in trade of the Treasury's Revenue Marine. However, the efficacy of this force was severely limited, because it numbered no more than seventeen vessels, none larger than topsail schooners, at its wartime peak in 1801.[5]

For example, in mid-1799 Secretary of the Treasury Oliver Wolcott wrote the customs collector at Boston that "Captain Decatur of the Navy during his late cruize [sic] near Cuba, met with the Brig *Dolphin* of Boston William White Master with 140 or 150 slaves for Sale procured on the coast of Africa." Wolcott directed the collector to "take requisite measures to enforce the law."[6] And, in April 1800, the secretary of the Navy passed along to the treasury secretary a short list, sent along by Captain Bainbridge of the USS *Norfolk*, of suspected slavers who recently returned from Cuban waters to Philadelphia.[7]

At the same time, the U.S. Consul at Parimaribo, Surinam, wrote of some of the attractions of the trade in the Spanish West Indies: "It is well known that the Spanish Governors in the W. I. will admit any Neutral to land

almost any cargo in their Ports—if the vessel brings 4 or 5 slaves. The profits of their trade is so alluring . . . [that] few people in Trade would scruple
or hesitate to adopt such a plan to gain admittance to a Spanish Port." He
further opined that the sole "criminality of it consists exclusively in the
inhuman treatment of the Slaves" and likened the trade in Africans to that
of transporting an "Irishman . . . and selling him for a season." [8]

With the enactment of the 1800 statute, the Navy immediately began seizing suspected slavers and sending them in for adjudication. The
first three were captured in the space of a month. The sloop *Betsey* of
Boston takes the dubious honor of being the first slave-trading vessel
captured by the U.S. Navy. Under the command of Capt. Bateman Munro
of Charleston, she was seized off Havana by the U.S. schooner *Experiment*, under Lt. William Maley. She had eighty-five slaves aboard, all
from Rio Pongo, Africa.[9]

Her capture set off a furor, as reflected in a letter to former Secretary of State Timothy Pickering from military intendant Samuel Hodgson
at Philadelphia: "Captain Maley has arrived, he has acquit [*sic*] himself
so as to meet the applause of all his last act was the capture of a vessel
from Charleston . . . with eighty five *slaves* . . . " The writer then raised
the issue of disposition of the freedmen: " . . . to be sold they cannot, both
Constitution and Law forbid this—what then is to be done—liberated
where they are or indeed any where else they cannot be for no Government would allow it—the only alternative is to return them to their own
Country . . . will it make the condition of the slaves any better? But Maley
has done right in making the capture . . . a great indignation is already
excited against the monsters that planned the voyage . . . " [10] The vessel
itself was condemned and sold at Charleston in October 1800.[11]

Betsey, captured on June 25, was followed by *Prudent* on July 19,
and *Phoebe* on July 21. Both were taken by USS *Ganges*, with 120 slaves
on board the latter and an unknown number on the former. The arrival in
the United States of *Phoebe* brought the following remarks on disposition of the freedmen from Secretary of the Navy Benjamin Stoddert: "It
was expected, no doubt, the captains making the captures would sell them
in the West Indies. . . . "[12] However, it appears from a later note from the
secretary that some of the freed blacks were taken to Philadelphia where
"the abolition society, much to their honor, took care of them, & I believe
provided them masters for a term of years . . . "[13]

Capt. John Rodgers, commanding USS *Maryland*, attempted a fourth capture, also in July 1800, but uncooperative local officials hampered him. The schooner *Ranger*, of Charleston, sailed into the Surinam River, and Rodgers pressed the local governor to turn the vessel and its sixty-two slaves over for prosecution. From July 9 through July 16, Rodgers awaited a response, but he was told the *Ranger* was unseaworthy . . . which he considered a ruse by her commander. In any event, the slaves were sold at Surinam and Rodgers departed without his prize.[14]

With the end of the hostilities with France, American commerce on the high seas rebounded, carrying with it the trade in slaves. Several factors contributed to this revival: First, the U.S. Navy fell prey to President Jefferson's anti-navalism and the blue-water fleet was cut back severely, supplanted by Jefferson's pet gunboats— single-masted, one gun vessels that were barely sufficient for harbor defense, no less action against swift schooners on the high seas. Second, of course, the Revenue Marine was cut back significantly, now that it was no longer cooperating with the Navy against France.

Meanwhile, other factors encouraged the trade, among them the wide use of the cotton gin and the Louisiana Purchase in 1803. The former vastly increased production, and the latter moved the slave economy westward to new lands. Additionally, the state of South Carolina, probably in anticipation of the coming end to the legal trade, in 1803 repealed its sixteen-year ban on slave importation. The result was a boom in which more than two hundred slavers landed their cargoes in Charleston during the ensuing four years.[15]

As the constitutionally mandated ban approached, Congress struggled to produce a workable law to enforce it. After significant haggling—particularly concerning the disposition of the freed blacks, the appropriate penalties, and the status of the coastwise trade—the measure was signed into law on March 2, 1807, to take effect the first day of the next year.[16]

The final law called for categorizing any violation as a high misdemeanor, with imprisonment and fines up to $20,000, and forfeiture of the vessels involved. Further, those who purchased illicit slaves were subject to fines of $800 per slave. The question of disposition of the freed slaves was left to the states, and coastal slave trading was banned in vessels over forty tons. As far as enforcement was concerned, the president was authorized "to cause any of the armed vessels of the United States to be manned and employed" against American vessels trading in slaves on the high seas. The authorization of prize money sweetened the job for both the Navy and Revenue Marine.[17] However, Congress did not specifically direct the Navy to institute any kind of formal enforcement unit solely for anti-slavery work.

Prize money, severe penalties, and an "official" ban on the trade had seemingly little effect in the next decade. Some of the reasons are obvious: First, the Navy continued to exist on minimal appropriations, despite the growing danger of another war with Britain. In fact, no new vessels were authorized until January 1813 . . . six months *after* war had broken out. Second, the War of 1812 saw the Navy concentrating on the enemy rather than trade violators. Third, after 1813 most of the Navy— as well as much of the sea-borne trade—was blockaded in American ports. After the end of hostilities with Britain, the Navy undertook an expedition against the Algerian corsairs of North Africa, then settled into what would become the major cruising stations for the foreseeable future: the Mediterranean, West Indies, and Eastern Pacific squadrons.

The West Indies and the southeastern territories that eventually became Florida became the locus of much naval activity as piracy grew, as well as strains between the Spanish and their colonies in the area. However, the first capture of a slave ship under the new legal regime was a fluke. The schooner *Kitty*, which left Charleston in 1806, departed from Africa in 1807 with thirty-two slaves. She met with desertion, hunger, and incredibly bad weather, bringing her to the United States *after* the 1808 law went into effect. The Revenue Cutter *Gallatin* picked her up "red-handed," but the court, due to the circumstances, exempted the vessel from the letter of the law. [18]

The secretary of the Navy, as far back as 1811, had noted the connection between illicit slave trading and the growth of piratical elements operating in Spanish Florida and ordered Capt. Hugh Campbell to cruise from Charleston southward, stopping all suspect vessels regardless of flag.[19]

Piracy and smuggling grew significantly in the post-war era, particularly in the Gulf of Mexico and the east coast of Florida. The Navy dealt with these problems with an *ad hoc* squadron under Commodore Daniel T. Patterson, which included one of Jefferson's little gunboats along with *Firebrand*, *Tickler*, and ketch *Surprize*.[20] Activities on the East

Coast were centered on Amelia Island, just south of the Georgia–Spanish Florida frontier, when the buccaneer "commodore" Luis Aury proceeded to take advantage of the vanishing Spanish authority in the area, and the island became a notorious center for piracy and the smuggling of slaves and other contraband across the southern frontier of the United States.

The operations against the island began with a blockade and the capture of the slaver *Tentativa*, with 120 slaves on board, by the U.S. brig *Saranac*.[21] The next step was the forming of a larger expedition and, consequently, a combined naval and Army force was dispatched to the island in late 1817. Commodore John Henley, on USS *John Adams*, plus the *Saranac*, *Enterprise*, *Prometheus*, *Lynx*, and *Gunboat 168*, joined an Army contingent to quash Aury and his band. The object was attained when Aury surrendered in December without bloodshed. The *Tentativa* was escorted into Savannah by the Revenue Cutter *Dallas* on November 19, 1817. [22] Unfortunately, it appears that the freed captives were "illegally bartered" by locals before the courts were able to determine their legal disposition.[23]

Shortly after the island capitulated, the British brig *Neptune*, not knowing the island's new status, attempted to land eight convict slaves from Jamaica and was captured by Commodore Henley. Henley suspected the slaves were to be smuggled into Georgia. This was further evidence that the island had not been subject to effective Spanish control, and therefore an American presence was necessary to put down lawlessness there, including preventing the smuggling of slaves into the United States.[24]

In the Gulf, slave smuggling was rampant at the mouth of the Sabine River between Texas—then Spanish territory—and Louisiana. In August 1817, the fourteen-gun brig *Boxer* under Lt. Commandant John Porter brought two slaver schooners into New Orleans with thirty slaves aboard. Later, in June 1818, the converted six-gun merchant ketch *Surprize*, commanded by Lt. Isaac McKeever, seized the slavers *Merino* and *Loise* and twenty-five slaves, and sent them to Mobile for adjudication. In the latter cases, the court moved slowly, neither forfeiting the vessels until 1822, nor deciding the fate of the slaves until 1824. It was 1827 before the case was settled, netting McKeever $419.45 in prize money, plus $3,000 reimbursement for his court costs in the case.[25]

One of the more unusual captures of the era was the "private slaver" *Antelope* (also known as *General Ramirez*) by the Revenue Cutter *Dallas*.

In 1819, a Venezuelan privateer, fitted out in Baltimore with an American crew, captured American, Portuguese, and Spanish slavers and appropriated their cargoes—an aggregate total of 280 Africans. The Venezuelan vessel was wrecked and the cargo and crew were transferred to one of the prizes, the *Antelope*. This was the vessel captured by *Dallas* and brought in to Georgia. While this supremely convoluted case inched its way through the system, the blacks were subject to local whims—including a lottery to determine their disposition—and their caretakers hired many out as slaves. The Supreme Court eventually ruled that the blacks captured from Spanish vessels be surrendered, and the remainder were to be returned to Africa. By the time of this ruling, due to death, disappearance, or other causes, only 139 blacks remained. One hundred were returned to Africa and thirty-nine were sold as slaves in Georgia. The case had taken nine years to settle.[26]

The Amelia Island incident, Gulf Coast slave smuggling, uncertainty over the legal method of disposition of recaptured slaves, and evidence of increasing numbers of vessels involved in the trade resulted in new anti–slave trade legislation. In 1819, Congress strengthened the 1807 act by authorizing the Navy to cruise on the African coast to suppress the trade, and by authorizing that one half of the proceeds from captures go to the captors, provided the slaves were placed under a U.S. Marshal. The most radical portion of the law authorized the president to "make such regulations and arrangements . . . for the . . . removal beyond the limits of the United States, of all such negroes, mulattoes or persons of colour, as may be delivered and brought within their jurisdiction." Furthermore, an agent was to be appointed in Africa to deal with the freed blacks, and $100,000 was appropriated for enforcing the act. [27]

The legislation was an improvement in that the blacks were placed under federal control rather being turned over to state jurisdiction—a situation which had hitherto often resulted in their sale rather than their freedom—and, for the first time, moneys were appropriated for enforcement. However, Congress was not finished: in 1820 a temporary act concerning piracy was extended and similar penalties were applied to the slave trade. As with pirates, convicted slave traders were subject to the death penalty. Three years later, the temporary portion of the law was deleted.[28] The application of the death penalty made the American law against the slave trade the most strenuous in existence.

THE FOUNDING OF LIBERIA

The 1819 law's provision for "removal beyond the limits of the United States," and for appointing an agent in Africa to facilitate the resettling of the freedmen, signaled a new phase in the struggle to end the slave trade and pointed to the eventual founding of Liberia. Indeed, one of the sponsors of the 1819 law was Charles F. Mercer, a Virginian and a leader in the American Colonization Society. [29]

The ACS had been founded in 1816 in Washington, D.C., under the leadership of Bushrod Washington, nephew of the first president. Other prominent supporters were Thomas Jefferson, Henry Clay, Daniel Webster, Francis Scott Key, and (later U.S. president) John Tyler. Though resettlement of freed blacks in Africa was their goal, the motivations of the ACS were mixed. Some saw this as a way to correct centuries of injustice to American slaves; others simply believed free blacks were a threat and should be removed from the United States. A third motivating factor was a deeply religious one, combining the creation of a Christian colony in Africa with a strong evangelical thrust. Finally, the active suppression of the trade had raised the controversial issue of the disposition of the freed blacks: If they were freed by the federal government and remained in the United States, it set a dangerous precedent as far as the South was concerned and smacked of general emancipation. On the other hand, it was felt that sending them back to Africa without some institutional support would likely result in their being enslaved yet again. The founding of a quasi-colony to receive freed blacks appeared to meet both of these needs.[30] Furthermore, such an entity would place an active American anti-slavery (and anti–slave trade) settlement on the African coast to complement the British colony at Sierra Leone, which had also been founded as a haven for freed blacks.

Carrying out the provisions of the law, by default, joined the U.S. Navy to the ACS. First, President Monroe's cabinet discussed the $100,000 appropriation: Secretary of the Treasury William H. Crawford, also vice-president of the Society, advocated turning the entire amount over to the group, and he was supported by Secretary of the Navy Smith Thompson. Despite Secretary of State John Quincy Adams's objections, it was done. The agent to be appointed in Africa was to supervise the disbursement of the funds, and during the 1820s much of it was used for transporting the freed slaves and building the colony. Little, if any, of the money was used by the Navy for suppressing the slave trade, but it was expected that the Navy would shepherd and support the society in setting up and maintaining an Africa presence.[31] In fact, Monroe announced in December 1819 that two ships—one a naval escort—with agents for the Society and a group of settlers would be sent to Africa to make preliminary arrangements for setting up a station to receive the freed blacks.[32]

The naval vessel was the War of 1812 prize frigate *Cyane*, under Capt. Edward Trenchard, which escorted the brig *Elizabeth*, the latter carrying eighty-eight blacks recruited by the Society, plus their sponsors. Arriving on the West African coast, the group initially settled on Sherbro Island, southeast of Freetown, Sierra Leone. It was a poor location, proving to be swampy and malarial. Additionally, the natives harassed and threatened the little group of interlopers . . . which they were at this point, as they did not yet have legal possession of the land. Almost immediately the group's leader, Reverend Samuel Bacon, asked Captain Trenchard to survey the coast and various headlands and "enquire whether the natives would be willing to dispose of a tract of land" for the settlement. This Trenchard did, leaving Midshipman John S. Townshend and a small contingent of his crew to assist the colonists in building houses.[33]

This voyage brought an unexpected reward. Off the Gallinas River in eastern Sierra Leone, *Cyane* surprised a little fleet of slavers and chased down and captured a total of nine vessels. The bag was mixed: *Endymion* and *Science* were from Baltimore. *Esperanza*; the former Revenue Cutter *Alert* from Charleston; and *Plattsburg* of New York were flying Spanish colors. Another brig was Spanish and three others were of undetermined nationality. Four of the vessels were put under prize officers and sent to New York; two vessels were released, the blacks sent to Sierra Leone, and the vessels destroyed. The three of unknown origin were also destroyed. It appears that the total number of slaves liberated was around seventy. There is no record of a trial for the Americans who were returned to New York.[34]

Continuing the original sortie, *Cyane* arrived at Cape Mesurado, farther east from Sherbro, in mid-April 1820. It was determined that the location was "the most elligable [*sic*] situation for a settlement"—according to Trenchard's lieutenant, Matthew Calbraith Perry. Perry, who was at the beginning of a distinguished career and would later command the first Africa Squadron, took measures to convene a meeting of local chieftains to discuss ceding land for the colony, and then *Cyane* returned to Sherbro.

From Sherbro, *Cyane* visited the Cape Verde Islands and was joined by the small, twenty-eight-gun frigate USS *John Adams* and the sixteen-gun brig *Hornet*. They returned to the African coast, and, despite outbreaks of fever and scurvy on board, seized two more slavers. *John Adams*, in company with the Royal Navy brig *Snapper* and a boat expedition, took the *Exchange* off Rio Pongas and *Hornet* seized the *Alexander*, but neither carried slaves. However, on *Hornet*'s return to Cuban waters in 1821, she captured *Le Pensee*, which carried 220 slaves, and sent her to New Orleans for trial.[35]

Returning to Sherbro, Trenchard found the little colony bogged down by the rainy season and decimated by disease and other causes, having lost twenty-six of the Africans and all save one of the white leaders. Additionally, the entire group of American sailors that stayed to assist the colonists had succumbed. The remaining colonists retreated temporarily to Sierra Leone, and the *Cyane* returned to the United States in December 1820.[36]

Six months later, Perry, in his new—and first—command aboard the schooner *Shark*, departed from Washington with the new American representative for the Sherbro colony, Reverend Eli Ayers. They were joined at Sierra Leone by the U.S. armed schooner *Alligator*, under Robert F. Stockton, who escorted Ayers to the proposed new site of the colony at Cape Mesurado, present-day Monrovia. Later, Ayers and Stockton were obliged to make a dangerous twenty-mile trek inland to round up the local chiefs for a "palaver" (negotiation) and to convince the most powerful of the native leaders, "King Peter," to discuss terms to sell the land. The Africans objected to the intruders, accusing them of "kidnapping Africans" and "destroying the slave trade"—rather contradictory accusations in any event. Through the force of Stockton's personality and an explicit threat involving a cocked pistol, the recalcitrant "king" was convinced to turn over an area which became much of the present Liberia, in return for a variety of trade goods—axes, hatchets, and cloth—valued at $300. Shortly thereafter a new group of fifty-two colonists arrived, as well as the Reverend Jehudi Ashmun, who would be the settlement's most famous early leader. These and all the surviving settlers from the Sherbro debacle were transferred from Sierra Leone to the new location, and the colony finally had the beginnings of a solid foundation.[37]

The appearance of American men-of-war seems to have had a considerable effect on the slave traders in the area, who then proceeded to favor the French flag for their activities. On the *Shark* Perry stopped two slavers, the first being the schooner *Ys*, owned by the governor of Guadalupe, and carrying trade goods suitable for bartering for slaves. Her papers were in order, however, and she was released.

The second vessel, the French schooner *Caroline*, was three days out of Cape Mount (south of the Gallinas River) when she encountered the *Shark*. On a relatively calm day, the chase involved wetting the sails, manning the sweeps, and sending out the gig and cutter to tow *Shark* in the calms. Finally, after more than six hours, the quarry hove to and raised French colors. Perry "hoisted Spanish colours and sent 3 officers and a crew on board . . . " W. F. Lynch, one of Perry's midshipmen wrote of her cargo:

> The overpowering smell and the sight presented by her slave deck, can never be obliterated from the memory. In a space of about 15 by 40 feet, and four feet high, between decks, 164 negroes [*sic*], men, women, and children, were promiscuously confined. In sleeping they were made to dovetail, each one drawn up to the shortest span, and the children obliged to lie upon the full grown [*sic*]. They were all naked, and to protect from vermin not a hair was permitted to grow upon their persons. Their bodies were so emaciated, and their black skins were so shrunk upon the facial bones, that in their torpor, they resembled so many Egyptian mummies half-awakened to life. A pint of water and a half pint of rice each, was their daily allowance, which is reduced if the passage be prolonged. The passage is performed in from fifty to seventy days.
>
> I never saw the sympathies of men more deeply moved than were those of our crew. Immediately after taking possession . . . we hoisted up a cask of water, and some bread and beef, and gave each poor slave a long drink and a hearty meal.

Unfortunately, her papers were in order and, as France had yet to sign the international treaty against the trade, she was released. But before doing

so, Perry, determined to slake his moral outrage, insisted her commanding officer sign a pledge to "abjure the slave trade forever." [38]

Lieutenant Stockton in *Alligator* was less impressed by paperwork,
and he captured four ostensibly French slavers in 1821: *Mathilde, L'Eliza,
Daphne*, and *Jeune Eugenie*. En route to United States, the first three
were retaken by their crews, and only the fourth reached Boston for adjudication. The result was a diplomatic uproar, including a theatrical confrontation between Secretary of State John Quincy Adams and the French
minister, in Adams's office. The Frenchman, Adams wrote, "dwelling
upon the word *guerre* with a long and virulent emphasis," threatened
open hostilities. Consequently, the vessel was released to her French
owners. Furthermore, the incident resulted in State Department orders to
American naval commanders to forbear capturing any ship flying a foreign flag.[39]

As has been seen, up until the slave trade suppression law of 1819,
American naval efforts against the slave trade had been strictly in the
western hemisphere and on an *ad hoc* basis—accomplished as the navy
was active in its other missions. American squadrons showed the flag
and protected American interests in the Mediterranean, the West Indies,
the coast of Brazil, and the Pacific and Far East, but prior to the imple-
mentation of the 1819 law and the founding of the American freedmen
colony on the West African coast, there literally had been no American
presence in or off West Africa.[40] In the next two decades, pressure would
build to transform that presence from a limited, almost casual one, to a
formalized, systematic unit specifically directed to suppress the slave trade.
The pressure on the Navy would emanate from home, particularly from
some abolitionist elements, as well as from abroad, especially from the
British, who were by default the leader in the movement to suppress the
international slave trade.

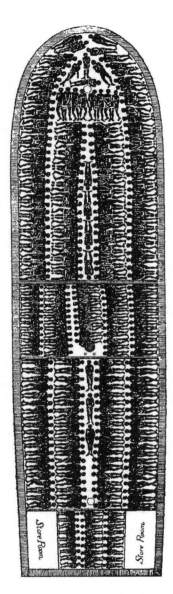

Slave Deck: appeared in a British history of the slave trade published in 1808: The ship Brookes *measured about 100' by 25' on the slave deck and the illustration shows approximately 290 slaves in an area equivalent to a modern four-bedroom house. (There were also diagrams of other decks on the vessel, and their complement of "black ivory".) Note that this illustration reflects conditions on the slave ships* before *the trade was outlawed in Britain. After the trade was prohibited, similar vessels carried significantly larger numbers of blacks confined in comparable spaces.* From History of the Abolition of the African Slave Trade, *by Thomas Clarkson, 1808.*

2

SPORADIC SUPPRESSION: U.S. NAVY ANTI-SLAVE TRADE ACTIVITIES 1822–1841

During the two decades between the initial settlement at Liberia and the establishment of the Navy's squadron off the west coast of Africa, the Navy's slave suppression operations were often referred to as the slave "patrol." The term implies an established, regular presence on station, though not necessarily a substantial force. It appears that even at the time, there was a general impression that there was indeed a naval vessel permanently "on station" off West Africa. This impression was reinforced by the fact that the Navy was receiving an annual appropriation for the suppression of the slave trade—though in fact this money went to the infant Liberian nation. The fact that the anti-slavery law of 1820 was the most strenuous national statute against the trade also encouraged the popular but totally rose-tinted idea that the slave traders had simply given up sailing under the American flag for fear of being subject to the death penalty. As will be seen, the reality at sea off Africa was far different from the popular notions of the time.

In the early 1820s, other than the operations in support of the early Liberian settlers, the Navy's efforts against the slave trade were part and parcel with the anti-piracy campaign being waged in the West Indies and Florida. This connection had been evident in the construction of a new generation of small vessels specifically designed for anti-piracy work, which replaced several worn-out ships that had been acquired during the War of 1812. (After the war, the Navy's only remaining small vessels were the purchased schooner *Fox* and the clipper-brig *Spark*.) The new ships were built in 1820–21 and were the topsail schooners *Alligator*,

Dolphin, Shark, Porpoise, and *Grampus.* They were each armed with ten guns, one of which was on a mid-ship mounted pivot circle. According to one authority, *Grampus* was considered one of the fastest schooners of the day, and despite their ostensible anti-piracy role, two of the ships, *Alligator* and *Shark,* performed their first commissions off Africa.[1]

By the end of 1822, the Navy's West Indies Squadron consisted of the frigates *Congress* and *John Adams*; sloop-of-war *Peacock*; schooners *Spark, Alligator, Grampus, Shark,* and *Porpoise*; plus *Gunboat 158.* The brigs *Hornet* and *Enterprise* were fitting out for that service.[2] These vessels and their commanders were warned that there was to be a difference in the treatment of suspected piratical vessels and those stopped for slave trading. The commander of *Spark* was instructed: "You will not consider your general instructions . . . for the suppression of the slave trade, as authorizing you, at any place out of the waters of the United States, to search, capture, or, in any manner whatever, to interrupt vessels under any other than the American flag." [3]

Operations in the Gulf netted two slavers in 1822. The first was in March, when the *Porpoise* seized the American schooner *Mary* with seventeen slaves on board. However, the slaves were not loaded at or destined for American ports, and they actually were Spanish property. Therefore, they were returned to Havana. The second incident was even less clear-cut: *Hornet,* under Robert Henley, in July recaptured the French brig *Theodore* after she had been taken by a Colombian privateer, despite the fact that no Americans were aboard and the passage was not to an American port. The 160 slaves thereon were returned to their owners.[4]

By 1823 the Navy's campaign against piracy in the Gulf and Florida waters was in full swing, under Commodore David Porter. Using a chartered steamer and a "Mosquito fleet," Porter and his successor Lewis Warrington destroyed the major pirate strongholds.[5] These accomplishments also eliminated the havens where the slave trade had flourished after the War of 1812.

Meanwhile, on the African coast, observers reported that the slave trade had declined. Lieutenant Perry noted that he had heard of no "American slavers" on that part of the coast. President Monroe echoed this in stating that "not one" slaver had been taken during 1823.[6] The secretary of the Navy's report of December 1823 stated: "During the time that Captain Spence [USS *Cyane*] and Lieutenant Perry were cruising, they neither saw nor heard of any vessel under the American flag engaged in the slave trade. If citizens of the United States are still employed in that traffic, they seem to have been driven to conceal themselves under the flags of other nations." [7]

Several other contemporary sources seem to agree that this era was one of declining numbers of slavers. However, the two caveats were evident: there were few *under the American flag*, and *on that part of the coast*. The law allowed American naval vessels to stop American flagged ships only, thus an American could avoid notice simply by raising another flag. So, in 1827, when Jehudi Ashmun reported an increase in the trade, he mentioned "many slavers" on the coast, but all save one displayed Spanish colors.[8]

Of course the Liberians themselves contributed to making times rough for the slave traders in their vicinity. In a series of small battles, in some instances in self defense, the Liberians attacked and destroyed the "barracoons," or slave factories, which had been established as gathering points for slaves who were brought from the interior and awaited sale and transportation to their new owners. By the mid-1830s, the Liberian newspaper claimed—though with some exaggeration—that almost four hundred miles of coastline were free from the slave factories, with the only exception being those near the Gallinas River, northwest of Cape Mount towards Sierra Leone.[9]

The dearth of slavers undoubtedly influenced the Navy's policy toward the anti-slave "patrol" for the next two decades. In 1824, Secretary of the Navy Samuel Southard directed the commodore of the West India Squadron to send "one of the vessels of his squadron to the coast of Africa, to touch at Cape Mesurado, minister to the wants of the agency there, and return by the usual track of the slave ships." Furthermore, Southard elsewhere indicated his intention to have a vessel off Africa at intervals of three or four months.[10]

In fact, that pattern had been set in 1823 when the frigate *Cyane* hove to with supplies for the Liberians, and to lend assistance in building fortifications. During the visit, Captain Spence found a small abandoned schooner, the *Augusta*, and refurbished it. The vessel was to cruise the coast and Spence felt that "its presence was at that time essential to the protection of the agency, and might prove useful in preventing the traffic in slaves." However, the *Cyane*'s visit was cut short by the outbreak of fever, felling more than forty of the crew, and the ship departed.[11]

According to one study, in the years 1823 to 1841, there were twenty-two visits by U.S. naval vessels to Liberia. In six of those years (1826, 1829, 1830, 1834, 1838, and 1839), there were no visits; in seven years there were two visits each, and in one instance (1836) there were four visits. In at least four instances, the vessel dropped anchor en route to or from the Mediterranean or Brazil Squadron; though, in 1833 and 1834, *Boxer* and *Porpoise* were in pursuit of piratical vessels.[12]

In the secretary of the Navy's 1824 report, Southard wrote again that Porter, commanding the Atlantic and Gulf Squadron, had, "from time to time dispatched one of the vessels . . . to the coast of Africa . . . " However, Southard noted that, "None of these, or any other of our public ships have found vessels engaged in the slave trade, under the flag of the United States, and in such circumstances as to justify their being seized and sent in for adjudication. And, although it is known that the trade still exists, to a most lamentable extent, yet, as it is seldom, if ever, carried on under our own flag, it is impossible, with the existing regulations and instructions, to afford very efficient aid in exterminating it."[13]

Southard's realistic assessment prefaced a sentiment and solution to the problem which would not come to fruition for another eighteen years, though attempts at the objective were being made even as he wrote: "That object can only be accomplished by the combined effort of the maritime nations, each yielding to the others the facilities necessary to detect the traffic under its own flag." [14]

Thus the secretary acknowledged the international aspect of the suppression of the slave trade and highlighted the ongoing diplomatic struggle concerning abolishing it, as well as establishing the reciprocal Right of Search and Right of Visit among the major maritime nations. The process had begun with the Congress of Vienna, which ended the Napoleonic Wars. Britain, the acknowledged dominant force on the world's oceans, had led the struggle toward international abolition of the slave trade, as well as the negotiation of multi-lateral treaties allowing the signatories certain maritime procedures designed to annihilate the trade.

The initial fruits of this effort were the abolition of the slave trade by the Netherlands in 1814, and the abolition of trade north of the equator by Portugal in 1815. The next treaties were with Spain, which agreed to end the trade north of the equator in 1817 and to total abolition by 1820. Additionally, treaties on the subject had been signed by Denmark and Sweden prior to 1814.[15]

The Right of Search was the long-term sticking point that prevented the United States from joining on equal terms with the British in enforcing the abolition of the slave trade. The American position, which denied any other nation the right to stop and search an American vessel on the high seas, originated before the War of 1812—the era when British naval vessels, under the Orders in Council, were blockading continental ports and interdicting trade with Napoleonic Europe. Neutral American vessels were stopped and searched on the high seas, and in many instances sailors were impressed into British service. "Free Trade and Sailors' Rights" became one of the watch phrases that brought on the declaration of war.

Of course, there were other American considerations at work in addition to the principle involved. First was the suspicion that the British insistence on abolition of the slave trade was a smoke screen for commercial trade advantages and imperial aggrandizement. As Lewis Cass, later secretary of state, wrote: "Who can doubt, but that the English cruisers . . . with an unlimited right of search, and discretionary authority to take possession of all vessels frequently on those seas, will seriously interrupt the trade of all other nations, by sending in their vessels under very slight pretences. . . . A trade carried on under such unfavourable circumstances, cannot contend with the trade of a favoured nation."[16] There was little hard evidence to back up this line of thinking, but it was popular nonetheless. However, evidence to that effect was seen in the many treaties with African tribes where the tribes' agreement to end the trade was accompanied by the establishment of a virtual British protectorate over the treaty tribe. There were also incidents where refusal to come to terms with the British resulted in use of military force to settle the issue. [17]

On a more visceral plane, there were American objections simply because it was a British idea. Worse, in this instance, the opposition was wrapped in the religious-moral superiority of a worldwide crusade against evil. The fact that the British had abolished slavery, while the American South regarded the institution as its key to prosperity and its "way of life," exacerbated the negative feelings considerably south of the Mason-Dixon Line. And there were also British actions that seemed threatening to the slave-holding South. First was the emancipation of slavery in the West Indies in 1833. Second was the treatment of the slaves from the vessels *Hermosa* and *Creole*, who were seized while being shipped from one U.S. port to another. The vessels were taken to the British West Indies for adjudication and the slaves were freed. Later, in the 1830s, there were certain British abolitionist activities in Texas prior to its annexation by the United States.[18]

In any case, in the wake of an international congress on the slave trade in 1822, the British launched a campaign to bring the United States into a treaty that included a reciprocal Right of Search provision. Negotiations had resulted in a convention in which the British had agreed to denounce the trade as piracy, and that slavers were to be tried in their own country, that vessels under naval convoy from their own country would be exempt from search, and that citizens of a third country captured on a slaving vessel would be sent to trial in their own nation. In agreeing to the proposition that equated slave trading with piracy, the British maintained that enforcement of this proposition as the Law of Nations would require the Right of Search, but qualified it with the provision that captured ships be tried in their own country.[19]

The treaty went to the Senate in May 1824—an election year. Monroe praised it as the beginning of a system "to accomplish the entire Abolition of the slave trade," but the senators took exception to it and made modifications to exempt American waters from Right of Search, and to eliminate the Right of Search for citizens chartering a vessel of a third nation. Furthermore, it is noteworthy that the rejection came close on the heels of the Monroe Doctrine, with its broad implications for America's isolationist foreign policy. The British did not sign the mutilated treaty. Though the British eventually—in 1831—offered to sign it as amended, the Senate again refused, and Secretary of State John Forsyth acknowledged that the United States would not sign any treaty on the slave trade.[20]

With the rejection of the treaty, the United States became more and more isolated in its position regarding the trade. In 1824 Sweden agreed to the Right of Search with Britain, and in 1826 Brazil agreed to abandon the trade in three years. Additional treaties were signed with Denmark, Sardinia, Naples, and the Hanseatic League.[21] Thus, there were fewer and fewer flags on the high seas that were immune to the Right of Search, but the major holdout—and the nation which, by the Civil War, had the world's second largest maritime commercial fleet—was the United States. Consequently, many vessels, regardless of their national origin, began flocking to the American colors, knowing they were immune to search by other nations, and that the likelihood of capture by the on-again off-again American Africa patrol was miniscule.

In addition to the advantages provided by the cover of the American flag, American-built vessels, particularly those constructed in Baltimore, gained notoriety as the speediest in the world. One British merchant noted seeing an American-built vessel flying Spanish colors: "one of the handsomest models of a fast sailer I ever saw. . . . the shipbuilders of Baltimore will out match [the British cruisers] in the sailing qualities of their clippers." [22] These vessels had gained a reputation during the War of 1812 by evading British blockaders, and their speed as well as their relative cheapness to build and operate made them particularly desirable for the trade. They were typically ninety to one hundred feet in overall length, and eighteen to twenty feet beam, and they drew about ten feet of water. Their schooner or topsail schooner rig enabled them to sail closer to the wind than a typical square-rigged naval vessel, and their sharp underwater hull lines made for great speed.[23] The latter quality was useful for evading the law as well as for making fast passages to the markets, and thus reduced the cost of the voyage as well as losses in slaves due to attrition during the passage. The inexpensive initial cost meant maximizing the profits and making the vessels nearly expendable if it became necessary to abandon or destroy the ship under adverse circumstances. Stories abound of vessels being run ashore on Cuban beaches in order to avoid capture. Once the slaves were off-loaded, the vessel—and evidence—was burned.

In this era, in order to combine the advantages of a fast, American-built vessel with immunity from search, the slave trade became logistically complex. The selected American-registered vessel was chartered in Cuba or Brazil by a slave dealer and sailed to Britain or elsewhere to load a cargo particularly suited for the African coast trade: cheap muskets, rum, etc. On returning to Havana or Rio de Janeiro, certain "passengers" boarded and the vessel made for Africa. On this leg, though obviously equipped to trade in slaves, the American registry and flag created immunity from search by non-American cruisers. Furthermore, and not infrequently, the vessel needed to hover off the coast while the agents ashore gathered the human cargo. During this critical interval, the American flag was particularly useful, as there was little chance that a U.S. naval cruiser would happen by, but a large one that the enforcer would be British. Once the Africans were gathered and the night was dark, canoes were loaded with the slaves and rowed from shore to ship. Simultaneously, the slave deck—the most damning evidence of the vessel's purpose—was quickly laid in place. Then the ship was "sold" on the spot and become Spanish, Portuguese, or Brazilian, and the "passengers" previously mentioned conveniently turned out to be the new officers and crew for the fast passage back to the Western Hemisphere with the slave cargo.[24] Once on the open sea, American-bred speed secured them from apprehension by cruisers of any nationality.

Thus, given fast, American-built vessels; immunity from search; and growing profits, the trade was becoming "an American business."[25] (Though it should be kept in mind that the major markets in this era were Brazil and Cuba, and rarely were slave cargoes brought directly to the United States.) In 1825 Ashmun reported that the trade was booming under the American flag., encouraged by the infrequency of the American patrols. According to one author, American naval vessels captured no slavers between 1822 and 1830. The exceptions to this were three captured by the Revenue Cutter *Alabama*, operating out of New Orleans in March 1822.[26]

The next slaver taken was again in the Western Hemisphere: the American-built Spanish vessel *Fenix* was taken by U.S. schooner *Grampus* near Haiti in 1830. In addition to having harassed the American merchantman *Kremlin*, she was captured with eighty-two slaves on board.[27] Amazingly, though *Fenix* had Spanish papers, the East Louisiana district court ordered the slaves sent to Liberia, and the *Grampus*'s crew was paid a bounty.[28]

In the early 1830s the American visits to Africa continued the pattern set previously. In February 1831 the frigate *Java* called at Monrovia and remained six days. The brig *Boxer* dropped anchor in April 1832, followed by *Porpoise* in February 1833; the latter pair were in pursuit of the piratical vessel *Rayman*. Next was *John Adams* in December 1833. This was followed by more than a year with no U.S. naval presence.

Then, in the summer of 1835 *Ontario* and *Erie* arrived, the former detached temporarily from the Brazil Squadron with orders to visit specific points on the coast including Cape Palmas, the Island of St. Thomas in the Bight of Benin, and Bassa Cove.[29]

A high point of sorts was reached in 1836 and early 1837 when four American naval cruisers called on the coast at different times: these were the *Dolphin*, *Peacock*, *Enterprise*, and the frigate *Potomac*. Unfortunately, it would be 1840—more than two years later—before the next American cruiser showed the flag off Africa.[30] It should be pointed out that these were peaceful years, and the Navy had few pressing responsibilities except the routines associated with cruising on the various other stations.

By all accounts the last half of the 1830s marked a quickening in the slave trade, particularly to Cuba, fed by high prices and minimum interference from American cruisers. The British Mixed Commission at Havana reported the arrival of 240 illegal slavers during the years 1836 through 1839, fifty-eight of which were under American colors. And it was reported that a New York mercantile house had taken in $240,000 in profits on the trade in the space of fourteen months, and that slaves had brought ten times their purchase price at Havana in the same period. [31]

Specifically, the Sierra Leone Mixed Commissioners' report of 1839 listed more than sixty slavers brought before them and condemned, with 3,283 slaves emancipated as a result. Of these vessels, all but three were captured on the African coast: eight below the equator, thirty east of Cape Palmas, and twenty west of that place. As to American vessels in the trade, the commissioners reported eleven vessels brought before them including six from Baltimore, three from Mobile, and one from Philadelphia. As the report noted, these vessels were not "admitted to prosecution," as the United States had not "conceded to our cruisers the right of visiting, searching and detaining her vessels for any purpose whatsoever."[32]

Also noteworthy from this report is the following: "Three of the vessels condemned during the past year . . . continued under the protection of the American papers, with which they cleared out from the island of Cuba, until the very moment when they took on board the cargo of slaves which formed the ground of their condemnation."[33]

This report forms part of the background for the charges made at this time that the trade was being encouraged by the actions of the American consul to Havana, Nicholas P. Trist, a Virginian who thought the trade was beneficial to the Africans themselves because it rescued them from the "paganism and cruelty of the Dark Continent." He also felt his authority to hinder the trade was limited, and indeed he became notorious for signing papers for suspected slavers with "no questions asked." Furthermore, between 1838–39, Trist, as a favor to the Portuguese consul, authenticated many suspect Portuguese vessels clearing from Havana to Africa. His actions brought inevitable British protests, popular uproar, and newspapers calling for his removal. The above quoted Commissioners' report stated: "And if America should still decline to apply a remedy to this extensive evil, she must consent henceforth to be classed with those unhappy powers, who can only escape from the charge of wilfully [*sic*] violating their engagements and promises for the suppression of the Slave Trade, by confessing the total absence of authority and control in the Supreme Government." An investigation resulted in a critical report of Trist, but he remained in office until the next administration.[34]

As the decade drew to a close, British Prime Minister Lord Palmerston's efforts on behalf of the Right of Search had resulted in agreements with France, Haiti, Uruguay, Venezuela, Bolivia, Argentina, Mexico, and Texas, in addition to those listed previously. The Spanish flag had guaranteed immunity until 1835, when a convention allowed seizure of slavers even if they were *equipped* for transporting slaves. Then the Portuguese flag allowed immunity until a treaty was ratified in 1839.[35] The latter left the United States in the unpopular position as the last major maritime nation opposing the Right of Search and its use against the slave traders, and 1839 proved to be a turning point in the American attitude towards immunity from the Right of Search, as well as seeming immunity from involvement in any international effort against the slave trade.

In 1839 several incidents brought the slave trade into focus on the very doorsteps of the nation. In June, two Baltimore-built slavers, *Eagle* and *Clara*, flying American colors, were seized by HMS *Buzzard* off Lagos, Africa. Once it was determined that their papers were fictitious, the British cruiser put prize crews on them and escorted them in broad daylight into New York Harbor, complete with their slave cargoes. It was the first time since the American Revolution that British cruisers had brought captured American vessels into an American harbor. Shortly thereafter, HMS *Harlequin* captured the slaver *Wyoming* and also brought her in with a British prize crew on board. Finally, the *Butterfly* and the

Baltimore-built *Catherine*—the latter with 350 pairs of handcuffs, cooking arrangements for 300 people, 570 spoons, and both Spanish and English logbooks—were seized by the British cruiser *Dolphin*. *Catherine* was on approach to West Africa and flying American colors at the time. A prize crew took her to New York where the vessel was condemned, as were *Butterfly* and *Wyoming*. *Eagle* and *Clara,* however, were deemed Spanish property and released.[36]

Thus the British rammed home their charge that they were being forced to enforce the law upon American citizens because the United States was not doing so. This, along with another incident in Long Island Sound brought the slave trade issue to center stage.

On August 26, 1839, the Revenue Cutter *Washington*, on temporary loan to the U.S. Coast Survey and with a Navy crew, fell in with a suspected smuggler. Upon sending a boarding party, it was discovered that the smuggler was a Baltimore-built schooner under Spanish registry as *Amistad*, and there were two frightened Spaniards and fifty-three Africans on board. The blacks, newly imported from Africa, had risen, killed two whites, and taken the ship. The two Spanish hostages had contrived to navigate the vessel north, rather than back to Africa, as their captors had desired.[37]

The Spanish government immediately demanded return of the vessel and cargo, which were being held at New London, Connecticut, but the case landed in the American court system and under the scrutiny of the American press and public. The Supreme Court eventually freed the blacks, but the case had become a public airing of the monstrous injustices of the slave trade, and it underscored the American recalcitrance to cooperate in enforcing laws against the evil.

Also, late in 1839, fallout from the British capture of American slavers shifted to Baltimore. The British Foreign Office supplied evidence to the federal courts that implicated the *Catherine*'s original owners, who had failed to sell her publicly at Havana and whose names were still on her register. They were arrested along with the owner of another successful slaver, the *Elvira*, and at the same time two schooners being built for the trade were confiscated.[38]

The trials of these malefactors were unsuccessful for the government and for the circuit justice on duty, Roger B. Taney. The local merchants united to agree to the probity and good character of the defendants, and the cases were lost. However, Taney, who later issued the Dred Scott decision, severely berated the defendants and decried the connivance and violations of the law that were rampant in these cases. His ire, and the confiscation of the schooners, served notice to the merchants of Baltimore and ended the construction of slave ships at that city. [39]

As 1839 drew to a close, the repercussions from events in New York, New London, and Baltimore brought an appropriate response. President Van Buren directed that "a competent" naval force be stationed on the African coast. This had become patently necessary to prevent the British from continuing their embarrassing drive to enforce the law in the absence of American forces on that station. [40]

Thus, in early 1840, the brig *Dolphin* and the schooner *Grampus* were dispatched to West Africa, where they remained for several months. They returned and were sent out again in 1841. The two vessels cruised continuously on the coast, though they captured only one slaver, the *Sara Anne*, in March 1840.[41] This was the first slaver captured by an American naval vessel in African waters in nearly twenty years, and her master was convicted and sentenced to two years incarceration and a $2,000 fine.[42] Unfortunately, close-in cruising brought on the fever, which struck down nearly two-thirds of Paine's crew and five of those died.[43]

On the other hand, Thomas Botts, a crewman on board *Dolphin*, complained little of disease and more of boredom:

> We have been cruising this coast now for nearly two months. A most dull and monotonous cruise it is, the weather intensely hot & dry save only when the tornados or thunderstorms come in. These are the most violent & the peals of thunder & flashes of lightening [sic] are far more severe than I ever beheld in the United States. . . . We have as yet all remained in fine health . . . owing perhaps to the great precautions we have taken to avoid disease. None of us ever Sleep on shore during the night. As it is said that staying on shore one night is sufficient to ensure the African fever, which to the white man is quite as fatal as the yellow fever to the South. . . . We have seen as yet no American vessels here engaged in the Slave trade though ther [sic] are many in that traffic under Portuguese, Spanish & Brazilian colors . . . A noted slave dealer . . . by the name of Pedro Blanco a Spaniard has

lately retire [*sic*] from his occupation with a capital of four millions of dollars. . . . [44]

Note, however, that this was written early during the vessel's deployment on the coast.

In addition to extended cruising, the American commander of *Grampus*, Lt. John S. Paine, who had orders for "friendly" cooperation with the British, entered into an agreement for joint cruising between the forces, wherein each agreed to investigate and hold suspect vessels for the other's return. It was virtually a reciprocal Right of Search, and Washington hastily disavowed the action.[45] However, Paine and Charles H. Bell's report on the cruise would serve to prepare the background for the establishment of the Africa Squadron in the coming year.

3

THE SCENE IS SET: WEBSTER-ASHBURTON AND THE U.S. NAVY, 1840–1842

The growing evidence that the slave trade was flourishing and not dying, plus the traumatic events of 1839, brought an immediate response of the dispatch of two naval vessels to *maintain* a patrol on the west coast of Africa for the first time. This was a token move, to be sure, but renewed British diplomatic efforts forced the United States—now exposed as negligent in enforcing her own anti-slavery laws—to come to the negotiating table with serious intent, even though the sole motivation may have been to save face.

In fact, the negotiations were part of a larger picture that was related to Anglo-American relations in general. Besides strains resulting from the dispute over the enforcement of the anti–slave trade laws, a long-standing disagreement over the U.S.–Canadian border had Congress calling for fifty thousand men to settle the issue in the woods of Maine and New Brunswick in 1839. Fortunately the "Aroostook War" was put on hold with an agreement to settle the border issue diplomatically. This set the stage for the arrival of Alexander Baring (Lord Ashburton) in Washington, who was prepared to work out both the border and slave trade issues.

Lord Ashburton's assignment was not an enviable one, and recent events served to exacerbate, rather than ameliorate, U.S.–British relations. As recently as December 1841, a five-power treaty had emerged from Paris, wherein the right of search was emphasized and the slave trade was labeled piracy. The latter stipulation was seen in some American quarters as a step to an international law on the Right of Search, which might potentially overrule any extant treaty provision.[1] This possibility so alarmed Lewis Cass, American minister to France, that he began lobbying the French against ratifying the treaty—and he succeeded. The Chamber of Deputies' negative vote occurred shortly after Ashburton began his talks with Secretary of State Daniel Webster on the proposed Anglo-American pact.[2]

Adding to the disruptive atmosphere was the appearance of an article in England and France charging that British motives were not altruistic. The writer believed that "but for slave-labour in the United States, in Cuba, and Brazil she could produce cotton, rice, coffee, and sugar cheaper in India than it could be produced in the United States, Cuba, or Brazil." Somewhat later, another American writer echoed popular suspicions about British motives. He noted that the British kept cruisers off Gallinas and New Sesters, West African sites of two of the larger slave "barracoons," and, "If the cruiser can capture the vessels, the captors receive 5 [pounds] per head for the slaves on board, and the government has more "emigrants" for its West India possessions. Now, were the cruisers to anchor at the mouths of these two rivers the slavers would be prevented from putting to sea . . . and the trade be inevitably stopped. But, in this case, where would be the head-money and emigrants?"[3]

Capt. Charles H. Bell on USS *Grampus* noted another variation on the above theme. Noting that the British loitered out of sight of land, he also suggested close-in blockade, but he was rebuffed by the British commanding officers who noted the condemnation costs would wipe out any profit from the vessels taken without cargo. "We came out here to make prize money" was their refrain, and Bell was convinced they were not serious about ending the trade.[4]

Adding to the unsettled Anglo-American relations in mid-1842 were nasty—and inflammatory—rumors circulating that, in the event of the Canadian border dispute escalating into war, Britain would send West Indian soldiers to foment slave rebellion in the American South.[5]

Yet another example of the perceived untrustworthiness of the British attitude toward the slave trade was the *Creole* affair of 1841, previously mentioned. The vessel— an American ship—was taking slaves from Virginia to New Orleans, when the slaves mutinied and forced the crew to land in Nassau. There the slaves declared themselves free. The British colonial authorities agreed, despite American requests that they be returned to their owners.[6]

Also noteworthy was the appearance of a piece entitled "The United States and the Slave Trade" in the British *United Service Magazine* in 1842. The writer ("G.D.H.") noted that he had visited the United States in 1840 and read an American newspaper's description of the "successful resistance of two Cuba slavers to the boats of a British cruiser." He noted in the article a general tone of exultation "at the escape of the lawless traders," and went on to excoriate the U.S. attitude toward slavery and liken it to the American policies toward the Indians.[7]

The Right of Search dispute was at the center of the Anglo-American negotiations. Some expected the British might rescind their insistence on the impressment of seamen in exchange for American concessions on Right of Search, but this hope proved illusory. In the end, the only possible solution was to simply ignore the Right of Search question entirely. Rather, Article VIII of the document called for each nation to, as President John Tyler declared in submitting the treaty to the Senate for ratification, " . . . maintain on the coast of Africa a sufficient squadron to enforce separately and respectively, the laws, rights and obligations of the two countries." The agreement called for each squadron to be composed of vessels carrying an aggregate of eighty guns, and the squadrons would patrol independently of each other, though they were to act "in concert and cooperation." Also part of the agreement was a term of five years for the squadrons to be in place on the coast. Subsequent extensions of the squadrons on station would then be voluntary. The treaty was signed on August 10, 1842, and it was ratified by the Senate ten days later, despite significant opposition by Thomas Hart Benton and James Buchanan.[8]

The Webster-Ashburton Treaty, also known as the Treaty of Washington, set in motion the establishment of the Africa Squadron by the Navy. Therefore, the following will set the stage for this endeavor and set forth in detail the problems the Navy faced off the coast of Africa, as well as present a description of the U.S. Navy as it was constituted at the time.

The Navy's "eighty guns" would be required to watch an African coast of roughly three thousand miles. In the north, slavers were known to operate as far as Rio Pongas, near Cape Verga, at 10 degrees north of the equator, in present day Guinea. This "Windward Coast" angled to the east, becoming the "Leeward Coast" to the Bight of Benin and Bight of Biafra, where the coast again turned nearly due south. It was some 1,500 miles between these two points. This section of the coast included the British enclave at Sierra Leone and the Liberian settlement. Southward from the Bights it stretched to St. Paul de Luanda ("Loando") and beyond in present-day Angola, about 10 degrees south of the equator.

The first climatic characteristic of the area under consideration is the heat, particularly as the heart of the African slave trade—the Bights of Benin and Biafra—are no more than 250 miles from the equator. The intensity and duration of the temperatures, as well as the humidity, would color all aspects of the Navy's onerous job of patrolling the coast. Compounding the problem were the calms prevalent on a belt paralleling the east-west portion of the West African coast. Commander Louis M. Goldsborough, Chief of the Bureau of Provision and Clothing, noted this in response to an inquiry made by Secretary of the Navy Upshur late in 1842, while plans were being made for the squadron.

> Owing to a belt of calm ocean which lies close to and extends parallel with a considerable portion of the Western coast of Africa, vessels, in navigating that coast are compelled to hug the land, in order to avail themselves of the land & sea breezes. Those, at best, are but light & fitful, while the current is steady & strong. The performance of a voyage therefore, from one place to another & back again, although the distance be considerable requires a good deal of time, compared with the general notions of navigation. Occasional fair passages, regarded, however, as exceptions, are made under the influence of favoring harmattans.[9]

In the years to come, the besetting calms became another unpopular characteristic of the anti-slavery patrol.

Another letter, this in 1838, gives a second seasoned naval captain's experience off Africa, in this instance during the rainy season:

> The rainy season set in on that coast in the month of July & continues throughout the month of August. The wind prevails during this time from the S.W. occasioning a heavy swell in that sea which

is denominated by those who frequent the coast, rollers, and renders the lying at anchor disagreeable if not dangerous. It is therefore of great consequence that a vessel bound to that part of the world arrive and depart before the month of July or postpone its visit till September.

I have been at Siera [*sic*] Leone in the season above mentioned, and can assure you that he who has experienced what I did on that occasion can never wish to return to see or feel it again. It is true I was lucky in preserving the health of the crew, but might not be so fortunate again.

Imagine yourself on one of the most inhospitable shores that is known, the rain pouring down in torrents for three or four hours together, with scarcely a breath of air stirring, and the sun coming out at intervals of thirty minutes so hot as to make his rays unsupportable even with the aid of an awning. But this protection, ineffectual as it is, is not always to be enjoyed, tornadoes off the land being frequent, when all canvas must be furled.[10]

(Note the terms "harmattans" and "tornadoes" which refer to the desert-generated siroccos.)

A seaman on the Africa patrol noted another description of the prevailing weather patterns in the late 1840s.

We sailed from Porto Praya to Monrovia. . . . Calms, light winds, and heavy squalls off the land prevailed, and we were more than a fortnight on the passage, the weather being now very hot and oppressive. The squalls of which I spoke were very peculiar. The sailors call them "pompy-doodles." During the day we would crawl along, just in sight of the coast, with perhaps a faint sea-breeze, towards afternoon, to fan us a few miles farther south. But before sundown clouds would gather and bank over the land in a most threatening manner, with vivid lightning and distant thunder, and about nine or ten o'clock a dark-arched squall would rush out seaward, driving the spray and spoon-drift before it. There was nothing to be done but to reduce sail, point the ship's head to the westward, and run before it. Sometimes we had to run off fifteen or twenty miles before it was safe to bring the ship to, a distance which we would be the best part of the next day in regaining . . .[11]

The climate, unattractive as it was, was complemented, in a manner of speaking, by the vast unmarked littoral. A historian of the British effort in Africa wrote: "Apart from the heat, the fever, and the strenuous monotony of handling a sailing ship in tropical light airs and calms [they] had another hardship. . . . This was the sameness of the landscape . . . There is plenty of attractive country in West Africa, but it does not show itself from the sea . . . The coast [between Freetown, Sierra Leone and Cameroon] is generally flat, a ribbon of dull green scrub or forest, with no natural harbors and few conspicuous landmarks. . . . One river mouth is much like another; most of them are muffled in mangroves. We . . . find the enormous sameness of the West African coast oppressive."[12]

A more famous mariner and novelist, Joseph Conrad, described a passage along this coast in *Heart of Darkness*: "I watched the coast . . . This one was almost featureless, as if still in the making, with an aspect of monotonous grimness. The edge of a colossal jungle, so dark-green as to be almost black, fringed with white surf, ran straight, like a ruled line, far, far away along a blue sea whose glitter was blurred by a creeping mist. The sun was fierce, the land seemed to glisten and drip with steam. . . . Every day the coast looked the same, as though we had not moved; but we passed various places—trading places—with names like Gran'Bassam, Little Popo; names that seemed to belong to some sordid farce acted in front of a sinister black cloth."[13]

These climatic conditions are hardly bearable in modern times, and they can scarcely be imagined in the context of typical life on a wooden sailing ship in the mid-nineteenth century. Ventilation was practically unknown below decks on a sailing man-of-war, and the heat extremes literally bubbled the tar that so lavishly abounded on those vessels. And, as noted above, even awnings stretched across the deck did little except provide shade. All this, and the men were ensconced on their crowded vessel for months at a stretch, enduring this coast's heavy swells rolling in across the vast Atlantic and living on typical Navy fare: salt beef and pork, weevil-ridden hard tack, and dried peas.

More sinister and deadly than the diet and the climate was that unseen blight so common to the white man on the African coast: the "fever." It would be 1880 before the source of malaria (as well as dengue fever, a non-lethal malarial strain) was proved to be the mosquito, and a cure was even farther in the future. In the meantime, tropical climates like that off Africa brought death to hundreds, many of them sailors of the anti–slave trade squadrons.

British experiences illustrate the deadliness of the disease. In 1837 HMS *Éclair*, at Sierra Leone, saw an outbreak of the scourge. In the six-month period from April to September, sixty-five men died, sometimes as many as four or five a day. Of the 142-man crew, only twenty-two escaped the fever entirely.[14]

The story repeated itself three years later. An expedition up the Niger River brought death to forty-five of a 145-man naval contingent. Only *eight* of the crew evaded the ravages completely. (Ironically, a British captain, W. F. W. Owen, had attributed the fever to mosquitoes as early as 1823.)[15] It was duly noted that none of the native blacks with the expeditions were affected.

At this time there was no cure or effective treatment. Bloodletting was common, but in the context of the now long discredited concept of restoring the balance of the supposed "humours" of the body, as defined as far back as the Ancient Greeks. The only supposed prevention was avoidance of "bad air," from whence the disease had gotten its name— the Latin *mal* (bad), and *aria* (air). Consequently, the men were to avoid swamps and other "effluvia" or miasma. In practical terms this meant, among other things, avoiding the continent itself, a "solution" which would have serious consequences for the new American squadron.

In sum, the conditions facing the new squadron were daunting: a seemingly interminable coastline with few good harbors; an extreme climate; uncertain winds; strong currents; and the very real threat of incurable, fatal disease. The natural obstacles were only exacerbated by the man-made conditions: crews were in overcrowded, unventilated, unsanitary ships and were required to remain on station without let-up for months. In fact, the standard cruise length in this era was three years, but on this station it was reduced to two, simply because of the hardships of the climate.

Given this littoral and geographic backdrop and the specific task assigned to the U.S. Navy's new squadron, we should look at the resources from which the service would draw its men and vessels for this duty.

The U.S. Navy in 1842 was, by twentieth century standards, tiny. But in fact, the service would maintain its limited size up to the Civil War, expand explosively, and then drop back to its pre-war level. As the mission of the Navy during peacetime was for the most part to cruise on foreign stations, to protect American interests and commerce, and generally to "show the flag," the size of the fleet was predicated on the number of squadrons, plus vessels in U.S. Navy yards refitting in order to replace those returning from overseas duties. After three years on station, a vessel would return to the States for refit, and another would sail out to replace it.

Before the formation of the Africa Squadron, the Navy maintained squadrons in the Pacific, off the coast of Brazil, and in the Mediterranean. A Home Squadron had been formed as late as 1841 on the East coast. There were smaller naval units in the East Indies, West Indies, and Florida by 1842. Finally, from 1838 though 1842, four vessels constituted the world-circling Wilkes South Sea Exploring Expedition. These squadrons and smaller units totaled thirty-nine ships, ranging from small schooners to seventy-four-gun ships of the line, plus one storeship on the Pacific station.

Of course this was not the total number of vessels in the inventory. Also considered "in commission" were eight receiving ships, which acted as floating dormitories for new recruits in various home ports. Five other inactive vessels were "in ordinary" at the yards and were considered a reserve fleet. There were two additional storeships, which navigated among the squadrons as needed. Always on the Navy list were the ships "on the stocks,"—that is, awaiting completion—as needed or as funding permitted. There were ten of these in 1842. Thus, the total number of vessels capable of going to sea numbered fifty-three, plus the storeships.

The composition of the fleet was very much arranged around appropriate vessels for cruising on foreign station, as well as budgetary considerations. The ships of the line (having seventy-four or more guns) were the prestige commands, but each of these huge vessels employed crews numbering more than seven hundred, and thus they were expensive to keep at sea—a large budget consideration in peacetime. The Mediterranean and Brazil squadrons sometimes were considered appropriate venues for these vessels. Of seven on hand in 1842, only one ship of the line was at sea—in this instance, off Brazil.

The American Navy was particularly noted for its fine—and large—

frigates, ships such as *Constitution* and *Constellation*. These carried batteries of thirty-six to fifty-four guns, and they were large enough to be appropriate for squadron flagships. In 1842 there was one frigate for each squadron or unit, plus two on the Home station, and a total of nine available for service. The frigates were nearly as impressive as the ships of the line, and marginally cheaper to keep at sea. It is noteworthy that neither ships –of –the line nor frigates were really "necessary" to protect American commerce—smaller vessels could as easily and more economically carry out those duties in peacetime—but from a diplomatic power presence standpoint, they were very much the expectation and tradition among the reputable navies of the era.

The smaller vessels—sloops-of-war, brigs, and schooners—were much cheaper to maintain and operate for long periods at sea. These had batteries of twenty guns or fewer and crews of around two hundred or fewer. These vessels had other advantages over the frigates and liners: they were more maneuverable, drew less water, and, in the case of the schooners, could operate closer to the wind. Thus they were more suitable for close-in work. The schooners particularly had a speed advantage over the square-rigged vessels. In 1842, there were nineteen sloops-of-war capable of sea service, carrying from sixteen to twenty-two guns each. There were four brigs of ten guns or fewer, and five schooners. (Another four small schooners were being used against the Indians in Florida waters. These were on loan from the War Department.)[16]

By 1842, steam ships had been operating in American waters for more than thirty years. The first steamer had crossed the Atlantic in 1819 and the British had begun regular transatlantic steam passenger service in 1838. The Navy's first steamer had been the *Fulton* in the War of 1812, but she was essentially an armed, powered barge. A second *Fulton* was commissioned in 1837, but proved to be a design failure. In 1842 there were four steamers in service: *Mississippi* and *Missouri* were as large as frigates; *Fulton* was on hand, but she was being used as a weapons test bed; and there was a small side-wheel vessel, *Poinsett*, which was not suitable for blue water duty. There was still much resistance to steam power in the service, and, in fact, there were good reasons for this. First, steam power vessels were expensive to operate and required convenient coaling stations. Second, the technology was still in a state of flux and unreliable engines made many of them unsuited for overseas duties. [17]

It is probably appropriate here to summarize the organization of the service in this era. In 1842 the Navy instituted the bureau system, where each major department (Construction and Repair, Yards and Docks, etc.) was headed by a senior naval officer. There was no general staff, nor was there a senior naval officer in command of the fleet. The squadron commanders, as well as bureau chiefs, reported directly to the Secretary of the Navy. Other than the usual coterie of clerical personnel, this was the entire bureaucracy of the Navy.

The squadron organization was equally simple. The unit's commander was usually a senior captain, denominated the "flag officer," which was a position rather than a rank, and he would revert to normal captain's pay after he was relieved from squadron duty. (At this time, there were only three officer ranks in the Navy: lieutenant, commander, and captain, so the flag officer in the U.S. Navy was somewhat similar to an admiral in a larger navy.) The flag officer rated a flagship—usually a frigate in the U.S. Navy, but sometimes a liner—fitted out with flag living quarters. The commanding officer of the flagship, as well as those on the other squadron vessels, reported directly to the flag officer.

The typical squadron amounted to one flagship—in most cases a frigate—and several smaller vessels, the number being determined by the needs of the particular cruising ground. In 1842, when the Africa Squadron was about to be established, the squadrons numbered from eight vessels downward. The Home Squadron, just established the previous year, had eight, including two steamers. The Brazil Squadron numbered seven, and the Pacific, six. In the latter case, due to the distances involved, the squadron also was assigned a storeship. There were four vessels in the Mediterranean, two in the East Indies, and three in the West Indies. Captain Wilkes's Exploration Expedition had four vessels and returned to the United States in mid-1842. There were no steamers on foreign station.

The purpose and mission of all of the standing squadrons was, in peacetime, generic: it was "maintaining a presence" and "showing the flag," more formally termed protection of American commerce and nationals, and, of course, looking out for "American interests." Where it was likely that the American vessels would be "on display" in harbors and roadsteads frequented by larger navies, the larger and more impressive ships were assigned. Of course, these were prestige assignments for the flag officers.

The Africa Squadron would prove to be an anomaly among all the American naval units. In the first place, it was the only squadron established and maintained by congressional mandate based on treaty obligations. Not only was its existence determined outside of the Navy, its size and mission were imposed on the service. Vessels in other squadrons went from port call to port call with an occasional diversion to rescue a stranded mariner or back a local consul in a diplomatic quandary. Off Africa, the mission was *not* the port calls, but the sea time cruising. In fact, in attempting to maintain a quasi-blockade, the port call was counterproductive.

Furthermore, the standard squadron composition proved unsuited to the job. The frigate-flagship—calculated to awe the natives and having the advantage of comprising more than half the guns required by treaty—was impracticably large for chasing small slavers and hovering close to the coast. By the same token, impressing the locals at Monrovia or Gallinas was not in the same league with piping aboard a foreign admiral or dignitary off the mole at Gibraltar. It was soon perceived that the Africa Squadron was nearly the nadir in prestige assignments in the Navy.

As will be seen, the Navy proceeded to reinterpret the new squadron's mission by adding its traditional protection of mercantile interests off Africa to the anti–slave trade mandate. In fact, there was some justification for this. American trade with Africa was growing significantly in this era. The market consisted of cheap manufactured goods, usually made in Britain, in return for numerous African products. Though native African products included small amounts of gold, ivory, hides, dyestuffs, hardwoods, and coffee, by far the largest percentage of exports was palm oil, a popular ingredient for wax and soaps.[18] The growth in this trade was phenomenal: in 1827 it was 4, 700 tons, and by the mid-1830s it was 14,000 tons. In the 1850s it would grow to more than 40,000 tons per year. [19]

The American portion of the legitimate African trade can be estimated by figures for the 1850s. Exports to African ports amounted to $1.3 million in 1855, which was about equivalent to U.S. exports to Holland, but exceeding those going to Puerto Rico. In the same year, about $400,000 was imported from British African colonies, plus $1.3 million from other African ports. This was more value than total American trade with Russia at the same time.[20] For the decade of the 1850s, American trade to Liberia and other African ports amounted to about $10 million in imports in American hulls, and $8.3 million in exports in American vessels.[21]

As to the illegitimate trade at this time, the statistics are extremely unreliable, as might be expected when dealing with sub-rosa and illicit activities. Furthermore, the statistics on the trade need to be distinguished between those slaves imported directly into the United States and those brought from Africa to other points in the Western Hemisphere, most notably Cuba and Brazil.

Despite exaggerated claims of early writers on this subject, direct imports of slaves into the United States were not numerous. According to an early estimate, something like 250,000 slaves were imported between 1807 and 1862. However, recent scholarship has reduced this estimate to about one thousand per year.[22] Another applicable statistic, by implication, was the number of *native* Africans in the United States, as numbered in the 1870 census: 1,984. [23] This latter statistic would be much more useful had the ages of these blacks been known.

The exact number of slaves brought into the Western Hemisphere tends also to be a hazy statistic. This is illustrated by the statistics for slaves brought into the two largest slave markets: Cuba and Brazil. Imports into these two havens had numbered a half-million in the 1830s, with a ratio of 2 to 1 (Brazil to Cuba). In Cuba, British consular estimates for 1859 ranged from twelve thousand to thirty thousand, and when the British published similar figures for 1860, the Spanish government protested that the totals were merely five thousand to six thousand.[24] This huge discrepancy illustrates well the vagueness of even the contemporary statistics. As to the trade with Brazil, after a relative decline in the early 1840s, it rose to a record fifty thousand per year for the remainder of the decade. These numbers are appalling in the raw sense, but they are made more so by the apparently accurate assessment that most of the ships engaged in the horrendous commerce were American-built.

Putting legs on this commerce was its immense profitability. One of the major traders of the era, Pedro Blanco, was reported to have said that if he was to "save *one* vessel out of *three* from capture, they [would] find the trade profitable. . . . This can easily be believed [the writer continued] when slaves can be purchased at Gallinas for less than twenty dollars *in trade* and sold for cash in Cuba for three hundred and fifty." [25]

Finally, the new squadron would out of necessity be in close and constant proximity with the Royal Navy's anti–slave trade unit. Of course the British had been early in the field, after their abolition of the trade in 1807. Though they had sent two vessels in a trial run as early as 1808, it was not until 1811 that a five-vessel squadron was sent to the West African coast. This unit was short lived due to the final phases of the Napoleonic Wars, and it was 1816 before a permanent squadron was in place.[26]

In the 1820s the squadron numbered around seven vessels, but it grew steadily, reaching around thirty ships in the 1840s. The number fluctuated with Parliament's funding and naval needs elsewhere. (The first steamer did not appear on station until 1844.)[27] Of course the Royal Navy was the largest in the world and had dominated the seas since Trafalgar, hence, its ability to field and maintain a substantial squadron off Africa.

The squadron made use of the Admiralty Court at Freetown, Sierra Leone to adjudicate and condemn seized vessels, and the freed blacks were returned there. The place was not a popular one due to the endemic sickness common to the coast. The saying among the British sailors was that there were standing orders for parties "employed digging graves" and "making coffins until further orders." Another common ditty applied to the whole of the slave coast: "Beware and take care of the Bight of Benin. There's one come out for forty goes in." For the crews decimated by yellow fever, malaria, and blackwater (dengue) fever, they were sent to Ascension Island or St. Helena for relief.[28]

The British influence on the slave trade cannot be underestimated: the at-sea activities of the squadron were accompanied by diplomatic pressure, and the resulting treaties made the Royal Navy for all practical purposes the "international police force" on the coast. This was based on Right of Search and Seizure treaties with the major powers—excepting the United States and to some extent, France. As with the United States, the French suspected the British were more interested in interfering with their mercantile trade than in suppressing the slavers.[29]

The seemingly omnipresent British cruisers and their often-unpredictable attitude and actions against suspected slavers under American colors would compose a singularly unique problem for the officers of the new squadron. Though the number of incidents involving British cruisers stopping American vessels—or those suspected of using American colors to avoid British notice—decreased after the American squadron was in place, it did not stop entirely, and diplomatic and semantic hair splitting would continue to keep tensions high during the ensuing years.

Making practical application of the factors relating to the West African slave trade came to the fore in late 1842, after the signing of the treaty. Setting up an anti–slave trade squadron would involve decisions about the number and types of vessels to be employed, the geographical boundaries of their cruising, the location of suitable supply and hospital depots, and the development of specific policy instructions for carrying out the squadron's assigned mission. Furthermore, the American officers would need instructions for dealing with the naval and diplomatic relationship between the U.S. and the British anti-slavery squadrons.

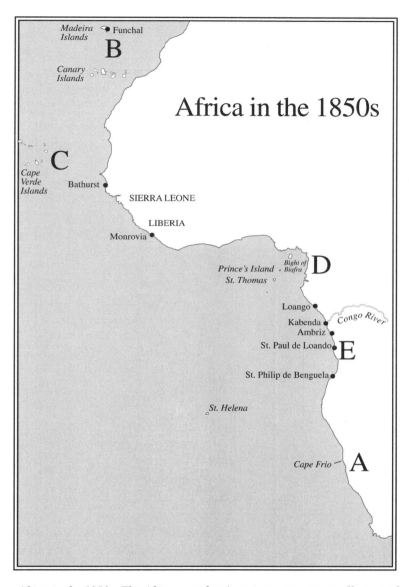

Africa in the 1850s. The Africa squadron's cruising area eventually ranged from Cape Frio in the south (about 18 degrees south latitude) [A], to Madeira [B] in the north. However, the squadron supply depot was in the Cape Verde Islands [C], approximately 2500 miles from the northern-most centers of the slave trade in the Bight of Biafra [D] and southward. The navy department did not move the depot location until 1859, when it was set up at St. Paul de Loando, in present-day Angola [E], about 8 degrees south latitude. At the same time the department put Madeira out of bounds for the squadron.
Original map in author's collection.

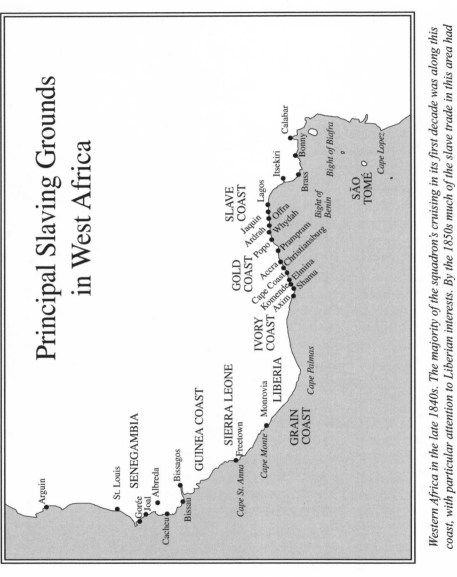

Principal Slaving Grounds
in West Africa

Arguin

SENEGAMBIA
St. Louis
Gorée
Joal
Albreda
Cacheu
Bissau
Bissagos

GUINEA COAST

SIERRA LEONE
Freetown
Cape St. Anna
Cape Monte

LIBERIA
Monrovia
GRAIN COAST
Cape Palmas

IVORY COAST

GOLD COAST
Axim
Shama
Komende
Elmina
Cape Coast
Christiansburg
Accra
Prampram
Popo

SLAVE COAST
Ardrah
Jaquin
Whydah
Offra
Lagos
Itsekiri

Brass
Bight of Benin

Bonny
Calabar
Bight of Biafra

SÃO TOMÉ
Cape Lopez

Western Africa in the late 1840s. The majority of the squadron's cruising in its first decade was along this coast, with particular attention to Liberian interests. By the 1850s much of the slave trade in this area had been eliminated by the British, based in their colony at Sierra Leone, as well as the Liberians. Original map in author's collection.

4

CAPT. MATTHEW C. PERRY AND THE FIRST AFRICA SQUADRON, 1843–1845

Secretary of the Navy Abel P. Upshur, a Virginian and a slaveholder, was now responsible for the task of creating a squadron within the parameters laid out in the Webster-Ashburton Treaty. Upshur had become the naval secretary under President John Tyler, in October 1841. He became known as an activist in the office. During his tenure, he instituted the department's first major reorganization and took significant steps toward adapting the service to steam powered warships, even to the point of subsidizing the construction of an experimental ironclad. Upshur established the Home Squadron and furthered reform in the education of naval officers. Added to his broad range of initiatives was the formation of the Africa anti–slave trade squadron.[1]

Upshur had a starting point for the latter task with letters on hand from Lieutenants Charles H. Bell and John S. Paine, lately from the African coast. Their report, which included the heretical idea of reciprocal search by American and British warships, emphasized small vessels. They recommended no less than fifteen—most of them lightly armed schooners—as a permanent patrol off Africa. Additionally, they suggested the utility of having a steamer in the squadron.[2] As the U.S. Navy possessed no more than four active schooners and two brigs at this time, and Congress was not likely to fund more construction, this recommendation fell flat.[3] The steam vessel recommendation was equally unrealistic, as there were only two commissioned steamers available at the time.[4] The reciprocal search idea was also an instant dead letter.

For other opinions on the new squadron, Upshur solicited advice

Secretary of the Navy Abel P. Upshur. Upshur, a Virginian in President Tyler's cabinet, was responsible for setting up the Navy's Africa squadron, as required by the Webster-Ashburton Treaty. Upshur essentially redefined the squadron's prime mission from suppression of the slave trade to the more traditional role of protection of American commerce off the coast of Africa.
Photo courtesy of the Naval Historical Center.

from senior naval officers and one of the respondents was Commander Louis M. Goldsborough, head of the Bureau of Provisions and Clothing. A more experienced sailor would have been difficult to find, as Goldsborough had thirty years of service and a tour of duty at the Navy's early hydrographic office.[5] Goldsborough's response included the description of the climate off Africa quoted previously, as well as the following observations on the proposed squadron:

> If the vessels [selected] be small, such as can carry not more than 10 to 15 weeks supply & the cruising ground be confined between the northern extremity of the slave coast & Cape Palmas, one depot at Sierra Leone or in its neighborhood would probably be sufficient, but should the cruising ground be extended as far as the Bights of Benin & Biafra, then a second depot at or about

the islands of Prince [today called Principe] or St. Thomas [Sao Tome] would become necessary. Should the cruising ground be extended still further so as to embrace the whole coast, comprehended between the northern limits . . . & the Cape of Good Hope, then a third depot, located at the latter place, would be found indispensable.

Capt. Matthew Calbraith Perry: First Flag Officer of the African squadron. Perry, later famous for the Japan Expedition, was diligent in instituting shipboard measures to combat the African "fever," but by the same token discouraged setting up a naval depot on the African coast itself; leaving the squadron dependent on a depot in the distant Cape Verde Islands.
Naval Historical Center.

Objections may be made to this multiplication of depots, but with small vessels & active cruising over such a range of sea, I do not see how they could well be reduced in number.

The number of men in the squadron which you propose sending . . . would be about 710. For that number, one storeship would be more than sufficient to keep each of the depots . . . supplied. She might after leaving [the African depots] touch on her return home at Rio de Janiero [*sic*], then deliver the remainder of her cargo [. . . to the Brazil squadron].

Supposing active & efficient cruising in *small vessels*, it would seem inadvisable to locate depots elsewhere than on the coast itself. The difficulties in getting to & from the islands which lie off the coast, even the Cape Verds [*sic*] which are the most contiguous, are such as to consume unavoidably, a great deal of time & this of itself appears to be a sufficient reason to deter us from adopting them as depots. In the event of serious & extended sickness . . . it might be highly advisable to run off the coast for change of climate and succor. Under such circumstances, Port [*sic*] Praya & St. Helena . . . would be most eligible places.

Concluding, Goldsborough noted that Monrovia had been suggested as a depot, in preference to Sierra Leone. He declined to recommend it, but on the grounds that he did not have sufficient information about the two places to do so.[6]

Goldsborough's November 1842 letter reveals a bit about the early thinking in the department regarding the squadron. First, it appears that the unit was to be composed of small vessels, as Goldsborough was not asked for information concerning the use of larger ships. By the same token, even including one frigate in the equation would have accounted for about 500 of the stated 710 personnel proposed for the squadron, leaving the balance of 210 to be apportioned among the four remaining vessels—an impossibility. This number was hardly sufficient for manning three ten-gun schooners. The proposed composition of the squadron at this point was, according to Upshur's annual report, two twenty-gun sloops-of-war plus three ten-gun brigs or schooners.[7] At any rate, it should be kept in mind that the Navy at this point had a surplus of sloops-of-war, and, as noted, only six active brigs and schooners. Furthermore, schooners were always in demand as dispatch and utility vessels for the squadrons, making it inadvisable to send them all to the African coast.

It should also be kept in mind that Goldsborough, as head of the Bureau of Provisions and Clothing was not being asked about the number of vessels or their types, but for his thoughts on the necessary supply depots and their locations. He rather pointedly objected to depots on the outlying islands, and this is of interest in light of the actual events.

These events included the monitoring hand of Congress, the authorizer of the annual naval appropriations. The cost of the squadron and its support as estimated and proposed by Upshur was around $440,000 for the vessels, $40,000 for initial repairs, and $240,000 annually for upkeep. Members of Congress from the western states—Thomas Hart Benton and others—objected, almost by habit, to naval expenditures in general, and they had been further displeased by the fact that the department had run out of funds in May 1842. In the event, the new budget was barely larger than the previous year's.[8] Indeed, Upshur had reassured the powers that be that it was "not proposed to increase the navy" to meet the treaty obligation.[9]

Final decisions on the composition of the squadron, its leadership, and the location of a depot were not forthcoming until early 1843, in part because the congressional appropriations had yet to be made.[10] On March 1, 1843, Upshur wrote and informed Capt. Matthew Calbraith Perry, then commandant of the Brooklyn Navy Yard, of his selection as squadron commander, effective March 10.[11] The frigate *Macedonian*, sloop-of-war *Saratoga,* and brig *Porpoise* were designated as three of the squadron's vessels, and Porto Praya (present day Pria) in the Cape Verde Islands was selected for a squadron depot.[12]

By the day of Perry's appointment as flag officer,* he was writing to Capt. Isaac Mayo on the frigate *Macedonian*, directing the fitting out of that vessel for duty on the Africa Squadron.[13] The flurry of missives which

---

* "Flag officer" was the official designation for a squadron commander in the pre-Civil War Navy. This was not a rank but a position, and the holder would simply drop the title when relieved of the duty. The terminology was necessary, as the rank of admiral would not be authorized until the Civil War. There were only three ranks in this era: lieutenant, commander, and captain.

followed reflected Perry's apparent enthusiasm for the assignment, as well as his conscientious nature. Having been in the service since the War of 1812 and from a noted naval family—Matthew was the younger brother of Oliver Hazard Perry of Battle of Lake Erie fame—Perry was an obvious choice for the assignment. However, as Africa was not considered a prestige assignment, there was some speculation that his selection had more to do with his family's party affiliation, which happened to be the opposite of the current Whig regime.[14]

Perry may well have solicited the assignment, as he considered himself one of the Navy's reformers and forward thinkers of the era, and a "liberal" in parlance of the time. He may have had a proprietary interest also. He and members of his family had long been associated with the American Colonization Society, and they supported its aims. Indeed, Perry had volunteered for service on the *Cyane*, which had escorted the first group of freed blacks to the African coast in 1820.[15]

As to the ships under Perry's command, in addition to the three vessels selected by March 20, a fourth, the smaller sloop-of-war *Decatur*, was also designated for the unit; however, it would not join the squadron until late summer.[16] Apparently the final decisions on the squadron's ships were not in place until at least mid-April, and the direction of Perry's thinking was obvious in letters of March 14 and April 7. In the former he requested the steamer *Union*, as "the services of one or more small steamer . . . will be almost indispensable to the performance of duties required . . ." In the latter note, he wrote Secretary Upshur asking for "one or two" small vessels: "By their easy draft of water and rapid movements, the frequency of visits to the various settlements . . . might be multiplied . . ." He also mentioned their advantages: effectiveness as consorts for the larger vessels, freer ventilation and therefore healthier habitat for the crews, and the possibility of disguising them as slavers. He noted that their light armament might not "cope always successfully with the large and heavily armed slavers . . . ," but they could travel in company with the squadron's larger ships. He specifically suggested the schooner *Phoenix*, a two-gun schooner built in 1841 that was operating in Florida waters.[17]

In the end, of course, these requests were denied. Perry may well have rued the request for the little steamer *Union*, however, had she been added to the squadron. She had visited New York early in 1843 and had apparently been seen there by Perry. The vessel was an experiment powered by Lt. W. W. Hunter's horizontal paddle wheels, a misbegotten alternative to the screw propeller. Though early reports on the vessel were enthusiastic, she proved horrendously uneconomical as well as unseaworthy and her service life amounted to less than two years before her engines were replaced.[18] The *Union*'s situation reflected the flux in early steam technology of the era, and particularly in the United States Navy at this point, all of which pointed to the unsuitability of steamers for extended overseas duties such as the Africa Squadron.

The squadron's vessels were an interesting group, though they were not necessarily appropriate for the task at hand. The largest was the second-class frigate *Macedonian*, one of only two small thirty-six-gun frigates in the service. She had been constructed in 1836 as a "rebuild" of the captured 1812 British frigate of the same name, and she retained some of the same dimensions and appearance as the British frigate, including her original figurehead. Her presence in the U.S. Navy symbolized to the British a thirty-year-old defeat at the hands of these same Yankees . . . and the ship may well have been selected for that very reason, given the large Royal Navy presence off Africa. She remained in the service until the 1870s.[19]

Second in size was the first-class sloop-of-war *Saratoga*, carrying twenty-two guns. She was fresh from the builders at Portsmouth Navy Yard but had nearly been scrapped from the squadron on her first cruise: the day after she sailed, a March gale caught and dismasted her. Back in service two months later, she would prove a longtime asset to the Navy, remaining in use until 1907.[20] At the beginning of the cruise, *Saratoga* was Perry's flagship, rather than the larger *Macedonian*, probably as a matter of convenience, as the latter vessel was refitted and sailed from Norfolk and Perry was based at Brooklyn at the time.

Decatur, a sixteen-gun sloop, was placed in service in 1840. After an initial stint on the Brazil station, she was refitted at Norfolk and recommissioned for Africa on August 5, 1843. She remained in service until 1865.[21]

Finally, the ten-gun brig *Porpoise* had already begun a notable career. Built in 1836, she had just returned from service with Wilkes's Exploration Expedition, a four-year odyssey during which the little vessel had circumnavigated the globe. After a needed refit she was again at sea. She remained in service until 1854.[22]

It has been averred by other writers on the Navy's Africa Squadron that the Navy sent their "decrepit" vessels and those in "bad condition" for African service, and this practice was part of the Navy's "deliberate attempt" to avoid enforcing the treaty.[23] These four vessels reflect the opposite: two were nearly new; the others were six or seven years old. *Porpoise* was the shortest lived, while two others had twenty years of useful service remaining, and the *Saratoga* soldiered on past the turn of the century. As to the selection of Porto Praya for a depot, Perry's thinking was indicated in a letter to Goldsborough: " . . . [provisions] cannot be well preserved at either of the American settlements on the coast, and that there is no place short of Port [*sic*] Praya suitable for a depot." [24] Two further considerations applied: there was an American consul in residence at the place and the port authorities allowed stores to be landed without special arrangements.[25]

A year later, other considerations had solidified Perry's opinion about establishing depots on the African coast: "There is no part of the west coast of Africa from the Gambia to the Equator where the annual mortality of unacclimated white persons living on shore would not be in the present uncleared state of the country from 30 to 50 percent . . . Hence there is no place suitable for a Naval depot." He continued, remarking that "such establishment would result in having men on shore . . . [and] take fever . . . [the British] never permit their men to land, but employ kroo [native] men." Further, he reiterated that there was no place in Liberia that could supply even a sloop-of-war and "cattle as well as other animals suffer with the fevers of the climate."[26]

It appears that there is some question about who was responsible for selecting Porto Praya as the squadron depot, though Secretary Upshur may have originally suggested it. Perry, in the letter mentioned above, also indicated that "the system of rotation of cruising so wisely established by the department enables one of the vessels . . . to be almost constantly passing along the coast of Liberia . . . ," a reference to Upshur's original instructions, which directed that a vessel be sent back from the coast to the depot every two months for rest and replenishment.[27] One of the contributing factors in the decision in favor of an offshore depot, in this case Porto Praya, may have been the fact that, unlike the small-vessel concept discussed earlier by Goldsborough, larger ships were assigned to the unit. Hence, their larger capacities for stores and provisions may have made a distant, offshore depot appear practicable. In any event, this selection of Porto Praya as the only squadron depot would have a crucial impact on the history of the unit.

These major decisions formed a backdrop for the hundreds of minor and immediately practical tasks that comprised preparing a sailing naval squadron and about 750 men for extended duty overseas. Perry, in the three months before the ships set sail, dealt with preparing the ships for sea, accumulating all the necessities to supply the men and keep them healthy, attending to the actual recruiting, and establishing squadron procedures and regulations.

Probably the most unusual set of preparations was the institution of a regime to deal with the dreaded "fever." Perry mandated an elaborate set of rules and procedures that he had actually used twenty years earlier on the *Cyane*, off Africa. He wrote at that time that the causes of the "diseases incident to that climate [were] exposure to the night air, the meridian Sun, intemperance, and fatigue. . . . " Consequently (though sometimes inexplicably), the men were to "wear flannel" and the officers were "never to allow them to sleep on deck, or to remain in wet cloathes [*sic*] for a moment if it can possibly be avoided, to pay the strictest attention to their cleanliness, and never to turn them out in the night unless absolutely necessary, to have fires burning upon the Birth [*sic*] deck a part of the day, for the purpose of dispersing the foul and introducing fresh air. To fumigate and, whitewash, the Birth [*sic*] deck every day, and to use every method of exhilirating the spirits of the crew . . . "[28]

Of course, this regimen was not original to Perry. A British physician, Sir Gilbert Blane, had written them in a medical journal in 1815. Another, earlier writer had added prohibitions against sleeping on and anchoring near any shore from whence "noxious exhalations" might emanate . . . such as those mangrove littorals of West Africa. Of course, any effective results of these directives were purely coincidental in the light of modern medical knowledge that the mosquito was the dangerous carrier to be avoided. From this perspective, the most effective portion of this regimen was anchoring off shore —beyond the mosquito's flying range. This was, again, coincidence, but in 1842 it was the latest medical advice.[29]

Accordingly, Perry directed Captain Mayo on *Macedonian* that it was "absolutely necessary that the hold of the vessel should be broken out and thoroughly cleaned . . . the ballast removed, cleansed and restowed,

not the smallest particle of matter should be left that could possibly cre-
ate foul air; a large quantity of . . . lime should be thrown among the
ballast and under the water tanks and every thing should be several times
whitewashed; this lime serves to prevent any accumulation of putrid matter for a good while."

Then Perry wrote that all the vessels of the squadron should have
duplicate sets of awnings, made to "haul down" to the hammock rails
with openings left for the rigging. Canvas hoods were to be fashioned for
the hatches to keep out rain. Then he mentioned looking for a band, a
chaplain, and a "good strong seine," as the "comfort of the men will be
much advanced by the catching of fish among the islands." All this, no
doubt, was part and parcel with "exhilirating the spirits of the crew."[30]

Perry then set about obtaining flannel for the crewmen, and one
assumes it would be lightweight material to, as he wrote, "prevent sudden perspiration on the legs . . . " These garments were "jackets and
trousers . . . longer than usual in order to cover the loins" to be used for
their night dresses . . . Their small cost would enable each person to have
a sufficient supply for change in rainy weather. Perry ordered 1,500 each
of jackets and trousers, in blue, providing two pairs for each sailor. [31]
Interestingly, Goldsborough replied that regulations did not allow blue
outfits, so Perry suggested supplying the material only, and the sailors
would make their own. Further correspondence with Goldsborough concerned Perry's request for "white" undergarments, because the traditional
red would "deceive the officers as to how often they were changed . . .
frequent changes [being] necessary for cleanliness . . . " Goldsborough
resisted this idea also, indicating red garments did not need to be washed
as often. Perry relented "for the present."[32]

On the other hand, Perry was more insistent about other portions of
his intended anti-fever regimen. The chief of the Bureau of Medicine and
Surgery was contacted about a "request for drying stoves" for the vessels. These were to be used constantly in the lower decks "during the
rains" and cost about six dollars each.[33] Shortly after this letter, Perry
requested an order to make the stoves for *Porpoise* and *Saratoga* and, as
late as May 11, he wrote Upshur reiterating his request.[34] The last appeal
finally had positive results, as one squadron officer later noted the use of
anthracite stoves between decks on the ships.[35]

The "air quality" between decks came in for another directive from

Perry: Fumigation by "Fuze Balls" made of "proportional parts of gun-powder, camphor, nitre, and chopped match rope, the whole mixed with vinegar and made into balls of ¼ lb. weight . . . " were to be used on lower decks—the balls to be placed "in a pitch kettle having a cover perforated by holes and in this way burnt . . . two or three men standing by with water to prevent accident by fire, and another . . . with . . . vinegar . . . to throw upon the blaze." All this was to be done with all hatches and tarpaulins in place "to prevent its escape into open air" and thus it "destroys or neutralizes any foul air . . . " In event of sickness appearing on board, this was to be done twice a day.[36] It seems the sailors were to be in for "foul air" regardless of the source.

Perry's correspondence reveals other facets of his concern for the health of his crews. He requested a storeship (*Lexington*) be detailed to Porto Praya as a hospital ship. No doubt for the morale of the crews, he suggested small copper boilers be made for making coffee and cocoa. To ensure the sailors would have no reason to go ashore, he requested permission to set up a "system" for hiring "kroomen"—the coastal natives—to handle the work as "messengers, Interpreters, Boatmen, and in communicating with the shore, in bringing off provisions, water, wood & etc. and in all these services of exposure to the climate; which the constitution of the white man is incapable of bearing." The system to be set up would regulate the number hired for each class of vessel, ranging from "20 nor more than 30" for frigates, down to "no less" than six for the smallest vessels.[37]

Another unusual request related to Perry's plans was one to Upshur asking permission to enroll "a few black seamen and ordinary seamen" for all vessels of the squadron. In Perry's opinion, the blacks were "more enduring in hot climates and are very serviceable to act as holders and as crews for the launches." Upshur responded immediately, and four days later Perry wrote the commander of the *Saratoga* that he was authorized to have "shipped for the Saratoga under your command fifteen or twenty black seamen. . . . You are therefore directed to fill up the complement of the ship of picked seamen of color not exceeding the number specified." [38] This order may well have been unprecedented, probably the earliest instance where black men, specifically, were actively recruited for the Navy. (We do not know, however, how many of these men were new recruits as opposed to blacks already on the Navy rolls.)

Besides the minutiae of Perry's health plans for the vessels, other more routine fitting-out tasks consumed these months. In March, Perry requested that four modern Paixhans-type shell guns be shipped in place of four of *Macedonian*'s eighteen-pounders, due to the "small caliber of the main deck guns . . . compared with those in general use at this time."[39] As the standard frigate's deck guns were twenty-four-pounders, *Macedonian* was certainly under-gunned, though how the more powerful battery would materially effect the anti-slave patrol mission is open to question. But then, Perry had just recently been in charge of testing these new weapons off Sandy Hook, and they were evidence of the Navy's modernity.

A few other time-consuming items rounded out the preparations: In April there were "certain alterations" to the internal arrangements of *Saratoga*. About the same time, Perry was informed that a "light poop" deck was being built on the quarterdeck of the *Macedonian*. Finally, as mentioned earlier, the day after *Saratoga* sailed from Portsmouth, New Hampshire, she was dismasted in a gale. This was March 17: it was May 3 before the ship finally departed for New York to complete her complement. The disaster changed at least one element of Perry's plans. *Saratoga* had been designated to transport supplies to Porto Praya, then the task fell on *Porpoise*. This arrangement was apparently unsatisfactory, as the schooner *Reinzi* was, in the end, contracted by the department to do the job. In any event, Perry did not break out his pennant on *Saratoga* until June 5, 1843, on departure from New York for Africa.[40]

The secretary of the Navy's instructions to Flag Officer Perry are relevant at this point, as the squadron finally made sail for the coast of Africa. They read, in part:

> The rights of our citizens engaged in lawful commerce are under the protection of our flag; and it is the chief purpose as well as the chief duty of our naval power to see that these rights are not improperly abridged or invaded.
>
>   . . . It is to be borne in mind, that while the United States sincerely desire the suppression of the slave trade, and design to

exert their power, in good faith, for the accomplishment of that object, they do not regard the success of their efforts as their paramount interest, nor as their paramount duty. They are not prepared to sacrifice to it any of their rights as an independent nation; nor will the object in view justify the exposure of their own people to injurious and vexatious interruptions in the prosecution of their lawful pursuits.[41]

This directive is probably the single most important document concerning the American anti-slavery squadron. It set a precedent and was passed down with little change as the squadron commanders succeeded each other on the station. (As will be seen, they were almost intact when transmitted to Capt. William Inman, the last commander of the unit, in 1859.) The most surprising provision, considering the purpose for which the squadron was formed, was the statement that the "chief purpose" and "duty" was that the "rights of our citizens in lawful commerce" were not to be "improperly abridged." Though this statement is couched in general terms about American naval power, its location in the document *before* mention of the slave trade makes the priority of protection of American commerce obvious. And, in fact, the phrases are pointed squarely at the British, the chief source of interference with American trade on the African coast.

Furthermore, in the paragraph dealing with suppressing the slave trade, it is, without any subtlety whatever, subordinated to protection of Americans in their "lawful pursuits." Thus, in two paragraphs, the secretary of the Navy turned the purpose of the squadron on its head. The official instructions to the unit's commander effectively discounted to a secondary position the purpose for which the unit was formed.

It should be noted, however, that in the political climate of this era, diminution of the anti–slave trade aspect of the squadron was not unpopular. Even the outspoken anti-slavery activist John Quincy Adams continued to harbor the belief that the British, in the Webster-Ashburton Treaty, were more concerned with furthering their mercantile objectives than in suppressing the slave trade. Therefore, Adams registered no objections to Secretary Upshur's emphasis in his instructions to Perry.[42]

The practical implications of these words for the men enforcing the nation's laws at sea are worth noting. From an accountability standpoint, it would appear that lack of success on the part of the squadron commanders in carrying out the anti–slave patrol mission would not be of vital consequence. On the other hand, failure to prevent a certain foreign power from stopping American merchantmen on the high seas, regardless of the reason given for the "interference," would constitute a serious failure on the part of the American squadron commander.

The instructions, which, incidentally, contained no reference to official dealings with Liberia, also established the cruising grounds for the squadron: from Madeira and the Canary Islands to the Bight of Biafra, and as far west as longitude 30 degrees. (There was some leeway on the southern extent of the area, as Upshur had indicated earlier to Josiah Tatnall that "if occasion should require, [cruising] still further south" was permissible.[43]) The depot was to be at Porto Praya in the southern Cape Verde Islands, about four hundred miles due west of the nearest point on the coast of Africa, near Dakar.[44] Thus the distances were formidable: it was one thousand miles north from Porto Praya to Madeira, and eight hundred to Sierra Leone from Porto Praya. To put this in perspective, with a steady wind, the ability to sail directly between the latter two places, and a typical average of seven knots, the trip was a little more than six days sailing. As will be seen, a steady seven-knot wind was not something that could be planned on, and sailing was rarely, if ever, as the crow would fly.

With the secretary of the Navy's instructions in hand, and presumably not without some trepidation at the uncertainties that lay ahead, Perry sailed from New York in *Saratoga*. The brig *Porpoise* had preceded him; Upshur had ordered her to sail across the Atlantic on January 28, "as soon" as the vessel was ready.[45] She actually departed on April 17, and the remaining vessels would rendezvous with Perry in September at the Cape Verdes.[46]

Perry arrived at Santa Cruz, Tenerife, in the Canary Islands in June 1843, nineteen days out of New York. He had bypassed a stop at Madeira in his haste to take up station. The passage had begun propitiously with *Saratoga* logging five hundred miles in two days, averaging about ten knots. However, sickness had set in and he lost one crewman, owing, wrote Perry, to the "dampness" of the ship.[47]

At Tenerife he met another "vexatious" delay: the authorities put the vessel in an eight-day quarantine. Despite his protests, Perry remained there until July 22, during which time he wrote yet another letter to Upshur requesting a storeship to be assigned as a hospital and storage vessel for "convalescents" at Porto Praya. During this short interlude, Perry also wrote John Foote, the commander of the British Africa Squadron, expecting "mutual acts of courtesy and friendship" between the squadrons and suggesting they establish a mutual code of "private signals."[48]

Once the quarantine was lifted, Perry allowed the crew liberty, in rotation, and took the opportunity to fumigate the *Saratoga*. That done, he sailed to the Cape Verdes, where he received a reply from Foote who agreed to cooperate as well as establish the signal code.[49] After taking on water and dealing with the Portuguese authorities to set up a depot at Porto Praya, Perry sailed for Liberia on July 22. Considering he had arrived at the Canaries around June 20, waited more than a week in quarantine, sailed some nine hundred miles from thence to the Cape Verdes, and dealt with the officialdom at Porto Praya, it appears Perry had been quite efficient with his time during this period. [50]

Perry arrived at Mesurado Roads, Liberia, on August 1, where *Porpoise* was already anchored. Here, Perry paid his respects to the president of Liberia, Joseph J. Roberts, rendering an eleven-gun salute and entertaining him and his cabinet in the ship's cabin. There, the conversations veered from diplomatic niceties to a discussion of the problem with the coastal tribes that had been plundering American merchant vessels. Next they turned to the dangers of remaining on that shore during this season, where the heavy swells could roll a vessel "scuppers under" and make transportation to the shore in small boats nearly impossible. No doubt Perry also discussed the state of his ships, which he described in a letter to the States: "The wear and tear of vessels on this station is very great owing to the prevalenced [*sic*] of strong winds and rain and the want of harbors of shelter." [51] Due to these conditions, it was decided that dealing with the misbehaving tribes would have to wait until November.[52] As far as the slave trade was concerned, Perry learned from the locals that the United States flag had not been used in "two years by any vessel in the slave trade."[53]

With the diplomatic hurdle run, Perry returned to Porto Grande, St. Vincent Island, in the northern Cape Verdes, to rendezvous with *Macedonian*, Captain Mayo, and *Decatur*, under Cdr. Joel Abbot. Here Perry shifted his pennant to *Macedonian* on September 9, 1843.[54] At this point the entire squadron was together for the first time. Shortly thereafter,

Perry allowed his commanding officers some leeway in application of the obviously stringent health regimen. If permission was given by the ship's surgeon, the crew was to be allowed relief from the constant fumigating. The requirement for frequent bathing could also be "intermitted" by surgeon's orders. On a minor note, the officers were allowed to wear straw hats, rather than the standard wool caps with visors.[55]

The squadron returned to the African coast and anchored at Cape Palmas, southwest of Monrovia, on October 19. Shortly after his arrival, Perry wrote letters to the local missionaries, desiring information about their relations with the natives, names of tribes among which they worked, and their observations on the treatment of traders by the natives. Most important, they were asked to relay to him information on the state of the slave trade in their areas.[56]

Once on the coast they visited the "Maryland" colony, which had been settled in 1827, with aims similar to that of the original enclave at Monrovia. (By 1838, three other settlements had been added on the coast, supported by other colonization societies in the United States; all were eventually folded into the nation of Liberia.)[57] After firing a twelve-gun salute and calling on the local dignitaries, the squadron returned to Monrovia, where they embarked President Roberts and other dignitaries and proceeded to Sinou (present day Greensville), between Cape Palmas and Monrovia, where the "Mississippi" branch was settled. This visit was a show of force to face down the Fishmen, local tribesmen who had heretofore been active as middlemen in the slave trade and whose enter-prises were failing due to the influence of the Liberians. Perry was there to make inquiries into the murder of two American crewmen from the schooner *Edward Burley*.[58]

Perry's approach to the negotiation (a *palaver* in the local language) smacks of a similar scene ten years later in Japan. As Purser Horatio Bridge described it:

> At 9 A.M., thirteen boats left the different ships, armed, and hav-ing about seventy-five marines on board, besides the sailors. En-tering the river, with flags flying and muskets glittering, the boats lay on their oars until all were in a line, and then pulled at once for the beach, as if about to charge a hostile battery. The manoeu-vre [*sic*] ... seemed to give great satisfaction to some thirty colonists

and fifty naked natives . . . assembled on the beach. The officers and marines were landed, and formed in line. . . . The music then struck up, while the Commodore and Governor Roberts stept [*sic*] ashore, and the whole detachment marched to the palaver-house.[59]

This seems rather overdoing it on Perry's part, but no doubt it was to hammer down a point: the U.S. Navy now was present—in force—off Africa, and the Liberians were special objects of its purview. (And, of course, the other "virtual" audience to be impressed was the British.)

The outcome of the negotiation was not that the murders were unjustified, but that the American captain had overstepped himself. He had kidnapped a number of natives in retaliation for a minor infraction by the tribesmen. In any event, the upshot was that the friendly tribes destroyed the Fishmen's village and ran them out of the area.[60]

The negotiations concluded with fine speeches, including one in which Perry pledged to see that justice was done evenhandedly in future disputes of this nature. President Roberts responded, and ritual gift giving concluded the proceedings.[61] The entire incident could be seen as simply defending American mercantile interests in the area, but the blow was also against the coastal tribe of middlemen in the slave trade. (It is noteworthy that the "assault" maneuver at the beach would have failed had it been attempted earlier, when the giant swells endangered any vessel approaching the beach.)

Perry's next object was settlement of yet other murders of American merchant seamen, news of which had reached the department before the squadron's departure. Two years previously, the Fishmen had murdered the captain and entire crew of the Salem schooner *Mary Carver* off Little Berebee, east of Cape Palmas. Perry set off with his squadron to punish this piratical "outrage" against American citizens and interests.

Going ashore with around two hundred men, Perry called together the local leaders and a major "palaver" ensued with, as one writer put it, "a great deal of lying on the part of the natives." Perry became disgusted with the dissembling of "King Ben Krako," headman of the offending tribe, and ordered the Marine Guard to approach. A shot rang out and a melee and chase ensued. Perry himself attempted to prevent Krako's escape by seizing his loincloth. Captain Mayo brought down Krako with a bayonet and the Fishmen were driven away. Their village and, later, three others participating in the piracy were burned by landing parties, with the men ordered to destroy property but to spare lives. There were no American casualties and a treaty was signed shortly afterward whereby the other native leaders—who now agreed that Krako was a "very bad man"—agreed to stop molesting American ships and missionaries.[62]

With the threat to American merchant seamen ended and secured with treaties, the immediate objects of the squadron's sortie to the African coast were completed. This coincided with a shortage of supplies, and Perry turned his ship west to Sierra Leone and then to Porto Praya via Cape Mesurado in December 1843 and early 1844, while the other vessels dispersed.[63] It is noteworthy that the squadron's surgeon reported on December 21 that the men's health was generally good, but they were suffering from "general debility" due to the heat of the climate.[64]

After restocking as best he could at Porto Praya, Perry on *Macedonian* returned to the coast in February, visiting Goree (now part of Senegal) near Cape Verde and the Gambia River. The news that the storeship sent from the States had been wrecked resulted in Perry's orders to sail to Funchal, Madeira, where food, as well as horse races and fine wine, could be had.[65] After two weeks at Madeira, there was a visit to the Canary Islands and then a return to Porto Praya in May 1844. In June and July, Perry was on the coast again at Monrovia, Cape Palmas, and Grand Berebee. The latter place, about two hundred miles east of Monrovia, was the farthest "down the coast" Perry ventured on *Macedonian* during his tour commanding with the squadron.

After a stop at Porto Praya at the end of July, a second trip was made to the Canaries, returning to the Cape Verdes in mid-September. November to mid-December was spent in and out of Porto Praya, in what today would be termed "training missions": out to sea to "exercise the great guns," practice small arms and short sword drills, etc. Perry's last trip to the coast was a short visit to Goree in mid-December 1844. Afterwards, he remained at the Cape Verdes Islands until turning over his command.[66]

Meanwhile, to follow the other vessels of the squadron, *Decatur*, under Joel Abbott, moved eastward and southward from Cape Palmas, sailing close to the shore. She arrived at the mouth of the Gaboon River, just above the equator, January 18. There, Abbott picked up a response to Perry's inquiry among the missionaries. William Walker, of the American Board of Commissioners for Foreign Missions, wrote: "The slave factories are on the west side of the river . . . sometimes 3 factories at a TIME. . . . probably from two to three thousand slaves carried out of the river anualy [*sic*] . . . It does not appear that the trade is carried on here under Am. Colours—though it is said by one who has been extensively engaged in the business that all their vessels are American built. The trade . . . is very dull at present & the people here say there are no slaves to be had at some of these places."[67]

Abbott then returned westward, arriving at Monrovia late in March. Here occurred an instructive example of Anglo-American cooperation, abetted by new technology. HBM *Penelope*, a large twenty-two-gun steam frigate recently converted from sail, lay at anchor there under Captain William Jones, the new commodore of the British Africa Squadron, which numbered twenty-two vessels. Jones informed Abbott that an American vessel was at Gallinas, more than one hundred miles west of Monrovia, which "might be going to take slaves." Jones very generously offered to "get up steam so as to start about sundown & will place your vessel at Gallinas at daylight tomorrow morning. . . . so about 6 o'clock P.M. the *Penelope* took the Decatur in tow, and although the night was very thick, dark & rainy . . . at about 7 A.M. we were dropped at the Gallinas & let go anchor close to the brig . . ." The thirteen hour tow had averaged over eight knots—no small feat in 1844—but yielded nothing: the suspect brig was the *Lima*, a legitimate trader from Kennebunk, Maine. Abbott informed Perry that Captain Jones expressed interest in meeting the American commodore and in further cooperation between the squadrons.[68] This small incident certainly highlights at least one "might have been"—the utility of paddle steamers on the African station.

Decatur then left the coast and Abbott recorded that the passage to Porto Praya was "unpleasant" with "no favorable winds" and was several days becalmed. "We have literally beat the whole way," he complained, and noted that all the white paint on the ship was a "light mud" color.[69]

After a short stay at the Cape Verdes, Abbott sailed southeast again in late June. This passage took *Decatur* as far as Loango, south of the equator and nearly to the Congo River. There, in late August, they gave chase to a suspected Spanish slaver. She "stood off, set skysails & crowded all sail. I gave chase. . . . After several hours chase finding I could not overhaul her . . . [and] stood for the land." This apparently was Abbott's only serious encounter with the adversary, and he then turned back north. By the time he reached the western coast of Africa, the heavy swells had set in and he wrote that one of the bullocks had died . . . some thought from seasickness. At the end of this cruise Abbott reported he had anchored sixty-one times since leaving Cape Mesurado, and, since leaving the U.S., "one-hundred & ninety times." [70] This was in the space of about fourteen months, a statistic that indicates a great number of short passages. He had also taken his ship farther south on the coast of Africa than any other vessel of Perry's squadron.

About a month later came *Porpoise*, under Lt. Thomas T. Craven, skirting the coast. She was ordered from Porto Praya on a four-month cruise if provisions allowed.* It was a routine cruise until Craven fell in with the Baltimore-built brig *Uncas* off Gallinas. On March 1, she was stopped and a short inspection revealed no slaves but a host of irregularities. The vessel had been registered at New Orleans with a crew of eight, and had made Havana where those were replaced by seven Danes and Italians, all with false names, and an Italian master with U.S. citizenship. She sailed from Monrovia with three passengers, one of who was "Castro" a "noted slave dealer," and cargo "suited to the slave marts." She had sold her cargo at Gallinas and had gratings for her hatches.

Josiah Tatnall, Perry's flag captain, noted that the vigilance of the Royal Navy brig *Ferret* had prevented her from loading her slave cargo. Indeed, officers from the British sloop *Alert* had boarded the vessel in February and found a host of irregularities, but they had foregone seizing the ship as it might "cause an unpleasant correspondence" between the two governments.[71]

However, Craven learned that on the last day of December the vessel's master had been murdered. Though the ship's papers were in order, the murder itself was sufficient cause to warrant her seizure and dispatch with a prize crew to New Orleans for adjudication. Evidence was insufficient, however, and the case was dismissed.[72]

Porpoise subsequently cruised with *Decatur* back to Cape Mesurado and Cape Mount, returning to Porto Praya late in April. Subsequently,

---

* Craven had replaced Captain Lewis after the latter had, without explanation, taken his leave of *Porpoise* at Porto Praya. Lewis is listed in the 1847 register of officers as having been on furlough since this date in 1843. Whatever arrangements had been made with the department for this had apparently not been communicated to Perry.

the brig sailed to Funchal and then the Canaries. On June 12, the vessel was back at Porto Praya. From June 28 through early October, she cruised on the coast as far east as Cape Palmas, at one point visiting the notorious slave operation run by Theodore Canot at Cape Mount. She made her last call at Porto Praya on October 16, and was back at Sandy Hook in mid-November.[73]

Perry wrote after *Porpoise*'s capture of *Uncas* that there must be a "want of proper vigilance at Havanna [*sic*] and perhaps at the Ports of the United States . . . in suffering a vessel to clear as the Uncas did from New Orleans." He went on to complain that the process of transmuting vessels from legal American merchant ships to slave traders on the coast under another flag "is the work of a moment." Once this administrative step was done the vessel would shortly be on the way to "Havannah" [*sic*] with a full cargo of slaves. Once the vessel was away from the coast the "risk of capture is removed."[74]

Also in March 1844, Perry wrote Secretary of the Navy David Henshaw that the "sales of vessels to be employed as slavers are not infrequent . . . though the transfers now generally take place south of the Equator, and without the limits . . . of the squadron, which is perfectly well known to slave dealers through their numerous agents along the coast . . . [the] whereabouts of the cruisers on the stations—of whatever nation, their respective force, rig, rate of sailing, appearance, etc." In consequence, Perry requested that the squadron's cruising grounds be extended "as far south as the most southern slave mart."[75]

Furthermore, Perry noted: "I cannot learn from all my inquiries that a single American vessel has for some years been engaged directly in the purchase and exportation of slaves from Africa, the only participation . . .is the sale of their vessels and cargoes to slavers."

In the same letter, Perry relayed to Henshaw that the British had informed him that they were assigning thirty fast vessels, including eleven steamers, to Africa, and that the French were establishing two coaling depots on the coast to supply their own vessels. This was, of course, in great contrast to the four American vessels, all of which were sailing ships. To make matters worse, Perry described *Macedonian* and *Porpoise* as "extremely dull" sailers, though he admitted that *Saratoga* and *Decatur* were "very fair" in that regard. Shortly after this he reminded the secretary that Upshur's "original design" had called for relieving the squadron vessels at "eighteen months or two years."[76] Perry had earlier in the same month requested he be relieved before the end of his second year on station, citing the "debilitating effects of the climate" on his health.[77]

The capture of the *Uncas* was the high point—such as it was—of Perry's command of the Africa Squadron. The low point was late in 1844 after the sloop-of-war *Preble*, a sister ship to *Decatur*, had joined the squadron. Her arrival on the coast was coincident with a threatened native attack on the British colony at Bathurst on the Gambia River. Heeding their call for assistance, Perry sent *Preble*. The brig's presence sufficed to stem the uprising . . . but at a great cost.[78]

Whether her commander, Lt. Thomas Freelon, was aware of Perry's health-related strictures or not, he certainly failed to heed them. He anchored for thirteen days within one-quarter mile of the shore and had the crew painting ship and sleeping on deck (wrote the squadron surgeon). Thus, they were exposed to the "verticle [*sic*] rays of the sun" and the "miasm of mangrove swamps and ricefields." The resulting outbreak left forty-nine sick and unfit for duty by mid-November 1844. By January, half her crew was at the naval hospital at Porto Grande, suffering from an "exceedingly obstinate" disease for which there was a limited supply of "quinine & other febrifuge." By early 1845, fifteen men had to be sent back to the States unfit for duty, and half of her crew had been replaced by men from other vessels of the squadron.[79] In total there were ninety cases of fever and nineteen deaths in a crew of 144.[80]

The *Saratoga*'s movements since the Berebee incident were similar to *Decatur*'s, though she did not venture as far south. After the return to Porto Praya in January 1844, she went on to Madeira, arriving January 21. She was back in Porto Praya about a month later and at Monrovia on March 3. Then she headed east down the coast, slowly, anchoring at, among other sites, Grand Berebee, Grand Lahou, Bassam, Assinee River, Axim, El Mina, Cape Coast, and Accra. From there she raised the island of St. Thomas, and from thence visited the Gaboon River, almost to the equator, near present day Libreville.

Departing from the Gaboon River at the end of May, she was back at Mesurado ten days later. During August and September of 1844,

Saratoga was in the Cape Verdes, then she spent three weeks back on the coast of Liberia and Sierra Leone. By the end of October she was at sea, returning to Hampton Roads. A study of her logs reveals very few boardings and certainly no encounters with slavers.[81]

One of Perry's last acts as squadron commander was the purchase of a plot of land at Porto Grande as a burial ground for the American sailors from the sloop-of-war *Preble*.[82] That accomplished, on February 20, 1845, he turned his command over to Captain Charles W. Skinner.[83] *Macedonian* and her pioneering captain arrived off Sandy Hook and New York on April 26, 1845, about two months short of two years since departing the United States for Africa.[84]

Shortly before ceding his command, Perry had written to President Roberts of Liberia that *Macedonian* would return to the United States without the "loss of life by the African fever . . . Such a result will be a strong argument against the prevailing opinion that the climate of Western Africa is pestilential in the extreme and that no care or precaution can guard against its insidious entrance on board ship." As to the disaster that had befallen *Preble*, he wrote, "I am led to believe that there has not been that precedence on board the *Preble* there should have been according to instructions."[85]

However, despite Perry's mixed success in dealing with the fever, the Africa Squadron's reputation would continue to hold a horror over those who were duty-bound to serve there. Typical was the comment found in a letter to Secretary of the Navy John Y. Mason in September 1844: The writer, in soliciting a purser's billet for a friend, implored the secretary to send the gentleman any place but Africa, as he was "too good a fellow to die on the Africa station." [86]

The squadron's effect on the slave trade was obviously negligible, *Uncas* having been the only "prize." The extent eastward of the cruising area for *Porpoise* and *Macedonian* was Cape Palmas, about two hundred miles east of Monrovia. As to the extended cruises, it appears that the slow cruise down the coast to the Bight of Biafra—as *Saratoga* and *Decatur* had done—was simply telegraphing his intentions ahead. It would have been a dull-witted slaver indeed who would not lay low at the news, and no slaver awaiting his cargo would hang about the coast with a naval cruiser in the offing.

As to Perry's actions in remaining so long at Porto Praya and other points farther from the coast, he may well have thought his frigate too large for the purpose intended. He had written in September 1843 that the " . . . services of a small vessel . . . are almost indispensable in visiting trading places of difficult and shallow navigation . . ."[87] Indeed, his actions as squadron commander and the sailing patterns of his vessels on the coast were certainly more suited to the traditional cruising squadron, rather than as a quasi-blockader on a foreign coast.

To put the new American effort into perspective, in 1845 Parliament ordered a report on the Royal Navy's West African anti-slavery squadron. It found that more than 385 men had died or been killed in action on the station, plus almost five hundred invalided out of the service. More than 600,000 pounds sterling was being spent supporting the squadron. Despite these efforts and expenditures, the estimated number of slaves exported had actually increased substantially: thirty thousand in 1842, fifty-five thousand in 1843, and upward. With thirty to forty vessels assigned to the squadron annually, they had seized forty-four slavers in 1843 and nearly double that in 1845. The report's conclusion was that the British Navy—even given their numbers of ships and men and their commitment to the mission—had no hope of stopping the trade altogether.[88]

"Kroomen" were the native tribesmen utilized by the squadron vessels for much of their communication with the African shore, in order to avoid sending the "fever" prone white seamen to the African coast. Each class of naval vessel was authorized a specific complement of these men. They were paid, subject to navy discipline, and shared in prize money. This is a rare photo of Kroomen on board the USS Sacramento on a visit to the Liberian coast shortly after the Civil War in 1867.

Naval Historical Center

Kroomen in the surf, circa 1848. This drawing, by captain's clerk Charles F. Sands on the brig Porpoise, *exemplifies typical conditions on the African coast: heavy swells which made any shore approach dangerous. These conditions also applied to the approaches to Porto Praya, making re-victualling exceedingly dangerous during some seasons.*
Naval Historical Center

5

COMMODORE SKINNER, THE FEVER, AND THE NOTORIOUS *PONS*, 1845–1846

Captain Perry turned over command of the Africa Squadron to his successor, Capt. Charles W. Skinner, on February 20, 1845, at Porto Praya. Skinner, like Perry, had been in the Navy since 1809, and in fact he was one number junior to Perry on the captain's list. He was born in Maine, appointed to the service from Pennsylvania, and called Virginia home.[1]

In common with all save one of the commanders of the Africa Squadron, Skinner would not see active service in the Civil War. Of the eleven commanders, four would die before the war and six would be retired before the end of 1862. One, Isaac Mayo, would be dismissed at the war's beginning. Only Francis Gregory, squadron commander from 1849 to 1851, held an active command during the conflict.[2]

Captain Skinner's squadron was somewhat more realistic in its composition than Perry's had been. The secretary of the Navy reported in 1844 that Perry had recommended "single decked vessels" as being "best suited" to the coast, due to their better ventilation.[3] Therefore, no frigate was initially assigned to Skinner's squadron, only three sloops-of-war and a brig.

As with the first squadron, two of the vessels were on their first cruises: the brig *Truxtun* had been launched in 1843 and sloop-of-war *Jamestown* had entered service in 1844. The other sloops, *Preble* and *Yorktown*, each carrying sixteen guns, were relatively new, having been commissioned in 1839. Their aggregate armament was eighty-three guns. Appropriately, Skinner flew his broad pennant on *Jamestown*, one of the few U.S. sloops-of-war with full-fledged carved quarter galleries appropriate to a squadron flag officer.[4]

Skinner's tenure began on a negative note: as noted earlier, the *Preble* was so ravaged by the fever that she was nearly useless—more than a third of her crew was downed by the disease. To relieve the crew, Skinner ordered her on a cruise to windward, northeast towards the Canaries. Later, in April, her commanding officer wrote Skinner protesting that the cruise had been without any "beneficial" effects, and that the vessel should have been sent directly back to the United States with her sick crew. Now, he insisted that she needed a complete new crew. Skinner finally consented to sending her home, and the *Preble* arrived back in the United States in late September 1845. Her total commission had been just over a year.[5]

The brig *Truxtun*'s cruise with the squadron was more profitable, but it ended with a similar story. She had departed from Philadelphia in June 1844, and after the usual stops at Funchal and the Cape Verdes, the vessel had gone on to the African coast and had patrolled off Monrovia in December 1844 with *Yorktown*.[6]

Then, in March 1845, Skinner learned that part of the crew of the wrecked slaver-schooner *Manchester* was at Monrovia, one of whom was Peter Faber, a slave dealer with a "factory" at Rio Pongas, northwest of Freetown, Sierra Leone. Faber had recently shipped slaves on the schooner *Hero* of New Orleans, which was seized by the Royal Navy steamer *Cygnet*. And now, Skinner was informed, another nine hundred slaves were at Rio Pongas ready to be shipped on the American schooner *Spitfire*. The *Spitfire* itself had, under the name *Caballero*, carried a cargo of 346 slaves to Cuba shortly before this. Skinner immediately ordered *Truxtun* to investigate and cooperate with the British squadron on site.[7]

An American officer, Simon Fraser Blunt, on *Truxtun*, afterwards wrote, as quoted in Andrew Foote's *Africa and the American Flag*: "Here we are in tow of Her Brittanic Majesty's steamer *Ardent*, with an American schooner, our prize, and a Spanish brigantine, prize to the steamer, captured in the Rio Pongas, one hundred miles to the northward. We had good information that there was a vessel in the Pongas, waiting a cargo; and on our arrival off the river, finding an English man-of-war steamer, arrangements were made to send a combined boat expedition, to make captures of both vessels."

Blunt, who was the boat officer on the expedition, continued:

On coming in sight, our little schooner ran up American colors, to protect herself from any suspicion, when our boats, after running along side [*sic*] of her, produced the stripes and stars, much to the astonishment of those on board. She proved to be the *Spitfire*, of New Orleans, and ran a cargo of slaves from the same place last year. Of only about one hundred tons; but though of so small a size she stowed three hundred and forty-six negroes, and landed [them] near Matanzas, Cuba.

Between her decks, where the slaves are packed, there is not room enough for a man to sit, unless inclining his head forward: their food, half a pint of rice per day, with one pint of water. No one can imagine the sufferings of slaves on their passage across, unless the conveyances in which they are taken are examined. Our friend had none on board, but his cargo of three hundred were ready in a barracoon, waiting a good opportunity to start. A good hearty negro costs but twenty dollars . . . purchased for rum powder, tobacco, cloth etc. They bring from three to four hundred dollars in Cuba. . . . The British boats also brought down a prize; and the steamer is at this moment towing the *Truxtun*, the *Truxtun*'s prize, and her own, at the rate of six miles an hour.[8]

Subsequently, Blunt wrote a lengthy description of the slave trade, in which he noted the conditions on the slaver ships: [on the] "slave deck they are packed by seating the first man in the remotest place from the hatch, and placing the next one between his legs, which are spread sufficiently open to allow the man in front to touch with his back the man behind him. . . . The rice is cooked on deck and handed down to the 'cargo' in tubs. The offices of nature are performed in large tubs, which when filled are brought on deck and emptied. A part of the 'cargo' is allowed to come on deck every good day, being well guarded . . ." He noted with—one hopes—sarcasm that in the case of the *Spitfire*, the cargo of 350 "was particularly comfortable." (Though he obviously did not observe this firsthand.)[9]

Blunt later betrays some of the attitudes prevalent in this era towards the slave trade and black Africans in general. "In Africa, the negro is the victim of the most repulsive and cruel superstition. Their system of paganism . . . teaches them none of the virtues or charities of life. When carried away in bondage they certainly are put in a way to learn something of the gentler feelings of the human heart . . ." As to the results of the anti-slavery squadron, he wrote: "The capture of every slaver adds to the profit of the dealers indirectly, the demand keeps up and being paid in cash, it gives them a quicker sale for their next cargo."[10]

In any event, *Spitfire* was seized and sent to the United States for adjudication. When the case reached federal circuit court in Massachusetts later that year, the long, convoluted story became record. The little schooner had been built in Baltimore and her first slave voyage, mentioned above, had ended with her interior being scrubbed and relieved of all incriminating evidence. She then sailed "innocently" into Havana, by now under Spanish colors (her ownership had changed at Rio Pongas), and then to Key West. There, one Peter Flowery purchased the vessel and thus the ship could again legitimately show American colors.[11]

Next, Flowery "borrowed" $7,500—which happened to be the "price" of the vessel—from Don Juan Scorsur, a Cuban with extensive property in Matanzas. Flowery then sailed to New Orleans where the vessel was "chartered" for an African voyage by none other than Don Juan Scorsur. In November 1844 the vessel sailed for Africa with a stop at Havana where "passengers" were shipped, including two men—a Spaniard and a Frenchman—described as "mates" on their passports. These gentlemen actually stood watch and kept their own "logs" of the voyage. The vessel's cargo manifest indicated the destination was the Cape Verde Islands, but bills of lading included Peter Faber—at Rio Pongas—as a consignee.[12]

As the vessel made passage eastward, the crew, who were signed on under the impression that this was to be an honest trading voyage, soon got wind of the actual nature of the enterprise—learning, for example, that the vessel carried a French flag for apparently illicit reasons. When they made land at Faber's establishment, the truth became obvious. They waited on board while the "mates" went ashore to make arrangements with Faber for shipping the cargo.

At this juncture, Faber refused back wages to Thomas Turner, a former crewman from *Caballero* (*Spitfire*), who was still ashore in Africa. He immediately denounced *Spitfire* to the blockaders, resulting in the ensuing boat expedition. Though the vessel had not been prepared to take on slaves at the time, Commander Bruce, on *Truxtun*, assumed Turner's testimony, as well as that of the other original crewmembers, would be sufficient for the case.[13]

In June 1845, the case appeared before the federal circuit court for Massachusetts, under Judge Peleg Sprague. In sentencing Peter Flowery the justice remarked: ". . . if you had gone one step further, and taken slaves on board, your life would have been forfeited by the laws of your country. Your offense originated in a cold, deliberate calculation of monetary gain; there was hardly a mitigating circumstance in the whole transaction." Despite this ringing condemnation, the jury's recommendation of mercy resulted in a sentence of five years and a $2,000 fine. Twenty-one months into the incarceration, President Polk pardoned the man, on grounds of his deteriorating health.[14]

Meanwhile, *Truxtun* continued cruising the African coast. This ended in October 1845. On the third of that month, *Truxtun*'s surgeon recommended against another African cruise due to sickness among the crew: "12 men sick today", he wrote, and many others were "hardly able to perform . . . light duty" and "very feeble."[15] Shortly thereafter, Skinner ordered Bruce to report the names of men who slept ashore at Princes Island, Porto Praya, and the coast of Africa. Ten days later he wrote the secretary of the Navy that he was sending *Truxtun* home, as the "principal officers" were medically unfit for duty, she was short of complement by eleven, and she had sick list of fifteen. Furthermore, the remainder were "much debilitated."[16] At the end of the month, *Truxtun* was at sea returning to Norfolk.[17]

Shortly after the capture of *Spitfire*, Captain Skinner was moved to write his opinion of the needs of the Africa Squadron. He maintained that the eighty guns should be divided among "as many vessels" of suitable rate as possible, noting that ten-gun brigs were quite as efficient as the sixteen-gun sloops. Thus, the optimum squadron would be composed of six ten-gun brigs and a twenty-gun flagship. Then four could be kept on the coast, while one was at the Canaries "recruiting" and the sixth en route to the coast to replace one of the four whose cruise was terminated.[18]

He concluded that *Truxtun* was "as efficient as any vessel of the squadron," and that small vessels were as healthy as large ones, and the loss of one would "not be as sensibly felt" in the squadron. Finally, the "flag would be shown" more often if there were more vessels available.[19] Of course, his recommendations were not to be carried out until long afterwards.

The cruise of the sloop-of-war *Yorktown* was to yield one of the most infamous captures of the entire era. The sixteen-gun ship, under Commander Charles H. Bell, departed from Brooklyn in October 1844, stopped at Madeira and Porto Praya, and raised the African coast in December.[20]

Bell cruised in the area west of Cape Palmas until January 1845, then went south, "standing along the coast," calling at Dix's Cove, Elmina, Cape Coast Castle, Accra, Quitta, Princes Island, Gaboon, Ambriz, Loando, and, finally, Benguela, in mid-April. There she reversed course and worked to windward, returning to Monrovia in May. From thence Bell sailed the sloop to Porto Praya, Madeira, and back to the coast in September. There, off Cape Mount on September 27, Bell captured the schooner *Patuxent* with no slaves on board. When sent back to the United States, the circuit court at New York dismissed the case.[21] *Yorktown*'s second passage down the coast brought her to the Gaboon River in late November.[22]

On the November 30, at 3 degrees, 26 minutes, south, and 9 degrees, 19 minutes east, about three hundred miles northwest of Kabenda, a barque was discovered standing to the northwest. The vessel showed American colors, but, as one crewmember reported, "her manner of steering being so wild that suspicion was awakened in the minds of the officers as to her legal character." After following for over an hour, she was hailed and a boat was sent on board.[23]

She proved to be the barque *Pons* of Philadelphia, under Captain Gallano. Gallano was obviously surprised to find an American cruiser had stopped him, and, on seeing the boarders' American uniforms, immediately replaced the American flag with the Portuguese. Next he pitched the ship's papers over the side. When asked to present his papers for inspection, Gallano brazenly responded, "I have none; I have thrown them overboard." When asked about his cargo, he admitted to "about nine hundred slaves." By this time, according to witnesses, the "jubilation of 900 shouting voices erupted" and the sound could be heard a mile away.[24] There was little left to do except seize the vessel.

Wrote Bell: "The stench from below was so great that it was impossible to stand, more than a few moments, near the hatchways. Our men who went below from curiosity [*sic*] were forced up sick in a few minutes. Then all the hatches were off. What must have been the sufferings of these poor wretches when the hatches were closed? . . . None but an eye witness can form a conception of the horrors these poor creatures must endure in their transit across the ocean."[25]

In what may have been the cruelest of slave voyages, the *Pons*, measuring some ninety-five feet head to stern and twenty-three feet in beam, carried 850 males in a space of less than two thousand square feet. (For comparison, a smallish modern three-bedroom house measures about 1,500 square feet.) And there was no slave deck: the blacks were quite literally piled on mats spread over bags of farina. Another fifty females were confined in the deck cabin. None had been fed in the three days at sea.[26]

It was later revealed that *Pons* had waited for twenty days in the Kabenda roadstead, watched by a British cruiser. Immediately, when the cruiser left her station one morning, *Pons* was loaded and put to sea, weighing anchor at about eight in the evening. All nine hundred slaves had been loaded, as well as water and provisions, in that short time.[27]

After the seizure, the sailors from *Yorktown* proceeded to feed the blacks and allow them on deck in shifts. They found that only about 250 could fit on the upper deck at any one time. With a prize crew on board, they sailed to Monrovia and in the fourteen-day passage 150 died. The Monrovia newspaper reported, "The slaves were much emaciated, and so debilitated that many of them found difficulty in getting out of the boats. Such a spectacle of misery . . . so excited our people, that it became unsafe for the captain of the slaver, who had come to look on, to remain on the beach."[28] Another newspaper account described the "demonstrations of . . . pleasure exhibited [by these] victims of an abominable traffic . . . Their songs of deliverance were borne upon the passing breeze, while they simultaneously clapped their hands for joy." [29]

The *Pons* was taken to Philadelphia for adjudication and confiscated by the government. She was auctioned off and the purchaser changed her name before returning her to commercial service.[30] Three of the *Pons*'s crewmembers were released when they were found to be Portuguese citizens.[31]

The remainder of *Yorktown*'s cruise was anticlimactic. After detailing thirteen men as a prize crew for the *Pons*, Bell cruised again off Kabenda and Loango. On December 15, he seized the 407-ton barque *Panther* off Kabenda. The vessel, which had cleared Rio de Janeiro in August, had been loitering about the coast apparently waiting for a suitable moment to run in for a cargo of slaves. In fact, later court testimony showed the vessel had anchored first off the Congo, then moved to Kabenda, Ambriz, back to the Congo, and finally, again to Kabenda where she was seized. All this inactivity was costing $1,750 per month, an amount hardly justified by the $2,750 worth of cargo brought from Brazil and the accumulated "trade" off Africa: two ivory teeth and fourteen gallons of palm oil.[32] *Panther* was nearly outfitted for the trade, and Bell took her in on the strength of these factors. She was sent to Charleston for adjudication and the result was mixed: the jury acquitted the commanding officer, Joshua Clapp, but the judge declared the vessel forfeit.[33]

In doing so, the judge, Robert B. Gilchrist, was making his decision based on the spirit of the anti–slave trade statutes, rather than on the "letter." That is, he did not consider it material whether the vessel had ever carried Africans into slavery. Indeed, he considered the vessel forfeit if it had only been "intended for that purpose."[34] As will be seen, through the next decades the attitudes of the presiding judges in these cases would vary significantly . . . and their decisions were not always consistent with their location above or below the Mason-Dixon Line. It is probably significant here, in South Carolina, that the jury acquitted but the federal circuit judge exercised his discretionary authority.

On *Yorktown,* Commander Bell, short-handed after detailing prize crews for *Patuxent, Pons,* and *Panther,* headed northwest for Monrovia, where he arrived in mid-January 1846. In early February she was at Sierra Leone, and at the end of the month she returned to Porto Praya. The sloop-of-war departed for the United States in early May and arrived at Boston at the end of the month. [35]

It was not until 1861 that the number of slaves captured on *Pons* was surpassed on a single vessel captured by an American cruiser on the African station. It is also noteworthy that two of *Yorktown*'s three seizures were taken below the equator, and that the third was on the southwestern coastline where knowledgeable local observers had consistently declared that the trade was moribund.

The cruise of the flagship *Jamestown* was nearly uneventful, at least in comparison to that of *Yorktown.* Captain Skinner had departed from the United States late in January and rendezvoused with Perry in *Macedonian* in February. After the change of command, Skinner made passage to the coast where he spent a week at Cape Mesurado. There he reported to the secretary of the Navy that Perry had provided him with five kroomen, and he had hired another eleven for transporting "wood and water" and other "boat duty requiring much exposure."[36] Here one crewman noted the bluejackets' penchant for applying "American" names to the various natives that would be nearly part of the crew during the cruise. Indeed, they were paid six dollars per month—equivalent to that of "boys," the lowest rank of regularly paid crewmen—and were subject to the same discipline as the regular crewmembers. Some of these slightly humorous appellations were Jack Will, Ben Coffee, Poor Joe, Jack Everyday, Jack Frypan, and Jack Crowbar.[37]

From Liberia Skinner sailed eastward along the coast, arriving at Princes Island, northwest of Gaboon, in late March. *Jamestown* arrived back at Cape Mesurado on April 22 and proceeded to Porto Praya. Skinner did not return to the African coast until November 18, 1845, dividing the time among Porto Praya, Porto Grande, Madeira, and the Canaries. It was during this interim that Skinner dealt with the situation on the sickness-ravaged *Preble* and *Truxtun*, meeting with the former vessel in August and ordering her return to the States. Similarly, *Truxtun* was ordered home in late October.[38]

In July, while at Grand Canary, Skinner reported to the secretary of the Navy an incident involving an American merchant vessel and the British cruisers. The master of the American barque *Madonna*, Richard Lawlin, complained that the British brig *Lily* had stopped and her officers had boarded his vessel without justification, though he admitted he had been the owner of the slaver *Atalanta*, which had been sold to slave dealers earlier in the year. The *Atalanta,* wrote Skinner, had arrived on the coast under American colors and awaited a "convenient moment" to board three hundred to four hundred slaves, discharge her American crew, and escape. Skinner, quite rightly, informed Lawlin that the British suspicions were justified, particularly since "it [was] believed on the coast that he conducted the entire negotiation."[39]

Lawlin, on his part, had written that the British vessel had flown American colors until she hailed and boarded *Madonna*. As to the *Atalanta*, that vessel had been disposed of "by her master to a person who did dispose of said vessel to one who made [a] Guineaman of her." Of course, Lawlin claimed this unlikely scenario had occurred while he was away somewhere "down the coast" in company with Commander Bell on *Yorktown*.[40] In any event, Skinner later wrote to Secretary of the Navy George Bancroft that the successful "maneuver" of the *Atalanta*, as well as the "escape of the master of the Spitfire from death . . . will . . . encourage other desperadoes to imbark [*sic*] in similar enterprises."[41]

When *Jamestown* returned to the African coast, Skinner first called at Cape Mesurado, discharged his kroomen and hired others, and proceeded to Cape Mount. There they met the sloop-of-war *Marion*, newly arrived on station. Both sailed to Sierra Leone, remaining there until December 4.[42]

The following day, Skinner wrote to Bancroft about his first capture of a slave ship. The Royal Navy sloop *Cygnet*, cruising off Sierra Leone, had detained the schooner *Merchant*, of New York. The vessel was released "coincidentally" as the American naval vessels entered the harbor. The *Merchant* had been sold to the Spanish "covered by our flag" and engaged in the slave trade. Skinner complained, again, of the "frequency of such dishonest practices" and that it "degrade[d] our national colors." On the other hand, he described the conduct of the British officers as "unjustifiable; something more than bare suspicion is necessary to authorize the capture of a vessel under the American Flag."[43] Conversely, the British authorities at Sierra Leone were pleased, both with this operation and the joint boat expedition which had brought in the *Spitfire*. They wrote that the American squadron, "having captured the schooners 'Merchant' and 'Spitfire'; and [exhibiting] the disposition to cooperate with our cruisers [*sic*] . . . cannot but tend, if generally acted upon, to break up that systematic assistance rendered to the slave trade by American citizens."[44] Indeed, the "bare suspicion" noted by Skinner was sufficient here to result in the government confiscating the vessel and jailing her skipper after court proceedings in the United States. Lawlin, however, was released in 1847.[45]

Skinner returned to Porto Praya on December 14 and remained in that vicinity through May 1846. There, supplies were available from the newly arrived storeship *Southampton* in February.[46]

January 1846 had brought Skinner his second capture in *Jamestown*. He had boarded, at Porto Praya, the schooner *Robert Wilson*, en route from Havana to Kabenda. The schooner had been driven into port by dirty weather. On surveying her papers and noting ten Spanish "passengers," Skinner determined she was a slaver, though the master disagreed. A search revealed "a box containing the cooking apparatus for slaves," kegs of water disguised as "aquadiente" (a type of Cape Verde rum), a "very large number of wooden slave spoons, and her slave deck partly laid." Confronted with this evidence, the master admitted the actual purpose of the voyage. After dealing with Portuguese authorities who wished to seize the vessel for false entry, Skinner seized the vessel.[47]

Robert Wilson was sent to South Carolina to the federal district court for adjudication. The vessel was confiscated and the master, William Von Pfister, was convicted. He received a three-year term and a $1,000 fine. In April 1847 he was granted a full pardon.[48]

Skinner spent the remainder of his tenure sailing in and out of Porto Praya in *Jamestown*. He departed for the western hemisphere on June 28, calling first in Cuba and from thence to Boston early in August 1846.[49]

The next vessel added to Skinner's diminished squadron was the brig *Boxer*. This vessel had originally been schooner-rigged in 1831, with a hull design based on the fast Baltimore "clipper" model. By the 1840s, however, the Navy had re-rigged the vessel as a brig—a more conventional naval sail plan, and one which reduced her speed. Her commanding officer in 1840 described her as a "dull sailer" with little room for provisions.[50] *Boxer* arrived at Porto Praya and met *Jamestown* and the storeship *Southampton,* in February 1846.[51]

Under commanding officer Lt. John E. Bispham, *Boxer* sailed south, calling at Kabenda in April 1846. While at anchor, a boat from the Royal Navy frigate *Acteon* came alongside with news that a suspicious American brig was in the bay. The *Malaga* was reported to be laden with slave goods and chartered by a "notorious" Brazilian slave trader, Manoel Pinto da Fonseca. Bispham boarded the vessel and seized her on April 13. This must have been a surprise for her crew: when they had heard an American warship was in the area, they reportedly did not believe it, boasting that "when they were captured, there would be icebergs in Kabenda."[52] Her cargo was brandy, muskets, dry goods, tobacco, farina, rice, biscuits, and salt beef. Bispham determined the vessel was involved in the slave trade as an auxiliary, bringing the trade goods to be exchanged for human cargo shipped in another hull. In fact, it was later shown that the Brazilian parties who had supplied *Pons* had shipped the goods.[53] Acting as an auxiliary in this manner violated the law of 1800 that declared it illegal "directly or indirectly to hold or have any right or property in any vessel" used in the slave trade.[54]

Malaga was seized and sent to the United States for adjudication, in this instance to the federal circuit court sitting at Boston. At this point the *Malaga* became the most important seizure to date. On July 17, Justice Charles L. Woodbury abandoned the lawsuit against the vessel. Despite the suspicious nature of cargo and shippers, he determined that the crew had no "personal financial stake" in the slaves that might be purchased with said goods, therefore they were innocent of "indirect [interest in the] property" as set down in the 1800 law.[55]

There would have been few consequences for the Navy had this release been the extent of the potential problem. However, the court did not issue a certificate of probable cause to protect the Navy's officer from civil liability. Almost immediately the *Malaga*'s co-owners billed Bispham $10,380 for damages incurred when their vessel was "unjustifiably" detained, sent to the United States, and held pending trial.

In mid-1847, when Bispham returned to the United States, he was understandably concerned, and he wrote the secretary of the Navy asking to be indemnified for the costs of his defense. He was told the service would not do so, nor "could it, in any event, give [you] relief if answered in damages," wrote Secretary Mason. Rather, Bispham's sole resort would have been application to Congress, "which has heretofore granted it when an unintentional trespass has been committed by a public officer."[56] No doubt this minimal level of support from the secretary of the Navy did little to assuage Bispham's concerns.

In the end, the department moved to provide defense for Lt. Bispham, but the outcome was not certain. Thus Bispham, with an annual salary of $1,800, was in a dangerous limbo until settlement was reached.[57] And the implications of this event—as well as the lukewarm support from the department—were not lost on the Navy's officers responsible for suppressing the slave trade.

In any event, Bispham continued along the coast, going as far as the Gaboon in May 1846. *Boxer*'s circuit was completed at Monrovia in June, and the vessel proceeded to Porto Praya. Bispham's remaining cruise in the squadron would be under the new commander, George C. Read.

The final addition to Skinner's squadron was the sloop-of-war *Marion*, another of the sixteen-gun *Dale* class vessels and identical to *Yorktown* and *Preble*. She arrived at Porto Praya November 14, 1846, and proceeded to the coast in early December. The sloop coasted east and south, "standing along the land" . . . "about 5 miles from the shore," arriving at Princes Island February 13, 1846. During this slow passage she chased a "suspicious" vessel that proved to be a Brazilian on legitimate business, and she was accosted by HM brig *Kingfisher*, which commanded her to "heave to." The British commander later apologized, explaining that *Marion* had been mistaken for an "English Barque." *Marion* was back at Monrovia in March, Porto Praya in April, and on the coast in May, where her tenure under Skinner ended.[58]

Skinner's term as squadron commander had been very profitable, bringing in seven vessels: five in 1845 and two in 1846. It would not be until 1859 that a similar number was taken by the squadron in the same length of time. It should also be noted that four of the seven were taken above the equator, indicating that the slave trade was not—as reported—moribund in that area.

As to the three taken below the equator, they proved the squadron was not reluctant to cruise the distance necessary to accomplish the mission. All of Skinner's squardron's vessels, excepting the sickly *Preble*, had made the passage east and south—most as far as Kabenda, with Bell in *Yorktown* sailing as far as Benguela—more than eight hundred miles below the equator. The results are also more significant given that during most of Skinner's tenure he was far below strength, owing to the ravages of the fever on two of his ships.

An appropriate postscript to Skinner's tenure is found in the secretary of the Navy's December 1846 report to Congress. Therein, Secretary John Y. Mason suggested construction of at least four sea steamers, armed "for their own defense." These would be of "great utility," he wrote, in Brazil and Africa—as demonstrated by steamers in other naval services.[59]

In fact, four large steamers were authorized in March 1847, but they were not completed until 1852 and none of them were ever assigned to the Africa station.[60] In fact, the outbreak of the Mexican War in June 1846 would overshadow the needs of the Navy in all other areas for the next two years.

6

FLAG OFFICER READ: THE FEDERAL COURTS TAKE A HAND, 1846–1847

Probably no greater contrast can be found between the tenure of Captain Skinner and those of the next three squadron commanders on the African station: Captains George C. Read, William C. Bolton, and Benjamin Cooper. From seven suspect vessels taken under Skinner, the seizure rate dropped to two seizures between August 1846 and April 1850.[1] This was certainly the low point in the history of the American naval effort to suppress the slave trade, and both of these captures occurred during the George Read's tenure: June 1846 through September 1847.

One factor that has been suggested to explain this drawdown was the playing out of the Mexican War, which was declared on May 13, 1846, and ended by treaty in March 1848. It might be supposed that other American naval forces, including the Africa Squadron, would be subordinated to naval needs of the war effort. Surprisingly, however, the war had little impact, except in the fall of 1847 when, for a short time, there were only two vessels on station, totaling thirty-two guns.[2] This decline in numbers had been discussed beforehand by Read and Secretary Bancroft and was an indirect result of the war effort.[3]

The Home Squadron, around which the Gulf of Mexico theater of operations was based, expanded significantly, numbering up to twenty vessels in 1847. Most of these vessels were pulled from the Mediterranean, leaving that important area completely denuded of American naval vessels.[4] To compensate somewhat for this, it was decided that some vessels from the African station would proceed to the Mediterranean after a year off Africa; in turn, other vessels would be sent from the United States as their replacements. In addition to reestablishing an American presence in the Mediterranean, this scheme would reduce the length of time the ships and crews would be in the "dangerous" African climate.[5]

In any event, when Read took command in mid-1846, his flag was on the frigate *United States*, and the balance of the squadron consisted of two ten-gun brigs (*Boxer* and *Dolpin*) and the sixteen-gun sloop-of-war *Marion*. These vessels carried eighty guns (though *United States*, rated a forty-four, actually carried fifty).[6]

This particular squadron composition was not the wish of the department. As noted earlier, the intention was to replace the frigates with sloops-of-war on the station. And, indeed, Secretary of the Navy George Bancroft—more noted as a historian than for his stewardship of the Navy Department—had written Read that he would command "three sloops of war & three brigs." Read disagreed, writing that he had sailed in a sloop-of-war on the Africa Squadron twenty-four years before, and therefore he "ought to" fly his pennant on a frigate "to command respect."[7] He apparently had also threatened to resign, though it may not have been in connection with the flagship situation. (Read was no doubt also looking forward to cutting an impressive figure later on in the Mediterranean.) Read, a veteran since 1804 with more than twenty years of sea service, was granted his request and was promised, tentatively, the nearly new frigate *Cumberland*.[8] In the event, *Cumberland* was sent to the war zone and *Brandywine*, Read's second choice (a ship of "superior force"), was under repair. Instead, Read was assigned the second oldest frigate in the service: "I must be satisfied with the frigate U. States," he complained.[9] The "U. States"—as she was invariably called at the time—of course was the famous veteran of the War of 1812 and sister ship to the frigate *Constitution*. She was, indeed, ancient, having been laid down in 1797, but she remained staunch and had recently completed a cruise as flagship in the Pacific.[10]

Read commissioned *United States* on May 18, 1846, and sailed for Africa, arriving at Porto Praya in mid-June. There he met *Dolphin* and reported that *Marion* and *Boxer* were already on the coast, and the latter was expected at the islands in July. There, *Dolphin* would be reprovisioning and then would join him off Africa.[11] Read also learned on arriving at the Cape Verdes that a fire had destroyed one of the provision warehouses being leased by the government. Inexplicably, he recommended that an-

other depot currently being operated at Monrovia be discontinued as un-
necessary, citing the availability of the storeship *Southampton*.[12]

Conditions at Porto Praya were not to the liking of another officer
on *United States*. Lt. John Rodgers wrote that the islands were where
"nature walks about dressed like Eve in her innocence—the hills and
plains being utterly naked—Not a blade of grass to be seen . . ." Later, at
Monrovia, he commented—reflecting the generally racist tone of the era—
that the place would be "more flourishing if the people would work
harder," and that his friends would be "horror stricken" if they found he
was in officially sanctioned social company with "a gentleman of colour"
there. Rodgers's attitude did not improve as his service continued, writing later that, "This is a d——l of a coast for want of interest and if
Jimmy Polk and the Mexicans had not fallen out so that we have bloody
wars to speculate upon I do not know what we would do." This attitude
had not been original with the lieutenant, as his brother Christopher
Raymond Perry Rodgers had written earlier that, "A cruise on the coast
of Africa is certainly no small atonement for one's errors." [13]

Read departed from the Cape Verdes and was in Monrovia on July
11. Here he began a series of letters generally critical of the entire
squadron's operations. The litany was familiar, but with some specifics to
add interest and variety to earlier reports. On the size and composition of
the squadron: "That the number of cruisers is not sufficient for the extent
of the cruising grounds, making it inconvenient to keep more than two
vessels on the coast at the same time" because the crews' "relaxed state of
mind and body" engendered by a four to five month cruise on the coast
resulted in the "absolute necessity" for "invigorating & strengthening"
them with a cruise to the Canaries (the "windward"). Thus he recommended at least another "thirty to forty" guns on the station to provide
"timely reliefs." He noted also that the French and British each had twenty-
six vessels on the coast, including several steamers, which kept station on
the various slave marts. However, he speculated that even an American
force of three times its current size would meet with "little success." [14]

As to the composition of the squadron, he implicitly reversed his
position on the utility of frigates. If the squadron could not be increased
in number of vessels, he recommended all vessels be of fourteen to sixteen guns, and that four brigs would substitute for a frigate.[15]

On a note related to the squadron's size, he complained about the "serious inconvenience" to the unit's commanding officer by the need to command "a force so scattered & the vessels at so great a distance from each other." He found himself detained at Porto Praya awaiting arrival of his other ships in order to communicate his orders and set up schedules for their movements.[16]

Read also discussed the attributes of his vessels. The two brigs and sloop-of-war "[cannot] sail sufficiently well to overhaul a slaver, nor can the two brigs carry provisions for sufficient time to let them remain on a distant station for more than a very limited period." This lack of celerity was also attributed to fouled hulls: there is massive sea-growth endemic to tropical waters. When the *United States*'s hull was scraped by the local kroomen–divers, the barnacles were found to be of the "enormous size of three & four inches in diameter."[17]

Of course, the distances involved in reaching Porto Praya, as well as the Canaries, from the coast were high on Read's complaint list, as this was directly related to the provision storage available on his ships. But the storeship *Southampton*, stationed at Monrovia, also caught criticism: Read found in October that the stores had been aboard for fifteen months and that of 750 barrels of pork and beef, only 450 were usable. Further, though she was sent as a permanent storeship and hospital, she was constantly "deluged with water" (no doubt from the heavy coastal swells), severely limiting her utility.[18] The fact that the vessel retained such a large portion of the stores over such a long period also illustrates the long distances and times involved when the squadron ships were sent far south along the African littoral.

The only positive point in all Read's verbiage was the health—as opposed to the condition—of his ships' crews. At Monrovia he met with the *Marion*, freshly returned from the south, and found that crew in "good health." In general, he admitted that all the health of all his crews was "remarkably good."[19] In that era, as well as this, the lack of liberty ports on the "sickly" African coast went far to reduce the sick list, given the high incidence of venereal disease associated with sailors free to roam in foreign ports. And, as long as the bluejackets avoided the fever itself, the worst they had to fear was the endless, enervating heat and boredom of the climate and stifling ships.

One of the major objects of Read's concerns was the brig *Boxer*, under Commander Bispham. Since taking the *Malaga* off Kabenda in April, the ship had returned to Monrovia, resupplied, and proceeded to Porto Praya. After a week there, she set off for the mainland and made passage eastward skirting the coast. She was at Princes Island on August 8 and rendezvoused with *United States* off Kabenda. There, Read ordered Bispham to cruise on the Bight of Benin as long as her supplies held out. Read later reported that she had cruised in company with the Royal Navy brig *Bittern* and discouraged the slavers in that area. The little brig hung about at St. Paul de Loando, Ambriz; the mouth of the Congo; and Kabenda until November 15, when she departed for Monrovia. Bispham had remained on station south of the equator for more than three months.[20]

For the remainder of her tour under Read's command, the vessel made two passages to Porto Praya, one in December 1846 and one in May 1847. In between these windward cruises, Bispham sailed down the coast again and met with the vessel *Senator*, but failed to seize it, as the evidence of guilt was no stronger in this instance than it had been with the ill-fated *Malaga* case. The result was tragic: After being released, the *Senator* loaded nine hundred blacks for Brazil. Three weeks later, only six hundred survivors landed on the shores of South America.[21] Afterward, there was another cruise down the coast, this one terminating at Benguela, far south of the equator. Despite the extended cruising, *Boxer* took no other prizes during this period.[22]

On the other hand, sloop-of-war *Marion*, under Commander Lewis Simonds, had taken a prize almost immediately after Read took command. Simonds had taken her from Cape Mesurado to Kabenda, arriving at the latter place at the end of July 1846. On August 2, she seized the brig *Casket* off Kabenda. The vessel had no slaves but was suspected of awaiting a slave cargo.[23] *Casket* was sent to Boston for trial.[24]

As with *Malaga*, the *Casket* became a snare for the squadron. Judge Peleg Sprague dismissed the charges, released the vessel, and failed to give Simonds a certificate of probable cause. Immediately the owner of the suspect vessel filed two lawsuits against the Navy commander. As with the *Malaga*, there was yet another pall hanging over the Africa Squadron's vessel commanders, one that would not disperse until the court system reached its decisions. In both instances, it would be 1849 before a settlement was reached. [25]

Secretary of the Navy John Y. Mason's* response to the *Casket* case is instructive. He wrote to Read: "Her officers have been released—not sufficient evidence to hold them . . . The number of cases of this description [in] the last year rendered it proper to call your attention to the subject . . . and prevent [its] re-occurrence . . . in order to avoid interruption of trade & complaints from innocent traders . . . it is desireable [*sic*] that seizures should be cautiously made and that, as far as possible, the judgement of the commanding officer of the squadron should be exercised upon each particular case." [26]

Here, the unrealistic expectations of the department—or at least of Secretary of the Navy Mason—were blatantly revealed, and Read responded appropriately, writing:

> If the commanding officer were always to be found, your directions that the circumstances of a case of capture should be referred to me, in order that I might decide upon the propriety of it, and that the report of the case should go through me to the Department, no doubt some mistakes might be avoided, but the numerical force under my command will not permit me to remain at anchor for a length of time. I am obliged to cruise to make up the deficiency of numbers, and it is utterly impossible to advise Commanders of vessels at the distance of two thousand miles . . .[27]

One cannot imagine the havoc which would have resulted if the secretary's order had been insisted upon. It is also difficult to comprehend how any knowledgeable naval secretary could have expected compliance.

Once Simonds sent the soon-to-be-snare *Casket* to the United States, he continued south to Kabenda and Loango, arriving at the former place on August 11, and the latter three days later. The ship turned north on August 20 and returned to the western coast at Cape Palmas the second week in September. The vessel logs recorded boarding seven vessels from May to September. At Cape Palmas Simonds met with Read in the *United States*, and the commodore ordered him to go to Porto Praya for provisions due to a shortage at Monrovia. Read later wrote that the sloop had

---

* John Young Mason of Virginia was secretary of the Navy twice: March 1844 to March 1845, and September 1846 to March 1849.

been able to remain on station for only nine days due to an "expected shortage" of provisions.[28]

Despite the shortage at Monrovia, Simonds remained there for a week before sailing to Porto Praya, arriving on October 9. He came back to Liberia in mid-December and started southeast along the coast. It was a long passage eastward and south, with no significant events but with stops at nearly every significant settlement. On an incidental note, one of their kroomen, "Jack Mast," was flogged for "fighting"—revealing that not only were the native quasi-crewmembers paid Navy wages, but they were under the same discipline as the bluejackets.[29]

Simonds arrived at Benguela on March 22 and reversed course, stopping at the slave mart of Molembo, Portuguese Angola, first. He then took the *Marion* to the open sea for the balance of the cruise. They arrived at Monrovia on April 20, 1847. They had been at sea, or skirting the coast, for more than four months.[30] The ship was replenished at Porto Praya. Simonds then learned of a diplomatic incident involving the Spanish seizure of an American merchant vessel in Barcelona, as well as the rumor that Mexican privateers were said to be operating in the Mediterranean. He was ordered to sail for Barcelona to deal with the situation. This ended *Marion*'s African duties. From Spain she made passage for Marseilles, as part of the movement to re-establish the Mediterranean Squadron. [31]

The last unit of Read's squadron, other than his flagship, was *Dolphin*, which had sailed from Norfolk in November 1845. She was at Porto Praya with *United States* when Read took command and sailed in company to Monrovia late in June 1846. A month later she was en route down the coast with orders to cruise the Bight of Benin and "to look in all the slave stations." Her commanding officer, Commander John Pope, however, apparently did little serious looking. In mid-August he was reproved by Read, who had arrived at the Gaboon River in the flagship: "Your late very short visit to the Bight of Benin compels me to require your immediate return to that gulph [*sic*]. The vessels under my command were sent here to cruise & not merely to go from port to port. Your former instructions confined your cruising principally to the Bight of Benin, for it was not supposed that American slavers would be found at the Gaboon River.

You will perceive that the omission to look into all the slave stations & examine all vessels found at them under the flag of the U. States, was not in accord with the spirit of your instructions. . . ."[32]

Accordingly, Pope returned to the Bight, but was back in Monrovia in January 1847. *Dolphin* sailed from Cape Mount to Porto Praya on February 16 and returned to Sierra Leone towards the end of March. On April 10, on a southeast by east heading near Cape Palmas, Pope encountered the vessel *Chancellor*. The boarding officer seized the ship as she was found "to have over twenty five thousand gallons of water, four or five hundred bags of rice, plank enough for the construction of a slave deck and a Quantity of bricks, supposed to be for a slave galley. Also that the vessel's rig has been altered from that of a Barque to a ship." [33] (The alteration of the rig was taken to be an attempt to disguise the vessel, or at least to confuse the authorities. American merchant vessel registration required a description of the vessel's rig and any unreported change was illegal.)

The *Chancellor* seizure involved the squadron in the downfall of the famous—or infamous—Theodore Canot (or, variously, Theophilus Conneau). This gentleman later wrote a memoir (*A Slaver's Log Book: Or Twenty Years' Residence in Africa*) extolling and exaggerating, no doubt, his exploits as a sort of picaresque hero who, by his own account, survived mutinies, sea battles, ship wrecks, slave revolts, and capture by pirates, and was unjustly—in his view—maligned and persecuted for his supposed dealing in the West African slave trade. In fact, he had owned a major slave barracoon at New Cess, west of Cape Palmas, and claimed that there were "five or six hundred slaves" there. He boasted that he was quite proud of the "most rigid rules . . . [he had enforced there] in regards to morality." He was obviously of the opinion that humane treatment of the soon-to-be-sold humans was of more importance than the crime of selling them as merchandise. By the date of the capture of *Chancellor*, Canot had, by his own "admission," retired from the slave trade. This self-interested conversion occurred in 1839, when he had voluntarily turned over a hundred slaves to the British cruisers which had harried his operation at New Cess, and who had begun putting pressure on him and other slave traders in the vicinity. The British made it easy on Canot by providing transportation on British vessels for him and all his goods to a new location at Cape Mount.[34]

As time drew on, Canot's innocent protestations were falling on increasingly unbelieving ears. The evidence seemed quite contrary to his words. For one thing, his schooner *Patuxent* had been taken by *Yorktown* in September 1845. The vessel had been released, but the judge had issued a certificate of probable cause. Canot claimed the "slave deck" lumber on board the vessel was timber for building a small schooner on his plantation at Cape Mount. In any event, Canot then sailed for New York, ostensibly to obtain another load of lumber. *Chancellor* was chartered and loaded with lumber and "assorted cargo for the coast," as Canot phrased it. When *Chancellor* arrived at Cape Mount, the British put a close watch on the vessel, having heard rumors of the suspicious cargo thereon. Shortly thereafter, Commander Pope in *Dolphin* seized the ship and, within a week's time, the British burned Canot's establishment on the coast.[35]

The question of Canot's innocence is called into question in light of statements by his contemporaries: Governor J. J. Roberts of Liberia wrote that in "my decided opinion she [*Chancellor*] is designed to carry off a cargo of slaves . . ." He had known Canot for ten years and reiterated his belief that he had been in the slave trade. As to her cargo, he noted that Canot had purchased bricks while at anchor off Africa, rather than in the United States. He also quoted a crewmember who had seen three hundred bags of rice on board and who also claimed Canot was intending to change the vessel's rig.[36]

Probably the nail which completed the coffin for Canot was a report to Read, also relayed by Roberts, that Canot had begun to manufacture "handcuffs & shackles" on his establishment. On April 7 it was reported that Canot had "taken on board the "Chancellor" rice sufficient for eight hundred slaves for six weeks; increased the number of his water casks; and prepared two slave decks . . . and changed the rig . . . to a ship."[37] Three days later, Pope seized the vessel; this effectively ended Canot's colorful career in Africa. He later came to the United States where—in Baltimore—he penned his rather self-serving memoirs.

The *Chancellor* was sent to the federal district court of southern New York for adjudication. Unfortunately the judge in the case, Samuel Rossiter Betts, was notorious for enforcing the letter rather than the spirit of the laws. Indeed, one recent authority on the legal aspects of suppressing the slave trade wrote: "To Betts, it was perfectly legal for a captain to sail his fully equipped slaver up to the beach and his waiting Africans; only after they came aboard could the captain be punished under the Act of 1800."[38] Therefore, since the Navy found no actual slaves on board the *Chancellor*, all other evidence was, as far as the judge was concerned, circumstantial, and the ship was released. Additionally, the jury freed the ship's captain.[39]

Meanwhile, Commander Pope turned the brig *Dolphin* eastward again, working toward the Bight of Benin. With stops along the coast, he was at Loango in mid-June and called at Kabenda on the 28th. The next day the brig was at sea and heading toward Liberia. *Dolphin* departed the African coast on July 22 and returned to the United States via Porto Praya and Porto Grande, arriving at New York on November 5, 1847.[40] The doughty little brig was to serve another term on the Africa Squadron in the mid-1850s.[41]

Read, on the brig *United States*, caught no slavers during his approximately fifteen-month command of the Africa station. He had come to the coast from Porto Praya in July 1846 and immediately turned his vessel east and south down the slave coast. He was at the Gaboon River in mid-August when he reprimanded Pope on the *Dolphin*, and at Kabenda on September 1 where he met with *Boxer*. He then turned northwest out to sea and arrived at Mesurado in the middle of the month. Later he called at Porto Praya and returned to the coast in December, arriving at Sierra Leone on the seventeenth. The balance of the cruise was in the Cape Verdes. Read took her to the Mediterranean in October of 1847, after leaving command of the squadron to William F. Bolton, on the sloop-of-war *Jamestown*.

Even before Read's departure, he feared the implications of the news he was receiving from the States, in particular from the federal courts dealing with the recent captures by his squadron. As early as October 1846 he had written of trying to "rouse the energies" of his officers who were apprehensive "of being made liable for damages in case of seizures . . ." This negative news was particularly disheartening, in that it was generally supposed that the courts were on the same side of the law as the Navy. Now that it was plain that this supposition was not necessarily true, it greatly increased the Navy's burden to prove beyond doubt that the suspect vessel was involved in the trade. Thus, "detecting those engaged in the slave trade" was a task made more difficult by the vagaries of the courts.[42]

Later, in December, Read wrote to Secretary of the Navy Mason that, "The liberation of a majority of the vessels seized & sent home for adjudication has created much disappointment among the officers on the station, and I fear will have a tendency to diminish their zeal. . . . They dread the trouble and expense to which they are liable to be put, and they will hereafter be so very cautious as to what they seize, that I have reason to doubt the probability of your having a capture being made." [43] Read would prove to be exceedingly correct in this assessment.

7

BOLTON AND COOPER AND THE NADIR OF THE SQUADRON, 1847–1849

As directed by the Navy Department on October 24, 1847, Commodore Read turned over the squadron. His replacement, Captain William C. Bolton, had anchored at Porto Praya on October 21 after passage from Norfolk in the sloop-of-war *Jamestown*.[1]

Bolton had been in the service since 1806 and was junior to Read on the captain's list. He was listed as British by birth but was a citizen of Washington, D.C. In forty years of service he had been at sea for eighteen, spent seven years on shore duty, and fourteen without an assignment. He served with distinction in the War of 1812,[2] and in 1829–30 he commanded the USS *Vincennes* in the first round-the-world cruise by an American naval vessel.[3] An odd addendum to his resume was his name change: his given name was William Bolton Finch, which he legally changed in 1833 to William Compton Bolton. He had been "awaiting orders" before his assignment to head the Africa Squadron.[4]

At Porto Praya, Commodore Read visited Bolton on October 22 on *Jamestown*, where they no doubt discussed the squadron's situation and arranged the change of command. Read sailed for the Mediterranean two days later. Bolton was left with only the brig *Boxer*; *Dolphin* having departed earlier that month for the States, and *Marion* having long since gone to the Mediterranean. And *Boxer* was a problem, having returned from an extended cruise below the Equator with a "want of serviceable sails." Bolton reported she might not be available for "some length of time," as the expected storeship—with sail cloth for *Boxer*—was long overdue.[5] At this point the squadron officially numbered two ships and thirty-two guns, though only the twenty-two-gun *Jamestown* was capable of active cruising.

Bolton wrote Secretary Mason that he intended to leave *Boxer* and sail south, to return to Porto Praya in January. He also requested, with good reason, an "addition to my command." He departed for Monrovia the next day and arrived there November 23, where he hired twenty-two kroomen (including "Jack Ropeyard," "Fourth of July," and "Half Dollar") and took on supplies.[6]

In December, Bolton wrote Mason again from Porto Praya: ". . . I intended to sail further south [from Monrovia] but did not have sufficient provisions and I also noticed a suspicious schooner which I thought might be waiting for me to sail in order to pick up a cargo . . . I then went towards Gallinas instead . . . and fell in with schooner and gave chase . . ." The British cruiser *Rapid* apparently had initiated this pursuit. The latter, as well as the schooner, outsailed *Jamestown*, and *Rapid* made the seizure. The schooner was a Brazilian vessel, "fully equipped" for slaving. Whether there had been any official communication or coordination between

U.S. Naval Brig Bainbridge. *Small naval vessels, such as brigs and schooners, were much more useful, and cost-effective, in suppression of the trade than large frigates. They usually carried 10 to 12 guns, but their strong point was speed—and the latter was more useful than armament as the slave vessels were rarely well armed. At about 100 feet in length, these vessels carried a complement of around 100 men. Other brigs used in the squadron were* Truxtun *and* Perry. *Two schooners on the station were* Porpoise *and* Dolphin.
Naval Historical Center

Jamestown and the British cruiser concerning this chase and capture is questionable, as there is no mention in the *Jamestown*'s logs of this event. At this point, Bolton decided that, "being so far to windward," he would continue on to Porto Praya.[7] *Jamestown* had been on the coast of West Africa one week.

Bolton remained at the Cape Verdes from December 13, 1847, until January 5, 1848. In this interval, he saw the arrival of the supply ship *Joseph Meigs* and the completion of *Boxer*'s sails. After overseeing a court martial and completing his resupply, Bolton sailed back to the coast along with *Boxer* on January 5, 1848, arriving at Cape Mesurado on January 16.[8]

Bolton wrote his intention to "touch at Sherbro, Gallinas, Monrovia, New Sherbro, Palmas, Elmina, Accro, Cape St.Paul, Little Po-Po, Grand Whydah, Lagos, and Princes Island," looking in to "the principal slave marts on the coast." Indeed, he took both vessels along the coast, though logs only report *Jamestown* calling at Cape Mesurado, Quitta, Whydah, and Princes Island; *Boxer* called at Cape Mesurado and Lahou. Indeed, the sweep eastward along the coast began January 24 at Mesurado and ended at Whydah on February 9. Bolton was at Princes Island four days later and sailed directly back to Monrovia on February 22, 1848, arriving there March 12. *Boxer* arrived back at Liberia three days later. Bolton had been on the coast itself for about three weeks.[9]

Bolton's limited cruising on the coast foreshortened any possibility of falling in with any reasonably resourceful slaver. A British officer during this period described the signal system employed to forewarn of the approach of any anti–slave trade cruiser: ". . . a line of signals is constantly kept up. Thus a single light means that the coast is clear . . . two that the whereabouts of the cruiser is doubtful; three . . . great danger, which if it increases is shown by repeated flashes. Should a cruiser be off the port at the time a vessel is expected, a bonfire is lighted, and every half hour a quantity of gunpowder is thrown in it. These flashes are seen twenty miles off. . . . With the protection of the American flag and the correct espionage and line of signals . . . it is impossible [that] the coast be effectually guarded."[10] Given this kind of wily adversary, only diligent cruising and some measure of stealth could be expected to bring effective results on this station. And it is obvious that Bolton was not willing to exert that kind of effort during his command on the station.

This cruise was the last of the brig *Boxer* on station. After the return to Mesurado, she sailed for the United States, arriving in May 1848. She was then surveyed, found not seaworthy, and sold that August. She had been in service since 1831.[11]

Captain Bolton sailed from Mesurado to Porto Praya on March 23, arriving on April 7. For the next week he dealt with the usual resupplying from the storeship and mentioned difficulties with this evolution due to "very high sea." He was anxious to leave, writing Secretary Mason that he hoped to get away from "this detestable place" and make for Madeira or Grand Canary for the crews' recreation. He was also concerned about the revolution in France, which had begun a few months before, and the possible implications for American interests in that nation during the unrest.[12]

Bolton sailed from Porto Praya on April 19 and arrived at Funchal, Madeira, on May 10, 1848. *Jamestown* remained at Funchal until July 1, then sailed to Porto Praya, where Bolton met the newest additions to the squadron: brigs *Bainbridge* and *Porpoise,* and the sloop-of-war *Decatur*. After four days at Porto Praya, Bolton went to sea along with *Decatur* and *Porpoise.* Again he returned to Madeira, arriving on August 17, only returning to the Cape Verdes on September 25. On October 17, Bolton was at sea again en route to Madeira, where he dropped anchor on October 26.[13]

The return to Madeira was due to Bolton's declining health. In late October Secretary Mason wrote to the flag officer the "deep lament" he felt at the "state of [Bolton's] health," and he approved the recommendations that had been forwarded to him from the fleet surgeon. Those included "temporary residence on shore in the Island of Madeira."[14] Therefore, Bolton remained at Madeira until his replacement, Benjamin Cooper, arrived and the change of command was accomplished. Bolton left Funchal on December 23, 1848, and sailed to the Mediterranean. [15]

Bolton had last seen the African coast on March 23 and had been at least four months—on three different occasions—at Madeira during the remainder of his tenure. The balance of the time had been at the Cape Verdes. His stays at Porto Praya lasted six, four, and five weeks, respectively. On the other hand, during his fourteen months as squadron commander, Bolton's total time on the African coast was about six weeks: one week in November 1847, and the balance in February–March 1848. And, of course, the flagship never sailed the coast beyond Whydah, at the western reach of the Bight of Benin. It appears that his concern for the health of his crews involved allowing them "relief" in more than equal proportion to their duty on station. Another question that comes to mind is how much "relief" was necessary from the rigors of the African climate when the crewmen rarely neared the continent itself.

It could have been that the troubles in France were of more concern to him than routine patrols off Africa. He no doubt decided that, if American interests in Europe were endangered by the impending revolutions, it would be better for *Jamestown* to be available at Madeira, seven hundred miles from Gibraltar, rather than another two thousand miles south. (Ignoring the fact that the frigate *United States* and sloop *Marion* were already in European waters.)

As has been noted, Bolton finally received his replacements in March 1848 with the arrival of sloop-of-war *Decatur* and the brig *Porpoise*. The squadron was back to strength with the arrival of the brig *Bainbridge* in mid-May. This brought the squadron up to sixty guns, now that the *Boxer* had departed.

Decatur, commanded by Edward Byrne, remained in Porto Praya until mid-March, then sailed to Monrovia. She sailed in the Monrovia–Cape Mount vicinity until June 10, and then returned to the Cape Verdes. On July 11, she departed for Tenerife, stopping there on the way to Funchal to join the flagship. She remained at Madeira until October 26, and then returned to Porto Praya. She was there when Cooper succeeded Bolton.[16]

Bainbridge, under Albert G. Slaughter, stayed at Porto Praya until May 19, and then sailed for Funchal, meeting the flagship there in June. A week later she sailed back to the Cape Verdes. On July 20, Bolton ordered her to make a sortie to the coast and cruise between Cape St. Anne and Cape Palmas. She arrived at Monrovia on July 25. Her stay on the coast lasted until September 21, and her logs record that her cruise was limited to the area from Cape Mount on the west to Grand Bassa on the east, a distance of about four hundred miles on the coast. The ship was back at Porto Praya through the end of 1848.[17]

The brig *Porpoise,* commanded by Lieutenant A. G. Gordon, sailed from Hampton Roads in January, stopped at Porto Praya, and was first at

Mesurado in March 1848, where she met *Jamestown*. She was back at Porto Praya in July, and sailed in company with *Decatur* and the flagship for Tenerife and Madeira.[18] She was back in the Cape Verdes in late September, from whence Captain Gordon took her to the coast again.[19]

The coast yielded a suspicious vessel: the schooner *Ohio*. Lieutenant Gordon reported that he had fraternized "all day with the darkeys on shore, listening to their tales of the slave-dealers and [who] under their information believed that every vessel flying 'the stars and stripes' was engaged in aiding and abetting the slave-dealers." The information he gained seemed to confirm his suspicions about the *Ohio*, and he sent a boarding party to inspect the vessel. Her papers were in order, however, and Gordon was reduced to simply setting a watch on her.[20]

The vigil was interrupted by a severe squall on the night of November 28, and they lost sight of the schooner. Next morning, another "saucy looking schooner" came in sight and a shot was fired across her bows. This was ignored and the vessel edged off. A chase ensued, but a diminishing wind resulted in sending the ship's launch to pursue and board her.

U.S. Sloop-of-War Portsmouth. *When the squadron flagship was not a frigate, a large sloop-of-war was employed for this role. These vessels carried about 20 guns each and were manned by crews of about 200.* Portsmouth *was one of the larger sloops, carrying 22 guns. Other 18 to 22 gun sloops on the squadron at various times were* Saratoga, Jamestown, John Adams, Germantown, St. Louis, *and* Vincennes. *(*Constellation *and* Cumberland *had similar numbers of guns, but were in fact the size of frigates.)*
Naval Historical Center

As the boat approached, the crew was seen hurriedly "throwing over-board . . . her coppers for cooking rice for the slaves." The commander of the boarding crew, Lt. Benjamin F. Sands, found she had "everything in readiness for her occupation as a slaver; the slave deck was laid . . . some forty of fifty water casks filled, etc., etc." The slaver's intention was to board three hundred slaves in the three-foot space between the slave deck and the weather deck. Unfortunately for Gordon, she was flying a Brazil-ian flag when boarded. Though a prize crew took her to Monrovia, Gor-don eventually decided the Brazilian flag was her protection and the vessel was released.[21]

Subsequently, *Porpoise* cruised off Cape Mesurado and by Decem-ber 12 had four officers invalided due to the climate, and the crew was "growing every day more weary of the duty." They were looking forward to an expected transfer to the Mediterranean, as the Secretary of the Navy had told them before they sailed that "one year's stay on this coast counted as much as two elsewhere." This expected boon was not to be, however, and after a few days at Porto Praya the vessel sailed to Santa Cruz in the Canaries, arriving in February 1849.[22]

Following this, the brig returned to Porto Praya in April 1849, then headed to Monrovia and the coast to the southwest. The run, skirting the coast from Liberia to Princes Island, consumed the month of June through early July. On July 26, the vessel was back at Monrovia after the change of command.[23]

It is noteworthy that early in *Porpoise*'s cruise, the captain's clerk was Charles F. Sands—brother of the vessel's executive officer—who was a talented artist. His sketches were admired by all, including "Old Com-modore Bolton." Many of those drawings now reside at the Navy Histori-cal Center, and some are included in this book. These are some of the rare "on site" contemporary visual records of the squadron off Africa. [24]

Among the squadron vessels in this period, the fascination with Madeira seems to have affected *Decatur* the most. The sloop-of-war re-mained there two and a half months, from August 25 through November 2, though there was a ten-day sortie out and back to Funchal in October. *Bainbridge*, on the other hand, was at Funchal only one week in June. The *Porpoise* apparently spent a couple of weeks there in September. As to their service on the African coast, the *Bainbridge* spent about two months between Cape Mount and Cape Palmas; *Decatur*, two months from April to June, 1848—again, not wandering far from Monrovia; and *Porpoise* about a month in late November.[25]

No American naval vessel ventured south of the equator, or even on the southwest coast east of Whydah, during this period. The farthest south reached was Princes Island, about three hundred miles out into the Bight of Guinea and two hundred miles north of the Line, by *Jamestown* in February 1848. At the same time, while the squadron was no nearer than two thousand miles away from the coast, the British reported extensive misuse of the American flag between Benguela and Mayumba; in January 1849, authorities in Loando reported not having seen an American warship in the vicinity for over a year.[26]

Captain Bolton left little advice to the department regarding the squadron. For reasons unknown, in April 1848 he directed his commanding officers that "none of our vessels should cruise jointly with any foreign man of war," and that they should "always fly our own colors." [27] It is possible that the commodore expected to cap his career with great things from his tour on the prestigious Mediterranean station. However, Bolton's lack of activity as flag officer must have been in great part due to his declining health. On February 22, 1849, less than two months after leaving for the Mediterranean, Bolton died at Genoa, Italy.[28]

It is somewhat ironic that, on the day of Bolton's death, Secretary Mason wrote to him, listing the letters he had received since September. (This was necessary procedure in those days when correspondence was sent by whatever ships were available and en route to the required destination.) The secretary, on the occasion of Bolton's ending his tour, officially "approved" his actions as flag officer of the Africa Squadron.[29]

Captain Benjamin Cooper was to be the squadron's shortest-term commander: he accepted the command from Bolton in late December 1848, and turned over the unit to a temporary successor on July 29, 1849.[30] In common with many of the older officers, he had been in the service since before the War of 1812, having entered in 1809. He had eighteen years sea service during his more than forty-year career, and he was listed in the Navy register as a citizen of New York.[31] His age at this time is unknown, but given his enlistment date, Cooper could well have been in his mid-fifties. However, one of his officers during this period wrote that his health "had long been failing."[32]

Cooper sailed from the United States on *Yorktown* and met Bolton at Madeira. He continued on to Porto Praya, where he hoisted his flag on the *Portsmouth.* He found his squadron numbered five vessels. These were the sixteen-gun sloops-of-war *Decatur*, and *Yorktown*, the twenty-two-gun *Portsmouth*, the twelve-gun brig *Bainbridge*, and the ten-gun brig *Porpoise*. This force totaled seventy-six guns and was made up of middle-aged vessels: the two smaller sloops had been built in 1838, the *Portsmouth* had been commissioned in 1844, the *Bainbridge* was commissioned in 1842, and the *Porpoise* in 1836.

The brig *Bainbridge*, under Lt. Edward W. Callahan, made one sortie to the African coast during Cooper's watch. Callahan was at Porto Praya until March 1849 and then sailed to Monrovia, arriving on March 19. Three days later he took her eastward, standing along the Ivory and Slave Coasts, calling at Elmina; Cape Coast Castle; Accra; and Quitta. This procession of about 1,500 miles consumed nearly three weeks. The *Bainbridge* sailed from the latter place on April 11 and arrived at Princes Island a week later. She then returned to Monrovia for four days and sailed to Porto Praya. She departed from the Cape Verdes on June 25 and arrived at Funchal, Madeira on August 10, having stopped at Santa Cruz in the Canaries for about two weeks. Of five months on the station only about a month was spent on the African coast. [33]

The sloop-of-war *Decatur*, under Edward Byrne, had been at Porto Praya with *Bainbridge* when Cooper hoisted his flag in December 1848. On December 23 Byrne sailed to Monrovia where he remained until February 3. Byrne arrived at the Cape Verdes on February 20 and proceeded to Madeira on March 6. He returned to Porto Praya in mid-May after a stopover in the Canaries.[34]

Decatur returned to Monrovia in late June 1849, after five months away on the islands, and sailed eastward on July 1, dropping anchor at Grand Bassa and Sinou. She continued east to Whydah, via stops at Cape Palmas, Elmina, Accra, and Quitta. The sloop left the coast on August 9, arriving at Princes Island four days later. A week later, Byrne turned her again to the coast, arriving at Grand Bassa on September 10. Three days later Byrne sailed west, beating up the coast to Monrovia. From the middle of September to the 22nd she was at Monrovia, then she headed to Porto Praya where she resupplied and departed for the States, ending her tour on the Africa station. The vessel had been on the coast about four months and had sailed no farther east than Quitta.[35]

Porpoise's service under Cooper began at Porto Praya, from whence she sailed to Funchal and the Canaries, returning to the Cape Verdes the first week in April 1849. Following this, there was an uneventful sortie to the coast, from Monrovia to Princes Island, and back to Liberia, occupying June and most of July. She was back at Porto Praya on August 10, after the command had devolved on Flag Officer Gregory.[36]

In contrast to the humdrum cruising by the other vessels of the squadron, *Yorktown* and her crew witnessed a pitched battle on the African coast. *Yorktown* had sailed from Boston in November 1848, carrying Captain Cooper to his new command. The crossing was a rough one, causing Cooper to write: "We have had a long a very disagreeable passage. . . . The present battery is much too heavy for the ship, twelve guns would have made the ship much easier and more efficient than the sixteen. . . . We have not had since we left Boston, a dry plank in any part of her."[37] This statement has been seized upon by a recent writer to prove that the Navy was "overgunning a minimum number of ships" to meet the eighty-gun quota for the squadron.[38] The truth of the matter was more mundane. *Yorktown* was one of a class of five "Third Class Sloops" built in 1839–40. This class included *Decatur*, *Dale*, *Preble*, and *Marion*, all of which were generally considered too small for their sixteen 32-pound carronades.[39]

In any event, after the tempestuous crossing, Captain John Marston anchored *Yorktown* at Madeira in late December. From there he sailed to Porto Praya, where Captain Cooper hoisted his flag on *Portsmouth*.[40]

Marston's first task on sailing to the African coast was to repair the ship's decayed rudder post, as facilities for this were not to be had on the Cape Verdes. This was done at Bathurst on the Gambia River, where an iron band was added to reinforce the rudder head. Marston then proceeded south to Monrovia. On arriving there, he played host to Liberian president Joseph Roberts—recently inaugurated as that nation's first chief executive—and was party to plans underway for an attack on a tribe on

the southern coast at Sinou, a strip of land that the Liberians had purchased previously. The offending tribal group in the area not only refused
to yield to the Liberian claims, but it was also harboring a Spanish slave
factory, where goods were gathered to pay for blacks captured in the
interior.[41]

When the small Liberian army was ready, they were loaded on boats,
towed by a French steam gunboat, and landed the next morning at Sinou.
Yorktown sailed in company with the expedition, with President Roberts
on board. Though the Americans did not participate directly in the battle,
Roberts requested that some of *Yorktown*'s crew accompany the battle
force "for effect." Thus, four of her boats were sent unarmed, giving the
men a "good view" of the engagement.[42]

With a French landing party and gunfire support, the Liberians drove
the enemy into the interior and captured the Spanish barracoon. *Yorktown*
hovered off the coast for several days as the engagement progressed.
Subsequently, President Roberts embarked again, took up residence "in
state" in the ships cabin, and the vessel made calls at Cape Palmas, Grand
Bassa, Tradetown, Cape Mount, and elsewhere.[43]

Once the military and political excitement had dissipated, *Yorktown*
sailed to Porto Praya, arriving in June 1849. There she replenished and
made for Cadiz, the closest port where her weakened rudder could be
replaced. Afterwards, Marston returned via Madeira and the Canaries to
Porto Praya. There, in October, *Yorktown* was caught by one of the islands' characteristic southwest gales—on a lee shore. Though normally a
vessel would go to sea to gain sea room, the storm had come up so swiftly
that the captain elected to ride it out in place. Through the perilous night
into the next day, *Yorktown*'s anchors barely held, with her stern not far
from the rocks at the base of a steep cliff.[44]

Another American vessel caught in the tempest was not as fortunate. The brig *Copperthwaite* dragged her anchors, went ashore, and
hoisted her colors union down. Marston sent a boat to assist, and after a
harrowing, stormy passage, the bluejackets managed to board her and
take charge. The men sent down the brig's upper yards and masts, and,
later, got out an anchor to windward. Once calm had returned, the vessel
floated with the next land breeze. The damaged brig was repaired by
Yorktown's carpenters and was back in service shortly thereafter. The
Secretary of the Navy subsequently commended the *Yorktown*'s crew for

their actions.[45] The susceptibility of Porto Praya to sudden, vicious storms was another constant which hampered the operations of the squadron throughout its existence.

The last of *Yorktown*'s service under Commodore Cooper was occupied with another cruise from Porto Praya to Monrovia in November 1849. She remained in Liberian waters until January 1850, when she departed for another cruise down the coast.[46]

Finally, the flagship *Portsmouth* began Cooper's command at Porto Praya in December 1848. Cooper took her to the coast and arrived at Monrovia at the end of January. The run down the coast to Accra, then to Princes Island, ended the first week of March, and she was back at Monrovia at the end of that month. Cooper was at Madeira in early June and sailed from there at the end of July, arriving at New York on September 3.[47]

Benjamin Cooper's short command—about seven months—marked the second period in which there were no slave ships taken, or at least none which were seized and sent back to the United States for adjudication. The two sloops and brig sailed to the African coast during Cooper's command, but *Yorktown* barely made it beyond the environs of Liberia. *Bainbridge* and *Decatur* each skirted the coast as far as Quitta and turned southwest to Princes Island. The flagship *Portsmouth* was on the coast during the month of February and left Princes Island on March 5 to return to Liberia. After four days there, Cooper returned to the squadron rendezvous, then, in June, reverted to Madeira.

Two other factors, besides lack of diligent cruising, may have contributed to the lack of results during these months. The first of these was the Royal Navy's treaty-making and enforcement activities in the years 1847 through 1849: Twenty agreements were signed with native leaders during these years, covering areas as large as a degree of longitude. As far as enforcement was concerned, in February 1849 Commodore Sir Charles Hotham assembled a fleet of seven vessels and sent three hundred men across the Gallinas River bar and burned all the factories and barracoons in the vicinity, destroying the trade goods that made the slave trade possible in that area. Hotham followed this by declaring a blockade of that part of the coast. The results were substantial: The local chiefs immediately turned out the Spanish slave dealers and threw themselves on the mercy of the British. By the end of the year it was reported that all foreign slave dealers had been evicted from Gallinas and Sherbro.[48]

Commodore Cooper was well aware of the British actions and, in fact, had been apprised of the blockade at its inception. He was able to write the secretary of the Navy in May 1849 that the blockade of Gallinas and destruction of the slave marts at New Cess "leaves the coast clear of the traffic," but that it would now be confined "to the Bight of Benin, near and at Whydah." He recommended a depot of supply nearer to "the only slave grounds within our limits for cruising."[49]

The second reason for the inactivity during this period may well have been the commodore's health. As noted earlier, one of his officers had referred to his failing health, and it was this which caused Cooper to turn over his command to Edward Byrne, commander of the *Decatur*, on July 29, 1849, and to return to the United States on *Portsmouth*. [50] The circumstances of the change of command seem somewhat ambiguous: the secretary of the Navy's report states that Cooper notified the department of his ill health in late August, which means that Cooper had turned over his command and departed from Porto Praya *before* the department was informed of his health problem and his request to be relieved. In fact, the secretary's letter relieving him of command due to his "continued ill health" was dated August 13, 1849. It further states that Cooper arrived at New York "before the departure" of Gregory for Africa. (Gregory's departure was August 17.) It appears in fact that Cooper returned to the United States, *then* requested to be relieved on health grounds. It was certainly unusual for a squadron commander to turn over his command to a junior commander and sail home before his official relief had arrived. The severity of Cooper's health problem can be judged by the fact that he passed away less than a year later, on June 1, 1850.[51]

With Bolton's death in 1849, two of the squadron's commanding officers had died within eighteen months of each other. This unusual co-incidence, of course, did nothing to reduce the general fear of serving on the Africa Squadron.

8

THE BRAZIL SQUADRON AND THE SLAVE TRADE, 1845–1849

Any study of the U.S. Navy's anti–slave trade mission should include activities of the Navy's Brazil Squadron. For a short period this unit was quite active, and it was in some respects an interesting contrast to the Africa Squadron.

The Brazil Squadron was formed in 1826 and was the American naval presence for the east coast of South America.[1] Generally, the squadron was entrusted with protecting American interests and trade, with no particular emphasis on suppression of the slave trade. The squadron's cruising grounds ran from above the equator to Cape Horn and included, nominally, both southern coasts of South America. As to the size of the squadron, it was rarely large: in 1847 it numbered two ships, a brig and a frigate.[2]

As has been mentioned, however, both Brazil and Cuba were the two major markets for slaves, and therefore they were destinations for the Atlantic slave traders. The slave trade had— nominally—been illegal in Brazil since 1829. However, the trade continued to thrive. For example, in 1837 the British Mixed Court in Sierra Leone reported ninety-two vessels landed around forty-six thousand slaves in Brazil. In the last half of the 1840s the numbers grew to more than fifty thousand per year.[3] Brazil would not begin the emancipation of slaves until 1871, and in the first half of the nineteenth century it had a slave population more than twice as large as that of the United States. This growth ended in 1850 with a turnaround of the Brazilian government's attitude toward the trade, in direct response to the British political and naval pressure. In fact, Royal

Navy ships actively boarded and seized slavers on the Brazilian coast, bringing diplomatic protests; but, of course, the predominance of British sea power was something few nations could flout with impunity.

As to American participation in the Brazilian trade, George H. Profitt, the American minister to Brazil, claimed—though with some exaggeration— that it was "almost entirely carried on under our flag and in American-built vessels." He added that the traders claimed they rarely saw an American cruiser on the coast of Brazil, and that if a British naval vessel approached, the slaver would simply run up the American colors. Henry A. Wise, a Virginian who actively fought the trade, succeeded Profitt in 1844. He made a nuisance of himself by hounding Congress and the Executive branch to act in direct response to this travesty. It was Wise who finally instigated active measures by the Navy in the mid-1840s.[4]

It is worth noting here the case of the American brig *Kentucky* as an example of the unbridled violence endemic to the trade, as well as the lack of American response. The vessel cleared Rio de Janeiro in March 1844 for Africa and returned with more than five hundred slaves. The blacks revolted but were subdued by the crew with gunfire. Summary "trials" were held on board, followed by quick convictions on trumped up charges of mutiny. Forty-seven blacks were hanged, shot. and thrown overboard. In some instances, in order to reuse the shackles, a convicted slave's leg was chopped off to separate him from his unconvicted companion.[5] In another instance, the brig *Senator*, which had been stopped and released in 1847 by the Africa Squadron's brig *Boxer*, had proceeded to load a cargo of slaves and land around six hundred blacks. This vessel had also cleared and returned to Brazil.

It was 1845 before the U.S. Navy's Brazil Squadron seized a suspected slaver. Prior to this, for example in 1843, when the charge d'affaires at Rio de Janeiro notified Brazil Squadron Commodore Charles Morris of the expected arrival of five suspected slavers under the American flag, Morris replied that, "Any effort to interrupt particular vessels with the Small force under my orders, upon a coast of two thousand miles in extent without any intimation of their ports of destination, would evidently have very small chances of Success."[6] For whatever reasons, Morris was ignoring the well-known fact that most of the slaves were being landed in an area no more than three hundred miles long, ranging from Cape Frio to Santos, with Rio in the center. By 1845 Morris had been replaced as squadron commander and the frigate *Raritan* made the first seizure. The offender was the brig *Porpoise*. *Porpoise* had made several slaving voyages, but most recently she had acted as a tender and decoy for the aforementioned *Kentucky*. When a naval cruiser would come in sight, the *Porpoise* would make to "escape" and lure the man-of-war away from the actual slaver.[7]

Wise arranged the vessel's seizure in January 1845, some three months after the brig had accompanied *Kentucky* on her infamous return to Brazil. The capture was not without controversy: it was accomplished while *Porpoise* was in the harbor at Rio. Apparently there was some miscommunication or misunderstanding beforehand, as Flag Officer Daniel Turner wrote Secretary of the Navy John Y. Mason that he had obtained permission for the seizure from the local customs officials who had first boarded the vessel.[8] The Brazilians apparently were intent on making an example out of the case and treated the seizure as a violation of Brazilian sovereignty. To enforce their point of view, Brazilian vessels surrounded the flagship frigate *Raritan* and demanded that the *Porpoise* and her crew be released. Later, Wise wrote that if extradition for the crew had been refused, he would have sent them back to the United States on the brig *Bainbridge* "at all hazards." This diplomatic rumpus, as well as political pressure from influential ship owners back home who claimed he was hurting American commerce in the South Atlantic, eventually ended Wise's tenure in office.[9] It is worth noting, however, that there was little material difference between Wise's actions in this instance and a policy instituted by Britain shortly after this, wherein British cruisers were authorized to capture suspected slavers in Brazilian waters.[10]

As an interesting side note, Turner wrote that "two young negro slaves [from *Porpoise*] were set at liberty" by the Brazilians. The two fourteen-year-olds maintained that they had been taken on board off Africa on the "pretext that they were Free Passengers" and they had "of their own accord" come on board *Raritan*. The two were apparently shipped to the United States on *Bainbridge*, but their final disposition is not known.[11]

Despite the ambiguous circumstances, Brazilian authorities eventually allowed the *Porpoise* to be sent back to the United States for adjudication, along with crewmembers from both *Porpoise* and *Kentucky*. The testimony of several unwilling sailors from *Kentucky* resulted in the court condemning the *Porpoise*. Cyrus Libby, skipper of the brig, returned voluntarily to Maine for trail and was acquitted. Minister Wise reaped contradictory rewards for his efforts. The British envoy at Rio wrote him to commend his "unremitting" "zeal and activity," and to convey "the gratitude" of his nation and "of all other nations embarked in this great cause of humanity." On the other hand, Wise's own nation officially reprimanded him for his role in ignoring diplomatic niceties in seizing the vessel.[12]

Another activist consul was responsible for the next seizure in Brazil. In June 1845, Brazilian authorities at Bahia seized the brig *Albert* of Boston at the behest of the American consul there. The vessel was put in the charge of Lt. Henry Walke of *Bainbridge* to sail to the United States for adjudication. It is interesting that the Brazilians cooperated in this instance, no doubt hoping to preempt precipitous actions on the part of the Americans. In any event, the case against the vessel was dismissed by the federal circuit court of Eastern Pennsylvania.[13]

The seizure of *Porpoise*, as well as the increased British anti–slave trade activities off Brazil, raised awareness of the problem back in the United States, and for the first time, late in 1845, the secretary of the Navy specifically instructed a naval commander to suppress the slave trade off that country. Secretary Bancroft wrote Captain Lawrence Rousseau warning him not to seize vessels within Brazilian waters, but to "use all your rightful and legal powers" for the suppression of the trade.[14]

This directive proved problematic for the squadron, as the force available for the task was being siphoned off for the Mexican War. There was little activity in the area in 1846, and by late 1847 the naval register listed only two vessels assigned: the sloop-of-war *Bainbridge* and the forty-four-gun frigate *Columbia* (a flagship from November 1845 to October 1847.)[15] Also, during most of the 1840s there was war between Brazil and Uruguay, in which British and French were involved. These factors added to an uncertain diplomatic atmosphere and discouraged the squadron from actions that might be construed as violating American neutrality toward the conflict.[16]

The only incident remotely related to the slave trade was the situation involving the barque *Fame* in mid-1847. This whaler had been damaged in a storm and had put into a Brazilian port for repairs. This done, the master—without reference to her owners—absconded with the vessel and took her to Africa. The barque returned with some six hundred slaves. *Bainbridge* was sent to retake the vessel on grounds she had been stolen—rather than having been party to the slave trade. This was sufficient to gain the cooperation of the Brazilian authorities and an American guard was placed on the ship. After further negotiations, the Brazilians allowed the vessel's officer, William Brown, to be returned to the United States for trial. The case against him, however, was predicated on violation of the 1820 anti–slave trade law. He was tried in Eastern Pennsylvania district court and acquitted.[17]

The year 1848 saw an abrupt change in the squardon's anti–slave trade activities. The new commodore, Captain George W. Storer, was directed to be more aggressive, and to help him do so he was given three additional vessels: the schooner *Onkahye*, the brig *Perry*, and the steamer *Alleghany*.[18] All three proved to be useful in the pursuit of slavers.

The little schooner was unique to the service. She had been built as an experimental yacht to a design by Robert L. Stevens—an avid innovator in both sailing and steam ships—and was stiff and fast. She was purchased by the Navy in 1843 and was armed with two guns. The schooner had first served in the Caribbean and Gulf of Mexico and arrived at Rio de Janeiro in December 1847.[19]

The brig *Perry* was similar to the *Truxtun* and had gone into service in 1843, mounting ten guns. As with the other Navy brigs of this era, she was over-hatted and laden with boats and equipment, and her battery had been reduced to eight guns by this time.[20] Before her service with the anti–slave patrol was over, *Perry* had six captures to her credit—more than any other vessel assigned to either the Africa or Brazil squadrons.

The most surprising addition to the squadron was *Alleghany,* the first steam ship to be involved in anti–slave trade operations. One wonders why the vessel was sent to Brazil rather than to Africa, given the unremitting requests by the Africa Squadron's commanders for steamers. It may well have been because she would be operating mainly out of Rio de Janeiro where coal was readily available, and she would not be expected to make extensive passages to obtain provisions. In fact, the *Alleghany* proved to be particularly voracious in her coal consumption. The vessel was an experiment, using "Hunter's Wheels." Essentially these were two paddle wheels mounted horizontally, on vertical axes, beneath the ship's waterline, with their paddles extending through apertures in the hull. The method worked, but the wheels tended to use as much power disgorging water from the wheel casings as in propelling the vessel. The result was a typical coal consumption of about one ton per hour—30 percent higher than other contemporary naval steamers. Probably the only advantage of the vessel, particularly in approaching a prey, was her appearance: except for a small smoke stack, the barque-rigged vessel looked like a sailing ship.[21] (Additionally, the barque-rig was traditionally a merchant, rather than a naval, rig.) It is also notable that the vessel was one of the first in the Navy with an iron hull, and she was commanded by Lt. William W. Hunter, the inventor himself.

With these vessels attached, the Brazil Squadron was, on its face, more appropriately equipped to deal with slavers than the Africa Squadron, not to mention that it had access to major ports and facilities. And, in fact, Commodore Storer had passed along to his commanders copies of Perry's 1843 instructions detailing the fine points of capturing slavers. Consequently, it was not long before there were results: on January 23, 1848, *Onkahye* seized the American slaver *Laurens*.

Afterward, Storer wrote that, "The circumstances attending the fitting out of this vessel, and the well understood object of her expedition, on shore, for a long period previous to her departure . . . together with the well authenticated [illegible] attending her capture, seem to warrant the belief that there can be no question as to the result of her trial."[22] Indeed, the case against *Laurens* was strengthened by the words of the first mate, who described the "criminal schemes" of the supercargo, and who also extolled the profitable nature of the slave trade. The outcome was not to be as obvious: the grand jury refused the indictment of the captain, but the vessel was condemned.[23] Unfortunately for the squadron, the small but lithe *Onkahye* departed from the coast of Brazil less than a week after this capture, returning to her permanent assignment on the West Indies station.[24]

Alleghany's term with the squadron was longer, ending in October 1848. However, just as *Onkahye* showed the utility of small fast vessels, *Alleghany* proved the utility of steam-powered cruisers in the fight against the slave trade.

In May 1848, Commodore Storer acted on information from the U.S. consul that the barque *Louise* was a suspected slaver. Her owner, Joseph Souder, had recently sent another of his vessels to Africa and sold her to slave traders. The consul kept an eye on the ship, and when she sailed, Lieutenant Hunter was ordered to pursue. Despite the fact that *Alleghany* was under repair and had no foremast or yards in place, Hunter slipped his moorings and pursued. Seven miles out, he fired a blank cartridge across her bows, brought the *Louisa* to, and sent a boarding party. No doubt the *Louisa*'s crew was caught off guard when approached by a vessel moving without sails or other visible means of propulsion.[25]

Hunter sent a boarding party that fairly scrutinized the barque, beginning by comparing the crew to the crew list and noting whether their wages were excessive. They were not, and the dozen or so extra men on board were described as passengers. The next step was examination of the cargo, which proved to be a mix of 161 barrels of farina, 320 barrels of gunpowder, 27 dozen planks, rum, rice, beans, beef, muskets, and barrels of salt water. The latter the captain claimed legitimately was for ballast.The cargo agreed with the manifest and there were none of the other expected accoutrements of a slaver: no apparatus to cook for a mass of slaves, no shackles, and no disinfectants. Hunter decided, reluctantly, that there was not sufficient evidence to "feel himself justified in capturing her."[26] Despite this, it was a historic event: it was the first time a U.S. naval steam vessel had stopped a suspected slaver.

In the next six months, Hunter and *Alleghany* stopped three other vessels on suspicion of participating in the trade. In June the *Juliet*, under Captain Nathaniel Gordon, was intercepted five miles at sea and subjected to an eleven-hour search by Hunter's officers. Again, the cargo was not particularly appropriate for a slaver and the vessel was sent on its way. It should be noted, however, that the same Nathaniel Gordon, fourteen years later, became the only American executed for violating the slave trade laws.[27]

Alleghany's last two stops were the brig *Venus* and schooner *Marion*, both in October 1848. The former was searched and was found to have nothing "indicating her character as a slaver." The *Marion* was bound for Loango on the African coast. Her master, anticipating trouble from American cruisers, had landed some of his manifested water casks, as he feared that they might "render him liable to seizure." Though the vessel was chartered to one who was "notorious" as an importer of slaves, there was, again, not enough evidence to warrant seizing her. [28]

Though none of Hunter's stops and boardings resulted in captures, when *Alleghany* departed for the United States, Storer was sorry to see her go. He wrote: "Her peculiar properties have enabled her to overhaul and examine all vessels suspected of being engaged in the slave trade, which have left here during her stay at this port; while the thorough and effective manner in which the search has been conducted, had done much to spread alarm among those concerned in that nefarious traffic."[29]

Alleghany then joined the Mediterranean Squadron, becoming the first American iron steamer to cross the Atlantic. Less than a year later the vessel was decommissioned and her strange and uneconomical propulsion system was removed.[30] *Alleghany* at least had proved, in principle, that steamers were useful in fighting the slavers, despite their cost and inefficiency.

The brig *Perry*, however, was significantly more cost-effective in taking on the slave traders operating out of Brazilian ports. Under the command of Lt. John A. Davis, she was first sent to investigate the vessel *Democrat* in early December 1848. The vessel was not seized, and Storer attributed this to the "inexperience of the officers of the *Perry* who had not been employed in this kind of service." [31] Shortly thereafter, Storer dispatched *Perry* to go after the barque *Ann D. Richardson* and included in his orders a few hints for Davis and his boarding parties. He wrote that the boarding crew pay attention to her charts, papers, number and description of passengers and "water casks (they sometimes may have false heads) hand and feet irons, chains . . . [and] materials for a slave deck . . . It has been ascertained that recently hand and feet irons have been stored in barrels of rice."[32] These instructions were in addition to a previous directive, in which he wrote that casks labeled "copper" might have cooking apparatus within and barrels of slave shackles might be labeled "iron ware."[33]

Ann D. Richardson was seized on December 11, 1848, off Rio, and Davis wrote that his justification for the act included cargo "undoubtedly meant for the slave trade": gin, brandy, boards, joists, rice, and farina; there was also a "discrepancy in the evidence of ownership . . ." Papers found on the vessel included authorization to sell the it on the coast of Africa for fifteen thousand Spanish dollars, and a letter from the American consul at Rio indicating that he had refused a sea letter for the vessel to sail to Africa, as the vessel had "ostensibly changed owners while in the harbour of Rio de Janiero . . ." A notorious American slave trader,

Joshua Clapp, was intimately involved with these transactions.[34] The barque was sent to the United States for adjudication, but the case was dismissed before a decision was made.[35]

Two days after taking the *Richardson*, Davis boarded and seized the brig *Independence*. In this instance, the circuit court of Eastern Virginia confiscated the vessel.[36] *Perry* had boarded three vessels in the space of two weeks, two of which were seized. This was a record for apprehensions for the Navy's anti–slave trade activities off Brazil.

The next intended victim for *Perry* was the ship *Flora*. Storer, having obtained information that the vessel's cargo was slave goods, had Davis keep a close watch on her as the vessel attempted to depart from Rio. For twelve days Davis hounded the *Flora*, moving his anchorage several times to forestall any attempt to escape. Additionally, the British naval commodore offered to tow *Perry* if it became necessary to apprehend the quarry. Finally the harassed captain, the aforementioned Joshua Clapp, caved in and brought lighters alongside to remove the incriminating cargo. Later, the vessel did sail and was reloaded at sea, only to be captured by a British cruiser and Brazilian customs officials.[37]

Perry's final capture while on the Brazil station was on January 6, 1849. This was the brig *Susan*. This vessel was sent to New York where she was confiscated by the court.[38]

With the exception of the surveillance of the slave ship *Imogene* in September 1849, the capture of *Susan* marked the end of American anti–slave trade activity by the Brazil Squadron. As mentioned previously, in 1850 the Brazilian government reversed its stance on the trade, and thereafter the government assiduously began to seize all Africans brought into the country as slaves.

In the short time when the squadron was active, four slavers had been seized and sent to the United States, and the squadron had certainly made its presence felt on the coast of that nation. Storer wrote the secretary of the Navy that the successful actions by *Perry* and *Alleghany* pointed up the need for an increased force in the area, "particularly steam vessels," and that the slavers were well aware that *Perry* was now the only vessel in the squadron that was capable of dealing with the numerous slavers coming into the area.[39]

The successes on the Brazil station during this period stand in stark contrast to the lack of activity on the eastern side of the South Atlantic;

certainly having a steamer and a small brig captained by a zealous commander contributed to the successes in Brazil. However, it should be pointed out that the two stations dealt with exactly the opposite ends of the trade and were faced with vastly different littoral situations. In Brazil it was a matter of monitoring the traffic in and out of a major port city and its environs. There was, in addition, an active American consul close at hand who fed the naval commanders timely intelligence on suspicious vessels, either in the harbor or about to sail. The American cruisers could simply wait out their quarry until the slaver made for sea, and then make the seizure. Off Africa, the number of points from which a slaver could emanate were scattered along a vast coast, and the cruisers had not the luxury of a convenient port into which they could resort when in need of supplies or respite.

9

COMMODORE GREGORY AND LIEUTENANT FOOTE REVIVE THE SQUADRON

Capt. Francis H. Gregory took up the squadron command in August 1849 at New York. Since Benjamin Cooper had departed from Porto Praya and left the squadron to a junior officer, Gregory was to depart immediately to assume his command. However, circumstances arose which required a delay, and Gregory was detailed to deliver dispatches to the Mediterranean Squadron, and then proceed to his assignment. Gregory departed from New York on September 20, 1849. [1] He finally arrived on station in the Cape Verdes in early November, after which Edward Byrne— the temporary squadron commander—departed in *Decatur* for the United States.

Captain Gregory, a native of Connecticut, was another pre–War of 1812 veteran, having been in the service since January 1809. Of his nearly forty years in the Navy, only four had been unassigned, while eighteen had been active sea service. His previous assignments included command of the schooner *Grampus* running down pirates in the Caribbean in the 1820s, and, more recently, command of the *Raritan* on the Brazilian station. [2] He was to end his career as general superintendent of the Navy's Ironclad Bureau during the Civil War. He was a highly respected and conscientious officer, and he was promoted to Rear Admiral before his retirement.

Strict enforcement of the squadron's primary mission—or at least the mission for which it had been established—was, as has been seen, something that had been lacking since Commodore Read departed in 1847. By the time Gregory assumed command, a few of the obstacles that had faced the earlier commanders were absent: First, the Mexican War ended in March 1848, allowing the Navy to redistribute its vessels more evenly on the various stations. Second, the longstanding lawsuits that had been brought against two squadron officers in 1847 for their acts in enforcing the anti–slave trade laws were dismissed in 1849.

The lawsuits had been of much greater concern to the Africa Squadron than to the officers of the Brazilian station, as the vessels seized by the latter were taken with the cognizance and information supplied by the local consul. (Though even then, Lieutenant Hunter's reluctance to seize vessels he stopped in *Alleghany* may well have been explained by this factor.) Therefore, the evidence of their guilt was more compelling and accurate than that available to the naval commanders off the African coast.

The case against Lieutenant Bispham in the seizure of the *Malaga* came before Judge John J. Kane of the Eastern District of Pennsylvania. Kane was aware that a naval officer off the coast of Africa could not thoroughly investigate the background of a suspicious vessel that had begun her voyage thousands of miles away. But, despite this lack of knowledge, the officer was still required to make a decision about the legitimacy of the vessel and voyage. Given these circumstances, the judge was willing to allow some leeway for these officers and allow the possibility of honest mistakes that should not be subject to legal penalties. Kane noted that the vessel in question, *Malaga*, which was chartered by a notorious slave dealer and carried a typical slave trade cargo, was, on these grounds, justifiably seized by Bispham.[3]

With the legal pall lifted, Gregory's squadron was freer to move about in areas where the slavers were most wont to operate—particularly south of the equator—and he did so. The squadron was again built up to full strength. During Gregory's tenure, the squadron consisted of the sloops-of-war *Portsmouth*, with twenty-two guns; *John Adams*, with twenty-four guns; and *Yorktown*, with sixteen guns; plus the ten-gun brigs *Bainbridge, Porpoise*, and *Perry*. (Later during his tenure, *Yorktown* was replaced by *Dale*.) This brought the number of guns to ninety-two on the station, and, more importantly, for the first time in the history of the squadron there were six vessels on hand.

Gregory's early months brought a welcome communication from the British Squadron commodore, Arthur Fanshawe, who wrote informing him that slavers under the American flag were operating on the southern coast in the Congo River–Benguela area, and that he hoped to see American cruisers active in that area again. Gregory replied positively and expressed the hope that the two forces could operate "in concert" in the endeavor.[4]

The first example of that cooperation was soon to occur. The sloop *John Adams* arrived from Rio de Janeiro in early January 1850. Her commanding officer, Levin Powell, met Gregory at Porto Praya for instructions and proceeded towards the coast on February 10. After less than a week in Liberian waters, she sailed directly to Princes Island, arriving on March 9. From there, Powell sailed to Ambriz and St. Paul de Loando. This passage marked a radical departure from the previous sorties to the coast, which usually had been characterized by a slow progress south down the coast from Liberia, then, methodically, eastward to near the equator, then a quick right turn away from the coast to Princes Island. Powell, conversely, sailed immediately to Princes Island, then eastward across to the coast near and below the equator. The British commodore's advice apparently was heeded in detail, and the squadron's reluctance to cross "the line" was suddenly gone.[5]

Off Ambriz, Powell found the British steamer *Cyclops*, under Captain Hastings, shadowing the polacca-brig* *Excellent*, which was under American colors at the time. On the arrival of *John Adams*, *Excellent* suddenly hauled down the Stars and Stripes. This was sufficient evidence to warrant sending a boarding party, accompanied by a British officer, to the suspicious vessel.[6]

Powell himself was with the party and found adequate evidence of the vessel's unsavory character: inaccurate crew lists, no shipping articles, no manifest, a "second slave deck laid," a cargo of farina, a large camboose (galley), a box of wooden spoons, and large supplies of rice and water. Thus, he deemed her in "complete preparation for the reception of Negroes." Powell seized the vessel and sent her to the States. The district court of Eastern Virginia confiscated the ship. The unusual vessel, however, was described as "very small and old," and thus her capture cost the traffickers little.[7]

Subsequently, *John Adams* cruised off the Congo River and contacted the British cruisers there for information on various American-flagged vessels in that vicinity, particularly the schooner *Oregon*. This

---

* A polacca (or polacre) was a typically Mediterranean craft with exaggerated overhangs fore and aft and masts made from single spars, thus having no tops or ratlines.

vessel was later found to be a slaver, operating out of New York, but at this juncture Powell could obtain no confirmation of this. After standing off the river's mouth for several days, *John Adams* sailed to Ambriz, then Loando. He finally departed for Cape Mesurado on June 12. The sloop had been on the coast south of the equator since early April, about two months on station.[8]

From Liberia, *John Adams* sailed to Porto Praya, then to Cape St. Mary's and Bathurst on the Gambia. In August Powell made passage to Funchal, then was back at Porto Praya in early October 1850. He returned to Norfolk via St. Thomas in November and remained at the yard for refitting until April 25, 1851.[9]

The brig *Perry* arrived at the Cape Verdes in December 1849, and her commander was ordered to Monrovia to pick up kroomen and supplies from *Yorktown,* and then to proceed to the south coast. Gregory put the southern limit to this cruise at thirteen degrees south latitude at Cape Saint Mary's (present day Cape Santa Maria). This was about one hundred miles south of Benguela.[10]

Gregory recommended sailing well off from the coast from Monrovia, keeping westward until across the equator. Only then would the vessel proceed to the coast and work northward, taking advantage of the prevailing winds in the area close to shore.[11]

Perry proceeded immediately to Loando and then to Benguela, anchoring there around March 7. In accordance with instructions, the commander skipped the leisurely tour down the coast and even bypassed Princes Island to reach the southernmost part of the cruising area.[12] This zealous officer was Lt. Andrew Hull Foote, who was to become the second most famous officer—next to Matthew C. Perry—to serve in the squadron. Foote, a dour Connecticut Yankee, was noted for his zeal in other areas, as well: he was a lay preacher with strong religious and reforming views. During his Navy career he was known for his temperance stance and the ships he commanded were "dry." With Foote's encouragement, the crewmembers voluntarily opted for monetary compensation rather than the standard grog ration. Certainly his reformist attitudes fueled his zeal in enforcing the laws against human servitude. Being religious, and in his early years a pacifist, did not inhibit his naval service, however: during the Civil War, where he rose to the rank of Rear Admiral, it was remarked that he "prays like a Saint and fights like the devil." (This remark was, in fact, attributed to Francis Gregory.)[13]

In any event, Foote set to work with a will. By March 17 he was back at Loando, writing: "having examined closely the intermediate coast from Benguela . . . our stay here will not exceed one week, which period is necessary to water ship, attend to the rigging, and [obtain] fresh provisions . . . [then] . . . we will cruise between this and the River Congo, where it is asserted that the Slave trade is now most actively prosecuted." At Loando, Foote learned that the British naval steamer *Firefly* had recently stopped a vessel—the barque *Navarre* from Rio de Janeiro—flying American colors. When the suspect vessel's captain was told by the British officer that his papers were forged and that the ship would be turned over to an American naval cruiser, he had a sudden change of heart: "He immediately ordered the mate to haul the American ensign down, to throw it overboard." It was replaced by Brazilian colors and he then claimed the vessel was Brazilian and gave up the ship.[14]

Though this action on the part of the British commander indeed brought a slaver to justice, it raised hackles with the Americans. Shortly after this incident, Gregory wrote Foote and cautioned him in no uncertain terms about relations with the British cruisers:

> . . . the English officers, when they have boarded vessels under the Flag of the United States, and not having the Right of Search. . . . Threats have been used of detaining and sending them to the U.S. Squadron. This is improper, and must not be admitted, or any understanding had with them, authorizing such acts—if they choose to detain suspicious Vessels, they must do it upon their own responsibility, without our assent or connivance.

He further reiterated that the enforcement of the law was the American squadron's responsibility only and "we have no right to ask or receive the aid of a foreign power."[15]

From Loando, Foote sailed to Princes Island, and then returned to the coast at Ambriz. Gregory had written him of the great importance of keeping one vessel on the Southern coast and, to that end, had ordered him to rendezvous with *John Adams* or *Portsmouth* for provisions. However, Gregory indicated both vessels were so low on their own supplies that they would necessarily turn back for Porto Praya by June 1.[16]

However, in the process of looking out for an American warship and his supplies, Foote spied a more interesting object. It was a large, ship-rigged merchant vessel with two tiers of painted ports. On approaching, Foote noted that "Martha" and "New York" were painted on the stern, and American colors flew at the peak. *Perry* had no colors flying when Foote sent a boarding party to investigate, and when they rounded the vessel's stern, the men on board noticed American uniforms. The effect was immediate: the American flag was replaced by Brazilian colors. Once on board, the boarding officer asked for her papers and was told by the captain, Henry M. Merrill, that there were "no papers—log—or anything else," and the officer noticed that "at this time something was thrown overboard." Another boat was sent over from the *Perry* and the floating object proved to be the captain's desk, which indeed had sufficient material to implicate the vessel. A part owner of the ship was Joshua M. Clapp, mentioned previously in connection with other slave traders. On board was overwhelming evidence: 170 casks of water, 120 barrels of farina, 20 sacks of beans, 4 iron boilers with bricks for building furnaces, iron bars to secure slaves to the deck, 400 wooden spoons, and a slave deck ready for laying.[17]

When Merrill argued that an American cruiser could not seize a vessel under Brazilian colors, Foote's lieutenant responded that a vessel with no papers could be seized as a pirate in any case. At this point Merrill capitulated and admitted *Martha* was a slaver and that his intention had been to load eighteen hundred slaves and clear the coast by the next morning.[18] Foote seized the ship and sent it to New York.

Later, the British commissioner at Loando congratulated Foote, remarking that *Martha* had been the largest slaver on the coast for many years; indeed the illustration that Foote used in his 1854 book *Africa and the American Flag*, and which is included in this volume, bears this out. Certainly the vessel must have been substantial if it was intended to accommodate eighteen hundred slaves—a number twice as large as any cargo captured by the American squadron in its twenty-year existence.[19]

The British diplomat also noted that Foote had sent the *Martha*'s entire crew— foreigners and all—to New York, a move that he was sure would prove a severe blow to the traffic. This was in contrast to the British practice in these cases, which was to land the slave ships' crews somewhere on the African coast.[20]

The U.S. District Court in New York condemned the *Martha*. The captain escaped justice by forfeiting bail, and the mate was sentenced to two years in the penitentiary. The foreigners among the crew were released.[21]

Lt. Andrew Hull Foote (shown here in a Civil War-era photo).
Foote, a conscientious evangelical Christian and lay preacher, was also a
naval reformer, advocating ending the grog ration on naval vessels. Also a
diligent abolitionist, during his tour on the African squadron he captured two
slavers and kept his vessel—brig Perry—*below the Equator for nearly a year.*
Naval Historical Center

Foote later wrote that the papers found in the floating captain's desk revealed many details about the trade and implicated various American citizens not previously suspected of participation in "such a diabolical trade." One letter writer discussed various slave ships as follows: "The *Independence* cleared for Paraguay; several of the American vessels were cleared, and had sailed for Montevideo, &c. [*sic*], in ballast, and as I suppose bound niggerly."[22]

After this relatively straightforward seizure, Foote, in accordance with Gregory's order, continued cruising the southern coast. His next encounter with a slaver was considerably more complicated. In August 1850, Gregory, who since May had been to Porto Praya and returned to Loando, received information from a British cruiser expressing suspicion about the legitimacy of the ship *Chatsworth* of Baltimore, anchored at Ambriz. Gregory ordered Foote there to investigate. Foote found that the vessel's papers were in order, but her cargo smacked of a slave trader: planking possibly for a slave deck, a large quantity of water, etc., was on board. Further, there was an order for the master to leave the vessel whenever the Italian supercargo directed. So Foote still harbored doubts, and he escorted her to Loando for Gregory to inspect. The squadron commander wrote the secretary of the Navy that he had the "general impression the vessel is a slaver," but felt that the physical evidence was lacking and released the vessel.[23]

Foote's doubts persisted and he kept the *Perry* in close proximity to the suspect vessel. He actually boarded her a second time near Ambriz, putting a thirty-two-pound shot across her bows to bring her to. Again, the boarding party found no additional evidence against her. However, Foote placed a boat nearby to report if any suspicious cargo was loaded while the vessel was at anchor. Foote's suspicions were confirmed when he later communicated with another American trader, *Louisa Beaton*, at Ambrizette. The master of the latter reported that both vessels had been at Rio de Janiero recently and that *Chatsworth* had arrived there with a slave cargo. He suspected she was on the African coast again for the same reason. At this point, on September 11, 1850, Foote seized *Chatsworth*.[24]

With appalling brazenness, the master and supercargo protested that the act was illegal and that the court would release the vessel. He then threatened to bring a lawsuit against Foote for $15,000 in damage. Foote acknowledged the "pecuniary responsibility" involved, but he persisted.

The vessel was put under a prize crew, sailed to Baltimore, and condemned by the court as a slaver. However, it sailed without the Italian supercargo, who found an excuse to go ashore at Ambriz and never returned. The foreigners who made up the crew were put ashore in Africa. [25]

The capture of *Chatsworth* was the third in the space of six months. All were seized near Ambriz, south of the equator. Two of the three were by the *Perry*, making her total seizures thus far five, including those as part of the Brazil Squadron. It is certainly obvious that, had the two previous squadron commodores sent their vessels below the equator, additional captures may have been made.

Subsequently, Foote remained in the area and called at Loando. There he met with an unusual legal obstacle when he attempted to board the *Louisa Beaton*, which was then lying in the harbor: the Portuguese authorities refused to allow American naval officers permission to board American merchant vessels anchored at that port. After Foote remonstrated against this in a letter to the local authorities, they backed down "in view of the friendly relations" then prevailing between the two nations. With this settled, Foote departed for St. Helena.[26]

Capture of the slave ship Martha *by Lieutenant Foote in brig* Perry, *June 1850. This vessel was one of the largest slavers of this era, though she was captured without a cargo. Her captain admitted plans to board 1800 blacks but escaped justice by forfeiting bail in New York.*
Naval Historical Center

Foote spent ten days at St. Helena, an island famous as Napoleon Bonaparte's place of exile in his final years. During this interval, Foote communicated with the British authorities concerning the specifics of the capture of the *Navarre*, mentioned above. A controversy ensued when Foote learned that the only evidence that the vessel's American papers had been false was the word of the British commander who had seized her. The "false" papers themselves had been destroyed. Consequently, Foote applied to the British court for copies of the Admiralty court proceedings in the case, for further information on the subject. If, indeed, the vessel was American—regardless of the legality of her trade at the time of seizure—the British had violated the terms of the Webster-Ashburton Treaty. Foote's request was at first refused, then acceded to, but the situation remained unsettled when he sailed *Perry* back to the coast.[27]

Returning to Loando, Foote cruised for a few days in company with the British steamer *Cyclops*, establishing "friendly intercourse" with the British officers and vessels. When *Cyclops*, shortly thereafter, departed for home, "the two vessels exchanged three hearty cheers." [28]

Foote then beat southward to Benguela, where he reversed course to Loando. Before the end of November, *Perry* had run to Benguela thrice, but found no suspicious vessels in the area. Instead Foote heard rumors that several suspicious American vessels had rounded the Cape of Good Hope into the Mozambique Channel.[29]

With his supplies running low, Foote sailed northward and anchored at Ambriz, where he communicated with the British commodore there. Their discussions centered around the *Navarre* and other disputed seizures. The British commodore attributed these seizures of American flagged ships to the "want of judgement" on the part of some of his twenty vessel commanders on the station, but he also suggested that the United States, "with [its] extensive commerce . . . ought to have more cruisers where we are so strong." The commodore related an anomalous situation where a British steamer had assisted an American merchant vessel in distress and later learned that the vessel was, at the time, running up the Congo River to take on a cargo of slaves. The continuing problem with the British was remarked upon in the November 1850 report of the secretary of the Navy: "Occasional instances have occurred of the interference of British cruisers with vessels bearing our flag . . . but in each instance the offence has been atoned for by explanations and apologies."[30]

Subsequently, Foote sailed for Monrovia, and thence to Porto Praya, reporting there in early January 1851. After consultation with the commodore in *Portsmouth*, Foote took *Perry* back to the coast in February 1851. Foote took her to the south coast cruising inshore to St. Paul de Loando. From there he cruised south to Benguela and remained on that part of the coast for the next few months. During this period, at Kabenda, Foote communicated with the British commodore, inquiring as to the state of the slave trade since the capture of *Chatsworth* the previous fall. The British officer reported having seen only one suspicious American vessel in the vicinity (on the south coast) during this interval, though another American vessel had reportedly boarded a slave cargo off Lagos on the northwest coast in the same period. As to the state of the trade in general, he reported that "it had never been in a more depressed state, a state almost amounting to suppression; and this arises from the active exertions of Her Majesty's squadron on both sides of the Atlantic, and the cordial cooperation which has been established between the cruisers of Great Britain and the United States on this coast . . . and latterly from the new measures of the Brazilian government." He further mentioned the breaking up of factories at Lagos, Congo, and Ambriz, and the large number of slavers captured by the British and American cruisers in the bights and on the south coast. His optimism was tempered by the continued existence of a "whole line of barracoons," which were reported to house many slaves awaiting transportation, and he fully expected "further attempts to do so."[31]

Perry's African cruise ended on May 17, when Foote sailed from St. Paul de Loando for St. Helena. Shortly before this, Foote wrote his commentary on the needs of any squadron on the African coast. He wrote: ". . . if even the commodore had a small-sized steamer—which is here wanted more than on any other station—in which he might visit the cruisers at points along the line of the slave coast, that we would no more hear of a slaver using the American flag." Further, "eight smaller vessels . . . two of which should be steamers, would not add materially to the expense, as coal at Loando may be purchased at ten dollars the ton . . . These cruisers might each be assigned two hundred miles of the slave-coast, having their provisions replenished by a store-ship and flag-steamer; and once during the cruise—which should never exceed twenty months—run into the trades, or to St. Helena for . . . the health of officers and men." Foote dismissed concerns about the health hazards along the coast, noting that he had had no deaths on *Perry* in sixteen months, and he was equally dismissive of the reputed dangers of the climate. Finally, he feared removing the squadrons would cause the breakup of the developing legal trade in the area— ivory, gum-copal, palm oil, copper, and caoutchouc (India rubber)—and leave the coast to the "tender mercies of the piratical slave dealers."[32]

From St. Helena, Foote sailed to Porto Praya, then to Madeira, spending seven weeks at the latter place. Back at Porto Praya, Foote received orders to return to the United States and sailed in mid-November. *Perry* was placed in ordinary at New York's Brooklyn Navy Yard on December 26, 1851.[33]

From the activity of Foote in *Perry*, we turn to the ill-fated remainder of *Yorktown*'s service in the squadron. The vessel, under Captain John Marston, departed down the coast from Monrovia in January 1850, calling at Accra, Elmina, Cape Coast Castle, Whydah, and Princes Island. At Whydah, *Yorktown* fell in with the brig *Bridgton*, suspected by the British to be a slaver, and was, in fact, being watched by a lieutenant in a launch from the British cruiser *Kingfisher*. However, when the American officers boarded her, the vessel's papers appeared to be in order. Subsequently, the British lieutenant reported that the *Bridgton*'s captain became very "cheeky" and would point to the American flag on *Yorktown* and boast that the Royal Navy could not "touch him now." In any event, it was later reported—after *Yorktown*'s departure—that *Bridgton* had successfully eluded the British and escaped with a cargo of slaves.[34]

While dealing with the *Bridgton* and the British lieutenant, Marston learned the story of an effective ruse used by one of the American slavers on that coast. The American captain found himself in port with two British cruisers and was at first under suspicion as a slaver. However, the gentleman's cargo was well stocked with liquor and cigars, and he became friendly with the naval captains, the three of them frequently dining together. During their last dinner, they discussed the relative speeds of their ships and the American suggested a trial of speed among them. This was agreed to, and the next morning the American sailed out, challenging them to the contest. At the end of the day, the British cruisers were obliged to return to their station and bid the American adieu. By the time they dropped anchor and learned that the American had escaped with a slave cargo, their friendly adversary was long gone. Whether this story was true or apocryphal is not known. [35]

From Princes Island, *Yorktown* sailed for Porto Praya, with a chronicler of her cruise reporting that the ship was "perfectly healthy the whole time we were on this station." They had been under Perry's original strictures concerning entering the rivers and staying ashore, and the writer considered the health of this station compared "favorably" with that of Brazil and the West Indies. He wrote that there was but one case of the "fever" on the vessel, and that patient recovered.[36]

In June, the sloop-of-war sailed to windward, beating up through the Cape Verdes to Funchal, Madeira. They remained there a month and "did nothing but enjoy ourselves," with the usual round of picnics and dinner parties hosted by the American consul. On August 1 they sailed to the Canaries, remaining there until the end of the month.[37]

The ship then departed for Porto Praya, where she was to meet her relief, the sloop-of-war *Dale*. The crew was in fine spirits, as might be expected as their cruise was over, and, as their chronicler had it: "We had lost but one or two men by sickness; there had been no courts martial, and nothing had occurred to break the harmony existing on board."

The high spirits ended less than a week into the passage. About dawn on September 6, while skirting the north side of the Island of Mayo in the Cape Verdes, *Yorktown* stuck hard on the reefs. She "fetched up with all standing," and within minutes her carpenter reported, "It is of no use to pump, the ship's bottom is knocked out." As she rose and fell on the heavy swells, her bottom was crushed in and the large water tanks in the hold were rammed up against the berth deck beams. They were about a mile from shore and the boats were hoisted out. There was time for the crew to escape from below before the vessel fell on her beam ends. The hull settled, but the port side remained above water. The crew manned the boats, carried a load of survivors to shore, and returned for the rest. None of the crew was lost.

For the remainder of the day, the crew shuttled to the hulk, salvaging what could be found. The kroomen proved particularly effective divers, finding the ship's money on the bottom and surfacing repeatedly carrying all they could hold in both hands and even in their mouths. With the salvaged material the crew patched together tents and remained on the beach for a few days, then they found and moved to a small town at the south end of the island. Thirty-three days after the wreck they were picked up by the *Dale*, which transported them to Porto Praya for transfer to the *John Adams* for the passage home. Captain Marston was court martialed for the loss of the vessel and was exonerated.[38] *Yorktown* was the only naval vessel lost during the two decades of the squadron's existence. (It should be noted that the sloop-of-war *Concord* was also lost off the Loango River in October 1842, but this was shortly before the squadron was set up.) The sloop-of-war *Dale* had arrived from the United States on September 7, calling first at Madeira. Commanded by William Pearson, she made for the island of Mayo in the Cape Verdes and picked up the *Yorktown*'s crew for transport to Porto Praya. She finally arrived on the African coast at Monrovia on October 31, 1850.[39]

Pearson took her eastward on November 8, calling or looking in at Elmina, Whydah, Badagry, Lagos, Oddy, and Jacqua (the latter about one hundred miles east of Lagos), before bearing southeast to Princes Island. At the end of December, Pearson was back at Quitta, then at Badagry in January. In mid-January he sailed to Princes Island and turned northwest, anchoring at Cape Mesurado on February 6, 1851. On March 7, *Dale* was at Porto Praya, rendezvousing with Commodore Gregory in the flagship and *Porpoise*. She departed on May 7 for Rio de Janiero.[40] *Dale* would return in late 1851 for another cruise, under the next commander of the Africa Squadron.

The brig *Bainbridge*, under Alfred G. Slaughter, had returned to Porto Praya at the end of 1849, meeting with Commodore Gregory as he assumed command of the squadron. Gregory ordered Slaughter to the coast, but not until March 1850, and then in company with the flagship *Portsmouth*.[41]

The two vessels sailed in company eastward, calling at Elmina, Quitta, and Whydah. At the latter place they separated, with the flagship sailing east along the coast and the *Bainbridge* going to Princes Island. From there, Slaughter turned north and sailed to Monrovia, then back towards the Cape Verdes. The *Bainbridge* and *Portsmouth* would rendezvous at sea on May 28 off Porto Praya. After just short of two weeks at Porto Praya, *Bainbridge* sailed home, arriving at Old Port Comfort, Virginia, on July 2, 1850.[42]

The third brig in the squadron during this time was the *Porpoise*. Early in Commodore Gregory's tenure the vessel was under the command of Alexander G. Gordon. She left Monrovia for Porto Praya toward the end of July, after the squadron devolved on Gregory, and remained in the Cape Verdes until November 1. Returning to Monrovia, the vessel encountered one of the more egregious examples of the frustrating weather patterns of this area. It consumed twenty-five days to reach Liberian waters, encountering several days where the logs record, "Calm," and "No headway." This was nearly twice the duration of her last passage on the same route in April.[43]

She was at Monrovia in late November and December 1849, and then proceeded eastward, making the rounds to Elmina, Accra, Quitta, Whydah, and Princes Island. After returning to Monrovia in late January 1850, she sailed to Porto Praya. At the end of February, by now under Lt. B. F. Sands, the vessel returned to Norfolk.[44]

Porpoise was out of commission for less than a month, and then crossed the Atlantic, arriving at Funchal on July 14 and Porto Praya on July 25. Now under the command of James L. Lardner, she arrived at Monrovia on August 7, 1850. Her next cruise down the coast brought the brig by Accra, Quitta, and Whydah, then to Princes Island. She arrived at the latter place on September 3. In early October she completed the circle and was back at Monrovia. She came back at Porto Praya in late October and remained there, supplying and provisioning, until December. On Sands's next coastal sortie, in December and January, he sailed *Porpoise* by Grand Bassa, Quitta, Whydah, and Lagos, before reprising her visit to Princes Island.[45]

February brought her return to Liberia, and a month later she was again at Porto Praya and in that vicinity, where she rendezvoused with the flagship. This visit ended in July, by which time Commodore Gregory had departed for the United States.[46]

The cruise of the *Porpoise* is the subject of one puzzling article written long after the fact by one of her midshipmen during this period. John Taylor Wood, famous for his swashbuckling exploits as a Confederate naval officer, wrote an article entitled "The Capture of a Slaver" for *Atlantic Monthly* in 1900—a full half century after his African service.

Unfortunately, Captain Wood seems to have been more interested in telling a good yarn than relating the probably much more mundane facts of the cruise off Africa. Though he has the names of the commanders of the vessel and squadron correct, he places the existence of the squadron from 1830 to 1850. He also relates some obviously personal experiences on board the *Porpoise*, as well as on and off the coast of Africa.

However, the body of the article is a detailed picture of the capture of a slave ship off the Niger River, carrying "about four hundred blacks bound to the Brazils." The seizure, in his narrative, comes only after an exciting sea chase in which he describes the boldness and skill of the adversary's ship handling. Indeed, the slaver is only brought to heel by the persistent and accurate shooting of the *Porpoise*'s bow chaser, which finally took down the brigantine's topgallant yard and gaff-topsail. Furthermore, to add to the swashbuckling theme, once the boarding party gained the slaver's deck, the slave captain instigated fisticuffs. According to Wood, "the struggle was desperate for a few minutes . . ." until the man was subdued on the deck. Once the slaver was in hand, Wood was put in charge of the prize crew to take the ship and slaves back to Liberia, and from there he returned to Porto Praya.[47]

Unfortunately, there seems to have been no such encounter or capture of a slaver by *Porpoise* while she was in Commodore Gregory's squadron. Though the logs mention various boardings, only once was there a chase with a shot fired. This occurred in February 1852—after Gregory had returned to the States. Further, the log does not mention any further contact with the vessel in question, indicating the chase was called off. Had a prize crew been assigned to a captured vessel, a list of the men detailed to the vessel would have been in the log.[48] In fact, disabling a slaver with gunfire and fistfights on captured vessels were almost unheard of on the Africa Squadron.

Commodore Gregory had raised his pennant on the *Portsmouth* at Porto Praya in December 1849 and remained in that vicinity until March 1850. In this interval, the supply ship *Relief* arrived on December 12 with provisions for the squadron. The new commodore met with the commanders of *Yorktown*, *Perry*, *Bainbridge*, and *John Adams* during this initial stay at Porto Praya. Also on hand in mid-January was the Revenue Cutter *Roger B. Taney*, which had returned from surveying duty in the Mediterranean.[49]

Gregory, having discussed his orders and expectations with his commanding officers, departed for Monrovia, arriving March 28, 1850. About a week later, he took the flagship eastward along the coast, accompanied by the *Bainbridge*. The sloop-of-war and brig parted after visiting at Whydah, and *Portsmouth* proceeded to Fernando Po, an island at the eastern extremity of the Gulf of Guinea. From there, Gregory sailed to Princes Island, where he met with Foote in *Perry*. By May 6, the commodore was back at sea, en route to Porto Praya.[50]

His stay at the Cape Verdes was less than two weeks, and Gregory sailed again for the coast. *Portsmouth* anchored at St. Paul de Loando on August 5, 1850. He spent at least three weeks at the Portuguese colony before sailing back to Porto Praya. It was during this interval that he had ordered Foote to investigate the *Chatsworth* at Ambriz. While returning to Porto Praya, Gregory boarded at least two merchant vessels, one of which was the British barque *Harrington*, said to be en route from Sierra Leone to the West Indies with "Black Emigrants" on board.[51]

At Porto Praya in early October, *Portsmouth* picked up survivors from *Yorktown* who were transferred from the *Dale*. After meeting with the *Porpoise* on December 1, Gregory sailed to Madeira. The stay at Madeira ended the day after New Years, when *Portsmouth* departed for Porto Praya. From January 11, 1851, through May, the flagship remained at the rendezvous at the Cape Verdes. During this period, *Perry*, *Dale*, and *Porpoise* called at Porto Praya. Gregory sailed for the last time from Porto Praya on May 25, arriving at Boston a month later, where *Portsmouth* was decommissioned.[52]

It is to be noted that Commodore Gregory, during his eighteen-month tour of duty on the Africa Squadron, made two cruises down the coast, one of which terminated at St. Paul de Loando, far south of the equator. The majority of the time was spent in the Cape Verdes (about eleven months). Unlike his predecessors, Gregory only resorted to Madeira for a total of one month—December 1850.

It is also significant that Gregory at least had attempted to circumvent the lack of a depot on the southern coast. This was evident in his orders to Foote to rendezvous with *John Adams* or *Germantown* to obtain supplies, which would enable *Perry* to remain far down the southern coast for an extended period. In the end, Foote was below the line for more than a year, excepting a month-long break in early 1851, when Foote resorted to Porto Praya.

As noted earlier, both the British and Americans were cognizant of the "lull" in the slave trade in late 1850 and 1851. This perception, in addition to the fact that the Webster-Ashburton Treaty included a clause allowing the anti–slave trade squadrons to be disbanded after five years on the station, certainly must have been considered by Secretary of the Navy William A. Graham in his report for 1851. Graham, a North Carolinian, wrote: "We are considering moving [the squadron depot] to St. Paul de Loando . . . but since the inhibition by Brazil of the African slave-trade among her subjects, it is doubtful whether it is necessary to continue this squadron as a permanent force, anywhere along the African shore; and it is accordingly proposed that notice be given to the British government of the termination . . . on our part, of the eighth article of the treaty." [53] To compensate for the Africa Squadron, Graham recommended strengthening the Brazil Squadron and dispatching an occasional vessel from there to the African coast to deal with the trade. Also, the Home Squadron would be asked to increase its vigilance in Cuban waters.[54] Graham's plan smacked of the pre-squadron approach to the suppression of the trade, and it was not acted upon.

As far as the causes of this "lull," it should also be noted that 1849 was marked by two important events that had drastic short- and long-term consequences for the American merchant marine. In January 1848 gold was discovered in California, and six months later the rush was on from the east coast ports. As many have noted, the pressure on the American merchant fleet was tremendous: "Any vessel that could move in a wind could find passengers;" even old whalers got into the business, and small sloops and schooners were pressed into service to take the gold seekers to the Isthmus of Panama, where they crossed to the Pacific side to catch another vessel to the California fields. The results were graphically shown in the famous photo of San Francisco in 1855: more than four hundred vessels were crowded the harbor, many of them abandoned.[55] Another measure of the extent of this trade was that in 1849, more than 775 vessels from the Atlantic coast cleared for California. Further, American laws required that only American bottoms could bring cargoes from the Atlantic coast.[56] These factors certainly draw one to the conclusion that the legitimate trade for the west coast, for a short while at least, drew a substantial number of American vessels away from the slave trade.

A less dramatic but more lasting factor was the repeal of the British Navigation Laws in 1849. For the first time, British merchants could purchase American vessels, and, more importantly, seagoing commerce with the British Isles was opened to American traders. This included the lucrative tea trade with China.[57] Between this and the California trade, the American merchant marine was undergoing a thorough realignment beginning in 1849, which, coinciding with increased British and American vigilance on the African coast, contributed to the "lull" in the trade.

10

CAPTAIN LAVALLETTE:
A LULL IN THE TRADE
1851–1853

In the midst of the prevailing calm on the coast of Africa in May 1851, Captain Gregory turned the squadron over to Elie A. F. Lavallette. Lavallette, another veteran whose date of entry into the Navy was 1809, was born in Virginia but listed his home as Pennsylvania. He was sixty-one years old when he took command of the squadron, and he was the son of Elie Vallette,* one of the first chaplains of the United States Navy.[1]

From 1842 to 1845, Lavallette had been commandant of the Navy yard at Pensacola, where an incident occurred which revealed a bit about the man and his attitude toward slavery. The story goes that a local government contractor, who had used slave labor in construction on the Navy yard, came to Lavallette complaining that some of his slaves had escaped while on the job. The contractor demanded that Lavallette detail sailors or Marines to join in the search, and Lavallette flatly refused. The result was an irate letter to his supervisors about Lavallette's lack of cooperation in the matter. As escaped slaves were considered fair game to all during this era, Lavallette's attitude was certainly unusual. In any event, Lavallette in his new command now found himself on the opposite side of the fugitive slave statute . . . returning slaves to freedom rather than pursuing them for recapture.[2]

When Lavallette raised his broad pennant, the squadron was composed of five vessels. The flagship was the sloop-of-war *Germantown*,

---

* Captain Lavallette had his name changed in 1840 from Elie A. F. Vallette to Elie A. F. Lavallette.

Captain Elie A. F. Lavallette, squadron commander, 1851–53.
*During Lavallette's tour two suspected slavers—*Advance *and* R.P.
Brown— *were seized, both of which had the poor luck to find themselves*
at Porto Praya in the midst of the American squadron.
Naval Historical Center

which was launched in 1847 and carried twenty-two guns, four of them eight-inch shell guns. The rest were the sloops-of-war *Dale*, with sixteen guns, and *John Adams*, with twenty-four guns, as well as the ten-gun brigs *Perry* and *Porpoise*. The vessels carried eighty-two guns, total.[3] However, it should be noted that *Dale* would quickly be detached from the squadron and sent on a mission east of the Cape of Good Hope, not to return to Porto Praya until December 1851.[4]

As Lavallette took command on this unattractive and reputedly unhealthy station, there were a few enlightening statistics available, as well as soon to be published, on this subject from the Bureau of Medicine. This bureau kept accurate count of sailors on the sick lists, as well as deaths in the squadrons. In 1850 the bureau published statistics on annual deaths, and the 1851 secretary of the Navy's report had enumerated the mortality rate as a percentage of numbers on the sick lists.

In the 1850 report, the number of deaths was listed for each squadron for the period 1845 though 1848. This number was then given as a percentage of the number of men in each squadron. The percentages ran from .82% for the Home Squadron down to .53% for the Mediterranean unit—this was during a period when the former was involved in the Mexican hostilities. Of the six squadrons, the Africa Squadron fell into fourth place behind the Mediterranean, Brazil, and Pacific squadrons. Only the East India and Home squadrons had higher death rates: the latter due to the war, and the former due to epidemics in the Far East. Actual numbers of deaths in the African Squadron ranged from a low of three deaths for 599 men on station in 1848, to eight of 751 men assigned in 1846.[5]

In the second document, which was published in the secretary of the Navy's report of 1851, the bureau calculated the percentage of deaths to the number of men on the sick lists. In this comparison, the highest death rate fell to the Brazil Squadron at .90% (Twelve deaths out of 1,286 sick); the second highest was the Pacific station (.75%); and next was the East India station (.72%). By these figures, the unit with the lowest death rate was the West Indies (Home) station at .19%. Significantly, the Africa Squadron had the second lowest death rate: six deaths out of 1,191 sick, a rate of .47%.[6]

These statistics do not support the thesis that the Africa Squadron was the least healthy squadron in the Navy. Overall, it seems rather to point to the East Indies as the assignment to avoid. It appears, also, that the sicknesses in the Africa Squadron were less likely to result in death than those ailments that were common in the other squadrons. However, statistics aside, the general opinion that an assignment to the Africa Squadron was a "death sentence" continued to prevail in the service. This reputation had not been helped by the recent deaths of two of its commanding officers in the space of eighteen months.

With his duty in mind, regardless of the drawbacks, Lavallette sailed in *Germantown*, under Cdr. James D. Knight, on April 14 from New York, arriving at Funchal on May 2. A week later he left for the Cape Verdes and anchored at Porto Praya on May 14. There, Lavallette met Gregory on *Portsmouth* and Lardner on *Porpoise*. About a month later, *John Adams*, under Cdr. Samuel Barron, arrived from Norfolk. The last element of the squadron, the brig *Perry*, was on the south coast of Africa during this period and would arrive at Porto Praya in early July. After

Gregory and Lavallette consulted and accomplished the change of command, the former sailed for home, departing May 22, 1851.[7]

Next to depart was *Porpoise*, which had been down the coast as far as Princes Island late in 1850, and had returned to Porto Praya in March. Lardner sailed to Funchal on May 19. Lavallette took *Germantown* eastward toward the coast on June 3, followed by *John Adams* on June 19.[8]

It is instructive to note Lavallette's instructions to Commander Barron, which were given immediately before they set out for the coast.

> I instructed Commander Barron that to encourage emigration alone it was necessary that perfect security . . . shall be insured [*sic*] to those who seek a habitation on the coast . . . & to impress upon the mind of the natives that the government of the U.S. consider all emigrants under its protection and will promptly use its power to secure it.
>
> I have also instructed Commander Barron to touch at Mesurado . . . once a month if possible . . . & to all principle [*sic*] settlements along the coast . . . and call [illegible] the kings and chiefs and represent to them the inevitable consequences and punishment in case of future injury to settlers.[9]

With these—and other—directives in view, from the end of June through September, *Germantown* and *John Adams* sailed in company down the coast. They stopped at Monrovia, Cape Palmas, Elmina, Accra, Cape Coast Castle, Grand Popo, Whydah, and, finally, turned west to Princes Island. On August 24 both ships made for St. Paul de Loando. Then on September 17 Lavallette sailed to St. Helena. At this time he wrote Secretary Graham that his crew had not been ashore in nine months and that they needed a short respite there.[10] After five days at St. Helena, Lavallette departed for Monrovia. After five days at the latter place in late October, he sailed to Porto Praya. Meanwhile, Barron took *John Adams* southward standing along the coast to Ambriz. He arrived at St. Helena several days after the commodore and left there a day before Lavallette departed.[11] This ended the squadron's first coastal cruise: no slavers had been encountered.

Back at Porto Praya, Commodore Lavallette wrote a report to the secretary of the Navy. No doubt reflecting on the lack of seizures or even sightings of suspected slavers during the cruise, he wrote: ". . . I found Commodore Bruce, commanding the English naval force . . . I also learn that the Slave trade is at least suspended, if not annihilated, on the West coast. From a knowledge of this fact, and of the apparent expediency of confining our cruising chiefly to the South coast, I . . . recommend . . . removing our Depot . . . to some point more convenient for our warships to rendezvous while cruising on the South coast . . . " He recommended St. Helena for the site.[12]

At Porto Praya, the squadron was reunited. By mid-November, *Germantown*, *John Adams*, *Porpoise*, and *Perry* were there, and *Dale* returned from her solo cruise on December 11.

Lieutenant Foote, in the *Perry*, had, on his arrival at Porto Praya in July, been given orders from the recently departed Lavallette that allowed him, at his discretion, to remain at Porto Praya or proceed to Madeira. Foote adopted the latter course and spent about seven weeks "recruiting" his "enfeebled" crew at the hospitable destination. Each day a portion of the crew was allowed liberty on the island.[13]

After the hospitality of Madeira, Foote returned to the Cape Verdes, where a diplomatic incident was brewing. The British consul there had denounced the American brigantine *Louisa Beaton* as a slave trader to the Portuguese authorities. Foote then took a hand and requested an explanation and enumeration of any evidence to that effect. The reply was that the British consul had believed the vessel had on board "irons, pots, and all other utensils" needed for the traffic, and that, ashore, a "load of slaves" was being purchased for the vessel's cargo. Foote then wrote to the harbor authorities emphasizing that the United States "would not permit an officer of any other government to interfere, officially or otherwise," with any vessel "entitled to wear" the American flag. He further suggested that the master of the vessel in question ought to be given a "pecuniary remuneration" in the case. However, the only tangible result of this exchange was an agreement that the local authorities would officially pass along to the American consul copies of documents concerning any further examples of attempted foreign interference with American vessels.[14]

Subsequently, in October, while still anchored at Porto Praya, Foote participated in the capture of a suspected slaver also moored in the harbor. Foote looked askance at the vessel, due to her "hull, rigging, maneu-

vering, and the number of men on board," and suspected her true character. He dispatched a boat to inquire further (he could not board a foreign-
flagged vessel in a foreign port) and was told that she was Brazilian, last
from Trinidad de Cuba, in sand ballast. Shortly thereafter, Foote learned
from the port authorities that the vessel's captain claimed smallpox was
on the ship, and therefore no one was being allowed on board. Foote
suspected a ruse and passed his suspicions along to the port officer, along
with a suggested plan of action. In consequence, the port official had his
boat rowed under her bows and requested her papers be handed down.
These documents turned out to be "too informal" to be legitimate, and
the vessel was boarded by the governor and collector of the port. No
smallpox was found and the vessel was seized. A contingent of sailors
from *Perry* was sent to assist in searching the vessel, moving her to the
inner harbor, and unbending her sails. [15]

The *Perry* remained at Porto Praya until orders were received to
bring the ship home. Thus ended the *Perry*'s eventful cruise in the Africa
station. On December 15, 1851, Foote sailed for the United States to the
sound of "three cheers" from the crews of *John Adams*, *Germantown*,
and *Porpoise*.[16]

The remaining squadron vessels dispersed individually from the
rendezvous at Porto Praya for the African coast, with the exception of the
flagship *Germantown*, which remained until March and then sailed for
Madeira. *John Adams* departed on December 19 and *Porpoise* on December 23. *Dale*, which had been at St. Iago, one of the neighboring
islands, when *Perry* sailed out of Porto Praya, departed on January 8. [17]
In late January, the squadron was augmented by the arrival of *Bainbridge*
from Rio. She departed on January 26 for the coast. [18]

The four vessels sent to the African coast cruised independently,
and for different purposes. *John Adams* was detailed to respond to a crisis developing in Liberia. In late 1851, President John J. Roberts had
written that the settlement at Bassa Cove had been attacked by a combination of Fishmen and Bassa tribesmen, resulting in a pitched battle and
their repulse by the Liberians. To assist in preparing for a second assault,
Roberts requested a vessel be sent to aid the settlers, and Secretary Graham ordered Lavallette to dispatch a ship for this purpose. Thus, *John
Adams*, under Commander Barron, was sent to Grand Bassa, arriving
there on January 1. Barron wrote in February that he gave assistance as

required, and the result was "the complete overthrow of the enemy." The specific kinds of assistance rendered by Barron and his crew is unknown, but it was probably more logistical in nature than active combat. Afterwards, on January 20, the sloop sailed to Cape Mount and she left the Liberian coast five days later. She returned to Porto Praya, and in early March sailed to Funchal.[19]

Porpoise had a less eventful cruise: she was at the Gambia River at the end of December and sailed along the coast to Monrovia via Bissao and Sierra Leone. She sailed from Monrovia on February 25 and arrived at Porto Praya on March 13. She remained until July 1 and sailed for home, where she decommissioned on August 3.[20]

Dale and *Bainbridge* each sailed eastward, skirting the coast. *Dale*, under James Lardner, was first, arriving at Monrovia on January 17. From there, the sloop called at the usual settlements: Elmina, Accra, and Lagos, then at Princes Island. Back on the coast, she was at the Gaboon River, then St. Paul de Loando. At the end of March, she left for Monrovia. Lardner kept her there about a week and returned to Porto Praya on April 10.[21]

A month after *Dale* had begun her sortie at Monrovia, *Bainbridge*, under Joseph Manning, followed in her wake. She called or looked in at Elmina, Accra, Quitta, Lagos, and, in the angle of the Bight of Biafra, the island of Fernando Po. Manning then took her back to Whydah and Quitta, and from there to Monrovia, reaching the latter place on May 12. He stayed a week there and was back at the Cape Verdes on June 7.[22]

During this cruise, Manning kept a running list of all boardings and "vessels seen," from February 11 to June 6, 1852.[23]

The listing shows a total of thirty-nine vessels, of which nineteen are named. The balance were apparently "seen" rather than boarded. Note the list includes several naval vessels, including four British, one Portuguese, one French, as well as the U.S. squadron's *Porpoise*. The largest number seen on a single day was at least nine at Lagos on March 20.

It is appropriate to note here that this is one of the few such listings found by the author in the research for this book. It was found not with the official documents but in Captain Lavallette's papers. In comparing this list to the *Bainbridge*'s deck logs in the National Archives, it is noteworthy that very few boardings or sightings were recorded in the logs. Also of note is the amount of traffic and its character on this portion of the African coast: thirty-seven vessels were seen in approximately four months, along about a thousand miles of coastline from Monrovia to Fernando Po in the Bight of Biafra. (The last two were recorded within two days of arriving at Porto Praya.) Further, a good proportion of the vessels seen were "regulars": vessels engaged in coastal trade or scheduled merchant ships, such as the "Hamburg Packet." Given this, it is obvious that any suspicious vessel would stand out and draw a fair amount of attention from the naval vessels (particularly the British) on the station.

At the end of May, Flag Officer Lavallette, in *Germantown*, returned to Porto Praya from Madeira. He was accompanied by Barron in *John Adams* and met the sloop-of-war *Dale*, which had arrived on May 10. *Bainbridge* arrived June 7. The brig *Perry*, now under Lt. Richard Page, returned from a short refitting at Brooklyn Navy Yard. She arrived from the United States toward the end of the month, about three weeks out from New York.[24]

With his squadron united again, Lavallette was in mind to put on a show, particularly with the national holiday in the offing. Thus, on Independence Day, amid salutes and cheers and with all five ships no doubt "shipshape in Bristol fashion," the squadron sortied in the sunshine from Porto Praya. *Germantown*'s deck log recorded that they "filled away: 'Dale,' 'Perry,' 'Bainbridge,' and 'John Adams' in company . . . the vessels of the squadron in their respective positions."[25]

At sea for the next few days, the squadron exercised. They practiced maintaining their positions, forming the line of battle and line abreast, and tacking in succession, among other things.[26] Of course, these sorts of maneuvers were totally irrelevant to the mission at hand. However, they were certainly justified in terms of maintaining a high level of seamanship and operational readiness. Also, it should be noted that while towering sails, glistening paintwork and brass, and sharp sail handling made for an impressive spectacle, the reality was that the year was 1852, and the age of the pure sailing Navy was essentially over. In less than two years, the Navy would launch its last major sailing vessel, the sloop-of-war *Constellation*. Steam power was now acknowledged as a necessity in all the navies of the world. And yet it would be another six years before the Africa Squadron was assigned a steam vessel.

With the show and exercises over, the squadron vessels proceeded to the work, though *Bainbridge* and *Dale* were off to Funchal, Madeira. Both would return to Porto Praya in early October. The other three— *John Adams, Perry*, and the flagship—made for the African coast. All three sailed into Liberian waters in mid-July. On July 28, *Germantown* sailed south directly to Princes Island, while *John Adams* remained in Liberian waters for another two weeks. *Perry*, meanwhile, started down the coast, calling at Cape Coast Castle, Accra, and Whydah before veering southwest to Princes Island. She was there by August 26 and remained until mid-September.[27]

Lavallette took the flagship from Princes Island to St. Paul de Loando in late August, arriving on September 13. There she met Barron in *John Adams*, who had arrived earlier that month. Their short rendezvous ended September 28, when Barron sailed for St. Helena, arriving there on October 3. Both vessels returned to Monrovia, the flagship on October 6 and *John Adams* on the 26th. Their next call was back at Porto Praya, with the latter arriving November 11 and Lavallette on October 27.[28]

The month of November 1852 found all the vessels of the squadron again at the Cape Verdes at various times, with *Dale* and *Bainbridge* dropping anchor on November 10 and 11, respectively, after returning from "R & R" at Madeira and the Canaries.[29]

Into the midst of the Africa Squadron now came the schooner *Advance*. The vessel had sailed from New York on September 18, and the squadron first took note of her on October 23, when she arrived at Porto Praya "leaking" and claiming to have on board a cargo of lumber, pork, and bread. *Bainbridge* sent an armed crew to board her "on suspicion" of being "an unlawful trader." Three days later, another armed party was sent "to secure her crew; who refused duty" and put them in irons at the request of the U.S. consul. While the vessel was thus under-manned, heavy weather set in and she dragged her anchor and went aground. In response, boats from the squadron's vessels "with kedges and hawsers were sent to her assistance" to bring her off. Apparently by this time, the Portuguese colonial port authorities were also involved with negotiations regarding her fate, particularly as she was an American vessel in a foreign port. Finally, on November 3, a party from *Germantown* seized the vessel "on suspicion of being a slaver." [30]

This conclusion had been reached when the inspecting officer, Lt.

VESSEL NAME	BOARDED OR SEEN AT	DATE	WHERE FROM/CARGO/ REMARKS
Arab	Monrovia	2/17	Cape Palmas Oil/ wood Anchored
Venus	Monrovia	2/18	Oil/wood
Spy	Monrovia	2/21	Cape Mount
Porpoise	Monrovia	2/22	Sierra Leone (USN Brig)
Constance	Cape Palmas	3/1	Anchored
Susan	Tafon	3/1	
Africa	Almina [*sic*]	3/6	Lagos Oil
Elizabeth	Almina [*sic*]	3/7	Anchored
(unk.)	Quitta	3/10	(Schooner)
(unk.)	Quitta	3/12	(French Naval Steamer)
(unk.)	Quitta	3/17	(Portuguese Brig)
Africa	Quitta	3/18	Accra
Jackall	Lagos	3/20	(RN Steamer/Blockading)
Africa	Lagos	3/20	Quitta
(unk.)	Lagos	3/20	("2 Brigs")
(unk.)	Lagos	3/20	("1 Schr.")
(unk.)	Lagos	3/20	("2 brigs")
(unk.)	Lagos	3/20	(English Barque)
(unk.)	Lagos	3/20	(English Brig)
(unk.)	Lagos	3/20	(Brig)
(unk.)	Lagos	3/20	(French Schooner)
Packet	Fernando Po	3/28	Oil Anchored
(unk.)	Fernando Po	3/28	(Barque) Anchored
Spy	Fernando Po	3/28	(RN Brigantine)
Bloodhound	Fernando Po	3/28	("War Steamer")
Jackall	Fernando Po	3/28	(RN Steamer)
(unk.)	Whydah	4/14	(Portuguese Sloop of War)
Vulture	Whydah	4/14	(RN Steamer)
(unk.)	Whydah	4/16	(RN Steamer)
(unk.)	At Sea	4/16	(Hamburg Brig)
(unk.)	Quitta	4/17	(Portuguese vessel)
(unk.)	At Sea	5/2	("Out of signal distance")
Liberia Packet	Monrovia	5/12	Cape Palmas
Venus	Monrovia	5/12	Cape Palmas Oil

John Nicolas, noted that Antonio Oliviera, a Portuguese subject with orders to proceed to Loando, "at which place the captain expected to sell the schooner," had chartered her. On the schooner was a light cargo of lumber and scantlings, water casks, rice bricks, and a boiler. After being told there was nothing stored under the cabin deck, the inspectors found bricks that the captain said were ballast. When asked about the small amount of cargo, the captain denied any knowledge of the freight, which, he alleged, was the domain of the charterer. He only wanted to "dispose of the vessel." [31]

The schooner was put under a prize crew and her cargo was reloaded from storage ashore. She was sent to Norfolk for adjudication. She met foul weather off Cape Henry and arrived—leaking again—after a thirty-day passage. The Federal district court of Eastern Virginia libeled the vessel for "being fitted out in port of New York and engaged in the slave trade." The vessel was confiscated and sold in May 1854.[32]

Following the rendezvous and seizure of the *Advance*, three vessels of the squadron again resumed duties on the coast: *Bainbridge, John Adams,* and *Perry. Bainbridge,* under Manning, was under special instructions from Lavallette to sail "in pursuit of a schooner I am informed was sent from New York" by the owners of the *Advance,* and which also was intended to be a slaver. He was directed to sail south as far as Kabenda in this quest, and then turn to St. Helena.[33] *Bainbridge* went to sea on November 6 and arrived on the 24th at Cape Mesurado. She stood along the coast to St. Paul de Loando, and then dropped farther south to Ambrizette and remained in those waters for about a week's time. From there, she sailed to St. Helena, then directly back to Liberia. By March 11, 1853, she was at Porto Praya awaiting the squadron's change of command.[34]

John Adams departed a month later from Porto Praya for Goree, and from there skirted the Gambia and Sierra Leone coast. She remained in those waters, including Monrovia and Grand Cess, until mid-March 1853, and then sailed first to Porto Praya where she stayed until May 9. She finally departed for Funchal, then to Boston, arriving July 22, 1853.[35]

Lieutenant Page took *Perry* to Liberia in December and proceeded along the coast, calling at various ports as far south as St. Phillip de Benguela, where he dropped anchor in March 1853. This was the farthest south any member of Lavallette's squadron ventured. After four days there (March 14–17), Page turned west to St. Helena. *Perry* was back in

Monrovia, then Porto Praya in May, ending her service under Lavallette.[36]

The fourth vessel of the squadron, *Dale*, remained in Porto Praya and environs nearby until March 2, 1853. From there she sailed to Boston, where she decommissioned in April.[37]

Also remaining at Porto Praya was Commodore Lavallette in the flagship, no doubt expecting an uneventful wait for his successor. This was not to be. On January 21, the schooner *Rachel P. Brown* dropped anchor at Porto Praya, forty-two days from New York. The next day, Lavallette, probably assuming this was the schooner he had dispatched *Bainbridge* to find, sent a party on her to determine her character. There was sufficient doubt as to her legitimacy that a party remained on her overnight examining her cargo. On January 24 a prize crew from *Dale* was sent on board the vessel. However, the next afternoon this contingent was withdrawn, no doubt due to complications involving the local port authorities. In the evening of the same day, Lavallette ordered a boat to anchor "near and inshore" of the schooner and await developments.[38]

Whatever information had prompted Lavallette to remove his men was accurate. At 8:30 that evening he learned that "the schr. had been violently boarded by a large party of Portuguese soldiers and the mate & his crew forcibly disarmed & possession taken. . . . the mate & his crew kept in strict custody."

At this point, regardless of the suspicions about the character of the schooner, Lavallette faced a situation where an American vessel had been violently seized by a foreign force. His first response was to set a close watch on her with an armed boat "rowing guard" around the vessel.

The next morning, Lavallette went active: after first sending an officer ashore with a "message" for the local authorities, he began preparations. The sailors on *Germantown*, according to her deck log, "beat to quarters— hoisted the colors, shotted the guns—got the boarders, pikemen & marines ready for landing with small arms—[and] put the boat howitzer on the launch—At 10:20 sent a boat alongside the American Schooner Rachel P. Brown to assist getting her underway—at 10:30 she got underway and stood out of the harbor. Called all hands—up anchor and stood out in chase of her."

Two hours later, outside the national waters of the Cape Verdes, the *Rachel P. Brown* was found under the lee of the *Germantown*. A boat was sent alongside with orders for the officer on board to "take charge of her and follow us into port." At 3 PM, the schooner anchored close to and inshore of the sloop-of-war back in the harbor of Porto Praya.

Under an American prize crew the schooner was then sailed to a nearby island to communicate with the Portuguese governor-general, who ostensibly was not cognizant of the situation. Three days later, the *Brown* returned with the governor-general on board. This was followed by a diplomatic dance, where Lavallette visited the governor-general; the governor-general visited Lavallette on *Germantown* and, in the end, mutual twenty-one-gun salutes were fired.

With the crisis defused, the schooner was thoroughly searched and suspicions were confirmed. On the vessel was an "unusual quantity of provisions, especially bread and rice, the former all in casks that would hold water, also the exact quantity of lumber and carlines to lay a slave deck . . . an extra caboose [galley] house, the necessary quantity of bricks and lime to put up a slave boiler and the fuel to use with it . . . and her whole ground tier is stored with casks, now filled with rum but which . . . . would contain probably six or seven thousand gallons of water." Additionally, there was red and yellow bunting to make a Spanish flag, a chart for the passage from Benin to Cuba, "a [American] commander's uniform cap of the new Regulation pattern . . . three swords, etc. . . . which would enable them successfully to deceive British cruisers on the coast, by representing the vessel to be a prize to an American man-of-war, or in the event of being met by one of the latter, to display the Spanish flag." [39]

The schooner was placed under Lt. George Sinclair and sent to Norfolk for adjudication. As with the *Advance*, the Federal district court at Norfolk libeled the ship as a slaver and condemned the vessel.[40]

Having deftly and boldly settled this final problem, Lavallette finished his service as flag officer on March 1, 1853. The two slavers captured at Porto Praya were the only fruits of his time in charge of the squadron. He did, however, during his tenure, make some effort to goad the department into reevaluating Porto Praya as depot for the squadron. He wrote: "It is quite as unhealthy as any part of the African coast, its anchorage is unsafe, it furnishes very indifferent supplies . . . the water is bad. The climate so much so as to cause great loss in our provisions, and the moth very destructive to clothing. The island itself has a very inconvenient position as regards our cruising, being in a region subject to tornadoes, almost constant rains, calms and currents, which present more obstacles to the navigation in making passages from thence to Monrovia and back, than are encountered on any other point on the entire coast."[41] Lavallette strongly suggested St. Helena for the site, and he provided estimates for purchasing supplies and provisions there. The department, however, favored a location on the coast at St. Paul de Loando.[42]

Of course, other than the two taken at Porto Praya in December 1852 and January 1853, Lavallette's squadron seized no slave ships. This may be attributed partially to the fact that most of the cruising done under his command was above the equator (though the two captures at Porto Praya seemed to contradict this). However, it is clear that there continued to be a "lull" in the traffic itself. An article in the London *Times*, reprinted in the *New York Daily Times*, noted—after describing the sharp decline in numbers of slaves taken to Brazil and a relatively small number going into Cuba—that: "We were not prepared for such an extraordinary falling off in the traffic as the figures before us evince. If things have gone this year as they went last year, the gross total slaves exported for the coast cannot exceed 6,000 or 7,000, a number wholly insufficient, we should imagine, to keep the trade in existence at all. The slave traffic demands large capital, swift sailing vessels, highly paid crews, depots on the coast, and organized connexions [*sic*] in the interior of the country all of which machinery can assuredly not be maintained by an exportation of eight or ten ship loads annually." The writer went on to note that the variations in numbers of slaves exported was "altogether irrespective of our blockading squadron . . ."[43]

The secretary of the Navy's report in December 1852 followed the logic implied in the above article to the next obvious step. Secretary John Pendleton Kennedy, after rehearsing the usual laundry list of complaints about the "arduous" character of service on the squadron, recommended that Congress inquire into the necessity of continuing the squadron at all. He noted that the traffic was now "driven into a comparatively narrow space on the southern portion of the coast," confined to north and south Guinea.[44] This, plus the recent turn around in the Brazilian attitude towards the traffic, seemed to him to signal a reconsideration of the Navy's entire mission off Africa.

It should also be pointed that political developments in the United States placed the Navy's efforts to suppress the trade in slaves in an invidious position. In 1850 the simmering conflict between the free states and slave states erupted in Congress, as legislation was needed to determine the slave status of the new territories acquired as a result of the Mexican War. The upshot of months of debate was the Compromise of 1850, passed in September of that year. A major element of this legislation was the Fugitive Slave Act, which called for severe penalties for anyone aiding an escaped slave and only required the statement of the owner to certify that the black was a runaway. With this determined, the slave would be returned to the state or territory of his origin.[45] Thus, the power of the federal government came down on the side of the slave owner and the slavocracy.

In light of this legislation, the term "ironic" is the very least that can be applied to the Navy's position off the coast of Africa. Here, the power of the federal government was involved in freeing blacks from their putative owners, the slave traders, many of whom were American citizens. Then, the Navy was not "returning" the blacks to slave-holding states, but to Liberia. Thus, under the strict interpretation of the Fugitive Slave Act, the Navy was violating the law.

11

COMMODORE MAYO AND THE *CONSTITUTION'S* LAST CAPTURE, 1853–1855

In 1853 the squadron came under the command of Capt. Isaac Mayo. Mayo was yet another veteran of the War of 1812, having come into the Navy in 1809. He was a native of Maryland, a slave state, but he had been associated with Perry in instituting the African Squadron in 1842. He eventually cast his lot with the Confederacy in 1861.[1]

Captain Mayo hoisted his broad pennant on USS *Constitution*, lying at New York, on December 23, 1852. However, the ship was undergoing renovation of the flag quarters and did not depart from the United States until March 1853—which was also the month Lavallette left his command at Porto Praya for the last time.[2]

When Mayo departed from New York to cross the Atlantic, his first stop was not Porto Praya. Instead, he was under orders to deliver the new U.S. consul, Col. Joseph H. Nicholson, to Tunis. Therefore, Mayo's first stop was Gibraltar, twenty-two days out of New York—a brisk passage for a fifty-six year old frigate. Subsequently Mayo did a three-month tour of the Mediterranean, including two weeks of sightseeing in Italy, calling at Spezia, Leghorn, Tunis, Algiers, and Tangier, before returning to Gibraltar in June. After a five-day weather delay at the Rock, the *Constitution* sailed to Funchal, meeting *John Adams* there and finally putting in at the Cape Verdes on July 12, 1853.[3]

Given this sequence of events, the squadron was without a commanding officer on station for about four months. In fact, the transition and replacement of vessels assigned was as follows: Lavallette departed in March in *Germantown*, followed shortly by *Dale; John Adams* left the

U.S. Frigate Constitution. *Though squadron commander Isaac Mayo complained about the high visibility of this big 50-gun-plus frigate, he captured the slaver* H. N. Gambrill *in it in 1853. This was the last capture by the famous "Old Ironsides." Given the Webster-Ashburton Treaty requirement for 80 guns on the squadron, concentrating 50 or more on one vessel sorely reduced the squadron's cruising capabilities.*
Naval Historical Center

Cape Verdes on May 9; and *Bainbridge* departed on July 24. *Perry*, which had been on the coast through early May, had reported in at Porto Praya during that month and gone to Funchal in July. The brig may have gotten orders there from Mayo, and in any event returned to the coast and remained a unit in Mayo's squadron. [4]

The only other new element of the squadron—other than "Old Ironsides"—was to be the sloop-of-war *Marion*, which arrived in late February 1853. Commanded by H. Y. Purviance, the sloop was the same class as *Dale*, mounting sixteen guns. Mayo's squadron was thus composed of that sloop; *Dale*, which returned to the squadron from refit in the States in October; *Perry*, with eight guns; and *Constitution*. At this time, the famous frigate mounted fifty-one guns (though it was rated a forty-four), giving the squadron a total of ninety-two guns.[5]

The assignment of the old *Constitution* to the squadron was the subject of some discussion at the time. In a report included in the secretary of the Navy's annual report to Congress, Commander W. F. Lynch wrote: ". . . I venture to say that the frigate Constitution is of little more use in suppressing that trade than if she were in the Bay of Fundy." He then emphasized the need for steamers on the squadron: "From Goree to Cape Palmas, ranging from fifty to eighty miles from the coast, is a misty region of alternate calms, light winds, currents, and tornadoes, with over-whelming torrents of rain. . . . In the "John Adams", we were ten days making a distance which a steamer could have accomplished in thirty-six hours. From Monrovia to the island of St. Iago [in the Cape Verdes], vessels are often forty days on the passage, which a steamer could make in five. In one direction along the coast it is a drift with the sluggish current: in the other, it is working up against it with light and baffling winds." He proceeded to describe the extent of the legal trade along the African coast. He declared that for this commerce —as well as the sup-pression of the slave trade—"the west coast of Africa needs the protec-tion of an efficient force—efficient more in its power of locomotion than in the number of its guns."[6] Also, though Lynch was most emphatic on the need for steamers, it is worth noting that the assignment of a big frigate to the squadron flouted the department's earlier pattern of making the largest vessel on that station a sloop-of-war.

Commander Lynch's report, incidentally, was a result of his own recent expedition to the coast of Africa. Officially sanctioned, Lynch, with the steamer *Alleghany*, was sent to find the best locales for "pen-etrating [the] interior" of the west coast of the continent. This expedition was to look into the commercial and mercantile possibilities offered by the African continent and locate a landing place for a proposed "explor-ing party."[7] (It is interesting that Lynch was given a steamer for this task— a fact that no doubt contributed to Lynch's report cited above.)

In connection with Lynch's expedition, it is also noteworthy that a second steamer was dispatched to meet Lynch as he returned from his explorations east of Liberia. This vessel was to be the *Vixen,* a small paddlewheeler used during the Mexican War. The steamer was to be-come part of the Africa Squadron when this mission was completed. Other considerations prevented this: *Vixen* was instead sent to Mexico with an investigative team to look into a criminal fraud associated with the late war. In other words, the small vessel did not become the first steam ves-sel on the station.[8] Shortly after this, Secretary of the Navy Dobbin reassured Mayo that if other demands made it "practicable," a steamer would be sent to the squadron.[9]

As an aside to this chronology of the Africa Squadron, the secretary's annual report for 1853 also included a description of one of the most horrendous individual acts perpetrated by the slave traders. A report from the commander of HMS *Medina* related that, as she approached a slaver, the only slave on board, a female, was chained to the anchor. The anchor was then let go.[10] It was a story that did nothing to improve the reputation of those participating in the trade.

With the newly reconstituted squadron, the first vessel to visit the African coast was *Marion*, which arrived at Monrovia on March 20, 1853. This would be a short visit, followed by a quick passage to Princes Island and a return to Liberia in May and Porto Praya in June. In late July Purviance was at Funchal, where the event of most interest was finding the Navy's school ship, the brig *Preble*, in the offing in a disabled condition. *Marion*, along with a British brigantine, came to her assistance and towed her into the harbor. *Marion* returned to Porto Praya in September.[11]

During this same period, Lieutenant Page was in *Perry*, which had reached the African coast in December 1852 at Monrovia. She made passage to St. Paul de Loando, arriving in January 1853, and remained "standing along the land" in the area of Kabenda south to Benguela until late March.[12]

While north of the mouth of the Congo, Page approached a suspicious vessel sailing out of Loango Bay. He determined to board the vessel, and "put [my] vessel in disguise." He found the ship to be the brig *Monte Cristo* of New York, whose papers were in order. The vessel's skipper, however, "was surprised when he [Page] revealed his true character." [13] It is not revealed what the lieutenant did to disguise his vessel, though any successful use of this "*ruse de guerre*" would have been the result of some effort and planning. It would not be last time this tactic was used on the squadron.

Page took the brig back to Monrovia early in May, after a stop at St. Helena. From mid-May to early October, Page took *Perry* to Porto Praya, Funchal, and Tenerife, and did not return to the coast until November 1, 1853.[14]

As has been seen, Commodore Mayo did not arrive at Porto Praya until July 1853. While there he met *Bainbridge* before that vessel returned to the United States, as well as the steam storeship *John Hancock*.

The latter was then part of Cadwalader Ringgold's expedition to the north Pacific, by way of the Cape of Good Hope. Subsequently, Mayo sailed for Africa. *Constitution* was first off Factory Island, then Sierra Leone. At the latter place he "sent the Marine Guard, Band, and Boys on shore to attend Church."[15]

A few weeks later, off Monrovia, Mayo wrote the department on various subjects, among them the status of the kroomen on the *Perry.* They had been on the brig during the capture of *Chatsworth* and requested a share of the prize money. Mayo wished to know if the claim was justified and, if so, requested authority to pay them. Surprisingly, the Treasury Department immediately authorized the payments.[16] On another subject, he remarked on the fact that the British had begun a regular steam commercial service from London to the African coast, and he perceived this as taking trade away from the American merchants who continued to ply the route under sail alone.[17]

Mayo continued down the coast, heard a report that the "coast was clear of slavers," and visited an American settlement at Sinou. There the local governor requested that the commodore use his good offices to end a long standing tribal war between the Barbo and Grebo peoples at Cavally. With that in mind, and probably remembering M. C. Perry's diplomatic efforts a dozen years before, Mayo made a show of force, sending two hundred men, a howitzer, and rockets ashore to overawe the warring natives. When the locals ignored mere threat, Mayo bombarded a Barbo town with the howitzer and rockets. Only one native was slightly wounded, but the demonstration brought both sides to the table, or, more accurately, to the great cabin of the *Constitution*. After the appropriate pomp and diplomatic niceties, a treaty of peace between the tribes was signed on September 6, 1853.[18]

After a visit to Trade Town, Sierra Leone, Mayo continued along the coast, calling at Elmina and points east and south. These were necessarily short stays: he went from Accra to the Lagos River in five days with three stops in between. At the end of September, *Constitution* was at Fernando Po; on the last day of October, the ship was at Kabenda. While in the vicinity of Gaboon, *Constitution* gave chase to a slaver, but called it off six hours later: her speed was no match for the small schooner.[19]

Three days later, at daylight, some sixty miles south of the Congo, a sail was seen ahead. The ship's log reads: "7:40, hoisted English colors

and fired a gun, the sail hoisted American colors . . . fired a shot to windward of the schooner . . . the schooner was brought under our lee . . . at 10
hauled down the English and hoisted the American flag." [20] The vessel
proved to be the American schooner *H. N. Gambrill* out of New York.

Lt. C. R. P. Rogers was sent aboard and found sufficient evidence
to seize the vessel. Though her papers were in order, there was no cargo
list. A new boiler was found, recently set in bricks, and a "deck of hem-
lock boards laid smoothly and carefully upon the tiers of casks, which . .
. were found to contain provisions and several thousand gallons of water." On interviewing the men aboard, there was a Spanish gentleman
who described himself first as a "supercargo," and then as a "passenger."
He then pleaded poverty, claiming he had been "kindly permitted to work
his passage" in lieu of cash payment. But the lieutenant found that his
trunk contained an ample stock of clothes and at least one hundred dollars, much of it in gold. Another questionable circumstance was the
captain's claim to have delivered one hundred barrels of provisions to a
buyer at Kabenda, though no receipts could be produced to confirm this.[21]

Lieutenant Rogers then interviewed the cook, who proved to be a
mine of information. He had signed on for an "honest voyage," but he
immediately became suspicious when the crew was not allowed to communicate with the shore for six days while they were detained in harbor.
When the cook raised questions about the large quantity of water aboard,
the captain finally admitted that it was to be a slaving voyage. After arriving near the Congo, they discovered the water in the casks was contami-
nated and it was necessary to empty and refill them with good water. Just
the day before their capture by the *Constitution*, the crew had knocked
down the bulkhead separating the forecastle from the hold, threw old
clothing and other impedimentia overboard to make more room, laid the
slave deck, and set up a boiler.[22] (Normally the forecastle was the crew's
berthing area, and, in this instance, the bulkhead removal was to provide
a single large area for the slaves.)

As to the circumstances of the capture itself, the cook explained
that the captain had seen the big frigate from the masthead but had mistaken her for a brig he had seen in the Congo. By the time he realized his
mistake, it was too late to escape.[23] (It seems that, in this instance, the
adversary was not expecting a vessel the size of *Constitution* to make an
appearance on the slave patrol.) One wonders, though, how a three-masted

frigate rigged to skysails could be mistaken for a brig probably not half its size and only rigged to topgallants.

The lieutenant confirmed much of the cook's story through the steward, found charts of Cuba and a quadrant in the Spaniard's effects, and learned from two kroomen that the mysterious "passenger" had recently commanded a slaver on the coast. Rogers concluded that, "Every thing I saw and heard stamped her unequivocally as a slaver, on the very eve of receiving her cargo." [24]

The schooner was seized, put under a prize crew, and sent to New York. The district court for Southern New York condemned the vessel.[25] The *H. N. Gambrill* was the last capture made by the famous frigate and veteran of three wars.

The capture drew out of Mayo a revealing letter to the secretary of the Navy on the state of the slave trade and the utility of his flagship on the station. As to the latter subject, he wrote that the old frigate was still staunch, but that "she is entirely unfit for the duty on which she is presently employed. . . . We have now 75 guns on this station, 51 of which are mounted upon this frigate, and . . . she can render no more service than the brig Perry, mounting but 8. . . . Added to this is difficulty in getting sufficient provisions . . . plus her towering sails makes her visible long before we see the small slavers . . ."[26] (It is not clear why Mayo was only counting three ships on the squadron; possibly he did not yet know of *Dale*'s arrival.)

Mayo also revealed his belief that:

> the Slave trade is reviving on this Southern Coast, and that the American flag is extensively used in its prosecution. Several cargoes of Slaves have been recently carried off in American vessels, which having regular papers, defy the English cruisers, and hope to elude the vigilance of our Squadron, knowing it consists of only Three Vessels, serving on a coast of great extent, and dependent for provisions upon our depot at Porto Praya, in going to and from which much time is unavoidably consumed.
>
> Information concerning the movements of all vessels of war, is carried along the Coast, by the Slave dealers, with wonderful celerity, and the masters of the Slave vessels, are provided with every expedient to avoid capture, by means of double sets of pa-

pers and flags . . . I have become convinced that the large force concentrated in the *Constitution* might be much more advantageously distributed, at the same expense, in several smaller vessels . . .[27]

After the seizure, Commodore Mayo continued south, met the *Marion* at Loando, and then sailed *Constitution* to St. Helena, taking twelve days to cover the 1,200 miles direct to that island. At St. Helena, a soiree was held on the frigate's quarterdeck, with the local British gentry in attendance. At the end of 1853, she was at sea, returning from Monrovia to Porto Praya. [28] Mayo spent two months there, where he hosted various entertainments for the locals and provided "official" transportation to the minor diplomats there. He then proceeded north, visiting Santa Maria Island in the Azores, about two thousand miles north of the Cape Verdes. Afterwards, *Constitution* sailed to Funchal and the Canaries, not putting back in to the Cape Verdes until May 15, 1854. While at Funchal, it is noteworthy that Mayo wrote the secretary of his desire to return to the States no later than September, due to the "death of a near relative" which required his personal attention. He mentioned that this would be the end of a two-year tour. How much he was really needed the relief is questionable, however, as the next day he put pen to paper and again wrote the secretary. In this instance, he wrote that he had heard of a possible conflict with Spain and volunteered to serve, regardless of "private interests." Mayo finally left Funchal for the next stint on the African coast on June 22.[29]

At this point it is appropriate to look at the functions of the flagship and the concomitant reasons for the flag officers' long—seemingly pointless—sojourns at the rendezvous at Porto Praya. Though there was a storage facility on shore at Porto Praya, there was no squadron headquarters structure as such. In fact, the flagship was the headquarters. The key difficulty for a squadron commander in this era was the element of sail propulsion. Because of the vagaries of the wind, it was rare that the entire squadron could be at one place at one time, and even then not for an extended period. As has been seen, the best that could be expected was for the flag officer to have most of his ships at the rendezvous, and then order them out to the African coast or elsewhere, to report back after a specified period—usually six months. This interval would correspond with the vessel's need to reprovision, as well as give sufficient time to make a circuit along the coast. However, as the pattern was to send the ships out in succession, to the coast and down, they would rarely reconvene during a short span of time. Once the ships were sent out, communications were more a matter of chance than plan. Any change in orders from the commodore would necessarily be sent via the next vessel leaving for the coast. But of course, both the recipient and the mail carrier were equally dependent on the wind. All this made for a communications system with total unreliability.

Thus, the squadron commander was often required, by such circumstances, to remain in one place for lengthy periods. This was especially true during the transitions between squadron commanders, as well as the periods on either side of the termination of the assigned cruises, overlapping the return of all the vessels sent out.

The flagship necessarily was the pivot point for the squadron vessels. It was the administrative center and it coordinated reprovisioning from both the stores on shore as well as the supply ships from the States. It was the funnel through which the squadron received orders from the department for everything from policy to personnel matters (detachments, dismissals, reassignments, etc.). The flagship was often the site for courts martial, which often required a larger number of court officers than were available on a single vessel. Also, it was the only place where men could be domiciled while awaiting reassignment, either to another ship in the squadron or home.

All these roles made the flag vessel an important "place" for the squadron. And if the flagship could not be found—if it were on a circuit on the coast for example— it made for, at the least, inefficiency. Fortunately, commanders of naval vessels were, by trade, quite independent and able to take care of most of their internal affairs while at sea.

In this context, it is worth reiterating that the advent of steam power could obviate a great number of the uncertainties mentioned above. It certainly would have greatly decreased the long periods of inactivity associated with waiting for the sail-powered ships to deal with the arbitrariness of winds and seas. And, as has been seen, the coast of Africa was certainly one of the most arbitrary of venues to deal with under sail.

While Mayo was back and forth among the islands, Lieutenant Page was on the coast sailing south from Liberia, and then east, reaching as far as Quitta in January 1854. During this time, Page participated in a "palaver" with the locals at Cavally, and the log noted "large fires on the coast"— no doubt communicating the brig's approach. In early March the brig was off the Congo, then off Loango Bay, near the point where Mayo had snared *H. N. Gambrill*. There he noticed an American brig. He hoisted English colors as a ruse but pointedly sailed in the opposite direction, knowing the rakish Baltimore-built brig could probably outsail him. The quarry, which at this point was farther from shore than *Perry*, relaxed their vigilance and continued moving toward the shore and the waiting cargo. Through the night Page shadowed the vessel, and at daylight he was positioned seaward of the suspected slaver and had her cut off from escape. Page wrote: ". . . I put out a fast pulling cutter and caught her . . . finding we were Americans she immediately burned a U.S. flag she had flown before . . ." Three blank cartridges were expended, and then the ship's cutter was dispatched to board her. The boarding party reported back that it was the brig *Glamorgan* from New York, "with a slave deck laid." Later Page noted that she "was found prepared in all respects for taking . . . a cargo of slaves." When the captain admitted she was on a slaving voyage, Page seized her and sent her to the States for adjudication. [30]

It turned out that the vessel had landed slave goods at the Congo and Ambriz, and the court condemned the vessel. Charles Kehrman, commander of the brig, was sentenced to six months in jail and a $500 fine. (He was granted a full pardon shortly after his release.)[31] Ironically, the Boston grand jury berated Page because he had released the Portuguese supercargo from the vessel, leaving him "at liberty to pursue his atrocious traffic."[32]

Less than two weeks after *Glamorgan*'s capture, Page, still in the vicinity of the Congo, was drawn to another suspicious vessel. In this instance it was a barque, the *Millandon* of New York. The lieutenant left a boat to observe her movements and board "if she [tried] to leave." The purser, in charge of the boat, reported that he found bricks, planks, water casks ("secret tanks of water 500 gal. each"), and bags of farina. However, though the purser's letter indicates his opinion that she was a slaver, there is no further indication that she was actually seized and sent for adjudication.[33]

Page spent another month on the south coast, and then headed north, including a stop at Whydah. This visit was unsettling for two reasons: He attempted to land his gig but found it impossible due to the high surf. Furthermore, he wrote, the natives would not assist him, as they were "almost entirely under the control of the slave dealers."[34] Page then returned to Porto Praya via Monrovia. *Perry* sailed out of the Cape Verdes on June 16, 1854, and ended her cruise on the Africa station. With the seizure of *Glamorgan*, her total number of captures was six, three of which were taken off Brazil. This was the largest number taken by any American naval vessel. *Perry*'s first was in December 1848; her last was in March 1854. She had been assigned to the Africa Squadron, excepting four months in refit, since November 1849.

The remainder of Mayo's tenure was relatively uneventful. The sloop-of-war *Marion* returned to the African coast in September 1853 after her stay at Funchal, where she had aided the *Preble*. She sailed as far south as Benguela and Ambriz. She remained in that area around the Congo and environs from late October through the first week in February 1854. At one point in November there was a rendezvous with Mayo at Loando. On March 5 she was at Monrovia again and departed for the islands five days later. Mayo found the crew "so much weakened by long service on the coast that [he] did not feel justified in sending her back to it, so he ordered her to the Cape Verdes to "look after distressed American seamen and the interests of the whaling fleet."[35] Purviance was at Porto Praya from April through mid-May and then sailed to Madeira, remaining there from mid-June to July 10.[36]

In August 1854 *Marion* returned to the coast at Monrovia and cruised as far east as Whydah. While there she came to in the midst of a harbor full of vessels. Her logs indicate she sent boats and boarded five vessels; four barques, and a schooner during the 4-to-8 evening watch, on September 12, 1854.[37]

Purviance continued down the coast and, off Loando in October, received information from the British commander on that station that two American vessels warranted careful watching: the brigantine *Wild Pigeon* and schooner *Oxford*. The former had arrived at Ambriz with a cargo consigned to the "notorious slave dealer" Francisco Antonio Flores. The latter vessel was rumored to be equipped for the trade and was to be sold to the slave dealers.[38]

Purviance acted on the information and had both vessels searched. He examined their papers also and found all correct and in order. Shortly after this he forwarded a letter indicating that the local Portuguese navy officers "found no ground of suspicion" for the *Wild Pigeon*, and that they had made the crew of *Oxford* dispose of all the water casks except those necessary for a crew of seven for their voyage.[39]

Shortly after this, Purviance returned northward and was at Porto Praya in February 1855. He was at the Cape Verdes when Mayo departed in March, and he remained until July 1855 and then returned to the United States.[40]

The sloop-of-war *Dale,* commanded by William Whittle, returned from Madeira in November 1853, stopped for a month at Porto Praya, and then sortied to Goree and the Gambia River. She beat out of the river on February 2 and was back at Porto Praya shortly thereafter. At the end of March she was in Liberian waters, followed by a voyage to Malemba and St. Paul de Loando. This occupied April through July, and she was back at Monrovia the first week in August. She was back at the Cape Verdes shortly thereafter and in Madeira for a month sojourn beginning the middle of September 1854. In October she was witness to an accident in which the ship *Osceola* collided with *Constitution* and sustained substantial damage, though "Old Ironsides" was only slightly injured. After contributing assistance to repair the merchant vessel, both *Dale* and the flagship sailed for the coast. They remained in company until November 23, and then the sloop sailed on to Monrovia and began a sortie south and east, spending several days in each of the major outposts as far as Badagry. Following a week at Princes Island, Whittle headed back southward, running the usual exercises en route, including timing the men at general quarters and target practice with the "great guns." Interestingly, the men used a 12 foot by 4 foot target at 545 yards, and out of five broadsides (eight guns each) there were four hits.[41]

Whittle cruised in the area around Ambriz and Loando for a month before returning to Porto Praya. He kept the vessel there for about two months, and on June 4, 1855, she was back at sea en route to Monrovia, this time under a new flag officer.[42]

Commodore Mayo returned from Funchal, the Canaries, and the Azores on May 15, 1854. After a month of administrative work at Porto Praya and the neighboring settlement at Porto Grande, he sailed *Constitution* to Monrovia. He took the frigate along the coast as far as Whydah, where he dropped anchor on July 27. While in this area, in the span of three days, boarding parties inspected at least eight vessels: one Spanish, one Dutch, one Hamburg, five British, and several Portuguese. All were released. Four days later, Mayo continued his career in diplomacy by engineering a "treaty of trade and commerce" with King Docimo of Lagos, who came on board with his retinue for the signing and ceremony. Afterwards there was an exchange of gifts, with the King becoming the recipient of a carbine, pistol, and ammunition.[43]

This done, Mayo visited Princes Island, and then sailed south to Mayumba and back to Loando. The seventy miles between the two settlements was exceedingly difficult, due to calms and adverse currents. Between August 24 and September 5, she anchored thirty-one times to prevent the current from carrying her back over her own wake.[44]

At Loando, the vessel's presence was sufficient to end an impending diplomatic incident. Two British traders had been kidnapped by a local king, who, upon hearing the frigate's morning gun, assumed he was the target and hastily released his hostages. Subsequently, a treaty was signed between the white merchants and the local king, with Lt. C. R. P. Rogers as witness.[45]

In early September, the frigate sailed northwest, returning to Liberian waters. Off Monrovia, one of *Constitution*'s bluejackets was killed; Ordinary Seaman James Lee was in an accident involving one of the ship's boats. After the burial, Mayo turned back towards Porto Praya. During this visit, the frigate was accidentally rammed by a whaling barque, losing her accommodation ladder. The whaler, however, was seriously damaged about the bows, and Mayo made the frigate's carpenters available to assist in the repairs. After this, the commodore spent Christmas 1854 and New Years 1855 at Funchal. Mayo made one more circuit to Porto Praya and the coast off Gambia and Goree before sailing into Porto Praya for the last time. He was in the Cape Verdes waters from late February until the last day of March 1855. Then the frigate weighed anchor and sailed west, ending Mayo's term as squadron commander.[46]

It is significant to note that the Bureau of Medicine and Surgery had a few significant comments about the squadron's aggregate health during Mayo's command. Their report noted that the *Constitution*, carrying 475 men and on station for nearly two and a half years, lost only one crewman to disease, though thirty-six were invalided home. The unit's other vessels were similarly free from high mortality rates. In fact the bureau's statistics showed that the Africa Squadron had the lowest mortality rate of all the stations, including the Home Squadron: .17%. In contrast, the *Cumberland*, which was in the Mediterranean for thirty months lost eighteen crewmen; the *St. Lawrence* in the Pacific, seven; and *Powhatan* in the East Indies lost fourteen. The report concluded: "It is remarkable, however, that the mortality in the Africa squadron should be so small . . ." The report concluded that this was due to the "excellent sanitary regulations" in force.[47]

It is worthy of note that some days out Mayo crossed paths with a merchant ship carrying news that war with Spain—over Cuba— was imminent, and that the Navy was concentrating a squadron off Key West. He immediately wrote the secretary of the Navy of his intention to join the force off Florida after reprovisioning at Havana.[48] Of course, hostilities did not break out and Mayo rerouted *Constitution* northward, putting in at the Kittery Navy Yard in Portsmouth, New Hampshire, early in June.

This was to be the venerable frigate's last operational tour of duty. Subsequent to a major refit, the *Constitution* was sent to Annapolis as a school ship and she remained in support roles for the remainder of her active career.

As to Commodore Mayo, he wrote some of his observations to the secretary of the Navy, James C. Dobbin, of North Carolina. First he noted that he had examined the whole coast, particularly the slave stations, and had seen no American flagged vessels. A British officer who had seen none in the Bight in several months confirmed this. A few months later, in a letter to Purviance intended to be passed along to Mayo's successor, he wrote: "The slave trade at present seems to exist only in very limited sections of the Coast. That part of the Bight of Benin between Quitta and Badagry required the greatest vigilance, as does also the coast between Kabenda and Ambriz, including the banks of the River Congo. . . . A few slaves are occasionally taken from the neighborhood of the Bonny and Calabor Rivers. On the other parts of the coast the trade seems dormant but may at any moment spring into activity wherever the European and American colonists have not established their supremacy."[49]

12

FLAG OFFICER CRABBE:
CRUISING TO NO REWARD,
1855–1857

Thomas A. Crabbe replaced Captain Mayo. Crabbe was born in Maryland but he was listed as a citizen of Pennsylvania. He was another forty-year-plus veteran with a pre–War of 1812 entry date: November 15, 1809. Of his long years in the Navy, during no less than seventeen he had been "unemployed," which was a mark of an undistinguished record. He would retire in 1862 and remained loyal to the Union during the Civil War.[1]

When Crabbe arrived on station at Porto Praya it was August 1, 1855, though he had left the United States in April. In the interim he had taken his flagship, the sloop-of-war *Jamestown*, to Key West to join the squadron forming there in anticipation of war with Spain—a circumstance resulting from the Ostend Manifesto, which attempted to justify American use of force to seize the island. When the crisis passed, Crabbe went on to Funchal, then Tenerife, before taking station at the Cape Verdes.[2]

Crabbe's squadron would consist of the *Jamestown*, the sloop-of-war *St.Louis*, and the brig *Dolphin*. The *Dale* would be on station until November, when she would be relieved by *St. Louis*. As the brig was carrying only four guns, and *Jamestown* twenty-two, the total number of guns on the station was forty-two when *Dale* was assigned and forty-six when *St. Louis* arrived.[3] With only three vessels, this was the smallest the squadron had been since its inception.

Again, no steamers were assigned; however, unlike the situation when the squadron was founded, there were now a substantial number of steam vessels available in the Navy. Furthermore, the state of the technology had advanced sufficiently to make it possible to find relatively reliable vessels to assign to overseas stations. In fact, the secretary's 1855 report listed fourteen armed steamers in the operational inventory. Five of these were on foreign stations, from the East Indies to the Mediterranean, and six were "vessels in ordinary, repairing and equipping, etc." Two of the operational steamers were storeships.[4] Also, given the fact that the British were regularly assigning steamers to the African coast, it is apparent that there was now no obvious reason the department should not follow suit. It is also noteworthy that Perry had had great success on the Japan expedition, which included three steam frigates.

As to the activities of the squadron under Crabbe, it is to be noted that during these two years no slavers were captured by the squadron off Africa. That the trade continued is clear, in that during 1856 five slave trading vessels were seized in the ports of the United States. The next slave trader captured by the squadron off Africa would be in November 1857, after Crabbe had relinquished command.

As the last remnant of Mayo's squadron, the *Dale*'s tenure only lasted until December 1855. She had been at Porto Praya from April 1855 to mid-June, when the sloop made a short visit to Monrovia. After her return to the Cape Verdes, she sailed to Madeira, where the vessel remained until October 18. After this period of relaxation for the crew, the *Dale* departed for Porto Praya. On the December 10, by which time *St. Louis* had arrived to replace her, *Dale*'s commanding officer raised her anchor for home. She arrived back at Norfolk in January 1856, and would return to the squadron a year later.[5]

The brig *Dolphin*, which had previously been in the squadron under Commodore Bolton, returned to Porto Praya in June 1855. After three weeks of reprovisioning, but before Flag Officer Crabbe arrived, the brig, commanded by Lt. E. R. Thompson, sailed to Africa. Thompson sailed east along the coast, turned to Princes Island, then continued south past the equator. From late August through October 10, the brig cruised as far south as Ambrizette, with most of her time spent near the wide estuaries of the Congo River.[6]

The highlight of this cruise came in the form of a cooperative effort with the British naval steamer *Scourge*. A boat expedition was mounted with the brig's first cutter, armed and given two days' provisions. The steamer towed the cutter thirty miles up the Congo River on September 23, and then returned on the 26th.[7] Other than adding to the record of cooperation between the two navies, nothing was accomplished as far as stemming the slave trade.

Shortly afterwards, Thompson sent another group ashore, this time at Ambrizette. In this instance, the marine guard was dispatched to "protect the property of American citizens against a threatened attack from the natives." [8] The move apparently settled the situation, as there was no further mention of this incident.

Dolphin sailed northward to Monrovia, dropping anchor there on October 24. Her next stops were Porto Praya, and Teneriffe and Santa Cruz in the Canaries. The stay in the Canaries was about a month in January and February 1856, followed by a return to the coast by way of the Cape Verdes.[9]

On this second sortie along the coast, while in Liberian waters, Thompson hosted a native "palaver" on his quarterdeck. Attending were the King of Rocktown and the ruler of Cape Palmas. Both agreed to a settlement of a local dispute, and "peace was agreed." This was in May 1856, and after which *Dolphin* sailed far to the south, anchoring at Little Fish Bay, some fifteen degrees south latitude, about two hundred miles south of Benguela, on July 6. This is probably the farthest south vessels of the squadron ventured. After some days there, the brig returned to Loando and remained in that vicinity until August 8, 1856.[10]

While hovering off the Congo River, *Dolphin* fell in with the Royal Navy steamer *Teazer*, and another expedition was sent upriver. In this instance, a dingy and three men were towed up the river and back. Again, there were no significant results, and the brig departed for Monrovia on August 8.[11]

Subsequently, *Dolphin* returned to Porto Praya, and then went to Teneriffe in December. From March to May 1857 she sailed to the Liberian coast, remaining in the area around Cape Palmas and Monrovia. During the last part of April her logs noted that she was leaking badly, but the vessel did not return to the United States until June. She decommissioned at Boston on July 21, 1857.[12]

Equally uneventful was the cruise of the sloop-of-war *St. Louis*, which arrived from the United States and anchored at Porto Praya on

December 10, 1855. Under the command of J. W. Livingston, she sailed for the coast near the end of the year and put in at Monrovia. On January 20 she was at Whydah in the midst of several merchant vessels. That afternoon, Livingston sent a boat which boarded and inspected five of these vessels. The next day, two more came under the scrutiny of *St. Louis*'s men. From there, Livingston took his command to Princes Island, then farther south. For about fifteen days they cruised on the Ambriz to Loando coast, but found nothing for their efforts.[13]

Livingston then sailed north, back to Monrovia, Porto Praya, Funchal, and the Canaries. *St. Louis* was back in the Cape Verdes early in August 1856. On her second cruise to the continent, she went to Princes Island, then as far as Little Fish Bay and Benguela. The vessel hovered off that south coast from mid-October to the end of November, before returning north. The only event worth mentioning in the vessel's logs was the accidental death of an ordinary seaman by gunshot wound while at Porto Praya in March 1857. He was buried at Porto Praya two days before she departed for Monrovia again.[14]

The stay at Monrovia was only two weeks in duration, and the vessel turned west again to Porto Praya, then Funchal. She was at Porto Praya when the squadron change of command occurred in July 1857. The sloop had put in about four months on the African coast during Crabbe's command.[15]

Commodore Crabbe, in *Jamestown*, arrived early in August 1855, but he sailed to Madeira without much delay. He wrote the secretary that he intended to resupply and depart northward, due to the fact that the "rainy and tornado season continues on the coast until some time in October." Furthermore, he added that a British officer reported that "the slave trade south of the equator had been entirely broken up."[16]

So, after a week in the Cape Verdes, he sailed to Funchal, then to Tenerife, not returning to the Cape Verdes until October 23. During his stay in the northern islands, he again wrote the secretary, requesting an "early relief and . . . return to the United States." This original letter is illegible in many places, but it appears that Crabbe was pleading a "severe domestic affliction . . . since my departure from home . . . [which has had an] unhappy influence upon my spirits, combined with other cogent reasons . . ." He intended to sail to the "southern limits" of the cruising area and would not be back to Porto Praya until March 1856. At that time he hoped to turn his flag over to the *Dale* and return to the United States, should his request be granted.[17]

At any rate, he reached Monrovia in late November, after two weeks at Porto Praya, where he met with *Dale* and *Dolphin*. Crabbe was visited by President Roberts while anchored near the capital of Liberia, and then he sailed east. He called at Cape Palmas, Elmina, among other ports, and was at Princes Island at the end of the year, ending his sweep of the coast at Loando.[18]

While at the latter place, Crabbe wrote the secretary: "After a thorough examination of the coast, which we were enabled to make by keeping it in sight from Monrovia to Whydah, a distance of nearly one thousand miles, and more particularly of the Bight of Benin, I have become thoroughly satisfied of the non-existence, at the present time of any organized traffic in slaves within the limits of this station." [19]

Back at Porto Praya in February, Crabbe met *Dolphin* and *St. Louis*, and he later wrote that *St. Louis*'s commanding officer had cruised the coast and found nothing "in the least degree suspicious or indicating much traffic in slaves." Shortly after this letter he determined that "recruiting the health of the officers and crew of the flag ship" was needed, and he sailed for Madeira. *Jamestown* was at Funchal for two months, when he again wrote the secretary that his intention was to depart from Funchal earlier, but "a virulent disease" broke out and the vessel could not get a clean bill of health "properly vised by the Spanish consul." So he "thought it proper, after deliberation, to proceed to some more northerly port for the purpose of obtaining one . . ." With this in mind, he took *Jamestown* to Tangier— about seven hundred miles northeast of Madeira— on July 25, and he returned on August 5. With this done, he sailed to the Canaries and finally returned to the Cape Verdes on October 2, 1856.[20]

Jamestown was back at Porto Praya for a month, and there was little to report, except meeting with *Dolphin* again. Also, one of *Jamestown*'s kroomen ("Peter Jarman"*) died, though no cause of death

---

*   In the vessel's deck log is a list of several "kroomen," giving the sailor's appellation for each. Some are quite droll, in the nautical sense: Jack Haultaut, Pea Soup, After Supper, Palm Tree, Upside Down, After Breakfast, Fill Away, Flying Jib, Brace Aback, Clear Hawse, Hen Coop, Hard Tack, Bow Gun, Port Anchor, Tar Bucket, and Last One.

was given in the logs. The native African died at 5 PM and was buried at sea forty minutes later.[21]

Through October Crabbe awaited a supply ship, and when none arrived he sailed for Sierra Leone for provisions. From thence, he made a "short cruise down the coast" from Monrovia, as far as Quitta, then back to Cape Mesurado. He wrote that the voyage was fruitless, as, after boarding many vessels, "nothing was seen to excite our suspicions." Subsequently he was at Bathurst, Gambia, from whence he departed for the last time from Africa on February 21, 1857. After a stop at the Cape Verdes, he sailed *Jamestown* to Philadelphia, ending his command on the Africa station.[22]

Crabbe, in his last communication from Porto Praya, conveyed to the secretary rather interesting information from papers taken in the seizure of the slaver *Flying Eagle*. (The author has not encountered information on this particular vessel, which was apparently seized by the British in November 1856). Crabbe wrote that it appeared that the trade was being carried on by "an organized company, of the members of which are residents of New York and Havana . . ." In late 1855, a brig shipped 479 slaves (called "volumes" in the papers) from the environs of Benguela and landed them at Havana for a payment of $85,000. This money was to be divided among forty-eight investors. It appeared that the vessels involved were Portuguese owned. They had obtained the right to use the American flag by maintaining residence in the States, and the vessels were manned by foreigners.[23]

With this information communicated to the department, Crabbe ended his tenure with the squadron. Though no slavers were seized, it appears that the ships of the squadron were all quite active and indeed sailed far south on the coast. There was definitely no lack of activity on their part, though it seems that Crabbe and *Jamestown* might have profitably curtailed their sojourns in the Canaries, Madeira, and, in one instance, Tangier. Crabbe's tendency to avoid the coast may well have been explained by health problems, as his official biography notes that after his tour off Africa, his health was "somewhat impaired."[24]

It does appear that the trade itself was at low ebb during this period. The years 1852 to 1856 were also a low period for the British squadron off the coast. (Part of the period also coincided with the British efforts in the Crimean War.) This has been attributed to the British clampdown in the area and the growth of legitimate trade, the latter encouraged by the appearance of regular scheduled steam merchant ships on the coast. [25] As has been seen, this followed the end of Brazil's turn against the traffic, so these were two effective blows against the illegitimate trade in the 1850s.

13

COMMODORE CONOVER AND COMMANDER MCBLAIR, 1857–1859

The command of the Africa Squadron now fell on Thomas A. Conover, the youngest man yet to hold the position. He was the first Africa Squadron flag officer with a later appointment date than 1809: his was January 1,1812, which still preceded the War of 1812 by six months. He was from New Jersey, had been a captain since 1848, and had a significant amount of sea duty on his record.[1]

The squadron under Conover's command numbered four vessels. The flagship was the *Cumberland*, which had just come out of the Boston Navy Yard where she had been cut down ("razeed") from a fifty-gun frigate to a twenty-four-gun sloop-of-war. The others were the twenty-gun *St. Louis*, which later would be replaced by the twenty-gun *Vincennes*, and the sixteen-gun sloops *Dale* and *Marion*.[2] The aggregate number of guns was seventy-six.

Conover would find that the slave trade was about to blossom again on the coast. In Cuba, now the largest slave market in the western hemisphere, there was a substantial expansion of the sugar industry, with its concomitant need for more workers. This need was exacerbated by a virulent cholera outbreak on the island, which killed sixteen thousand slaves in 1853–54. It was estimated that the trade grew to a figure of twenty-five thousand slaves imported in 1859 alone. For specifics, a British naval officer off Africa listed twenty-three ships that had reportedly escaped from the coast in 1857. Eleven of these had been boarded by Royal Navy ships, but "though they were known slavers, they were necessarily left unmolested through their being *bona fide* American vessels."

Cuba's political status was also influencing the American attitude toward the trade: there was a growing, strident movement for the annexation of the island—by force if need be. This was viewed by some to be the logical next step after the humiliation of Mexico in the 1846–48 war and the subsequent huge territorial gains by the United States. The slaveholding states were not subtle about their desires, either, as Cuba—which is nearly the size of Mississippi—would certainly have become a slave state had it been annexed.[3]

Other influences were not conducive to the Navy's efforts against the slave trade. Beginning in 1853–54, there was a concerted effort by radical southerners to reopen the trade itself. There was much attention paid in the press to the idea, and the governor of South Carolina devoted one of his annual messages to fostering the concept. Further acknowledgement of the movement came at the 1858 meeting of the Vicksburg Southern Commercial Convention, which came on the heels of a well-publicized rumor that a slave depot had been established on the Mississippi to handle the expected cargoes from Africa. The extremists in favor of the idea were using it as another cudgel in their agitation for secession.[4] Of course, the trade was not officially reopened, but there were to be major developments stemming from the idea during the next few years.

In a related foreign development, in 1857 the French government signed a contract to provide laborers for Martinique and Guadeloupe. The source of these workers was to be the Loango Coast and points along the Congo River. The scheme was termed "free emigration" and the blacks were called "apprentices," but it apparently was only a slight variation from slavery. It was state-sponsored, legal, and resulted in some fifteen thousand blacks being removed to the western hemisphere from officially sanctioned factories at Loango, Kabenda, and elsewhere.[5] To modern sensibilities, both this and the proposed reopening of the trade are movements that are striking for their transparently reactionary and immoral aspects, but, obviously, in 1857, in some quarters, they were simply considered "good business."

From the standpoint of the Africa Squadron's business, the most interesting and revealing correspondence to come out of Conover's command was that of Commander William McBlair, commanding officer of the sloop-of-war *Dale*. McBlair, a Marylander, wrote daily to his wife, Virginia Myers McBlair. Since his letters could not be mailed immediately on a daily basis, the result was a somewhat rambling chronicle—part letters and part journal—of McBlair's cruise. In it he discussed, sometimes in detail, the daily routine and operations of the sloop-of-war, as well as personal matters and reflections on his ongoing studies in the Bible, as he had recently been converted to Christianity. His attitude toward slavery is ambiguous, however, as Maryland was a slave state, and in the end he resigned to join the Confederacy.[6] Note: The next several pages are a narrative forged from a combination of McBlair's letters and the *Dale*'s deck logs for the period.

McBlair set the stage for his cruise by communicating portions of a letter from the commercial agent at St. Paul de Loando: "The slave trade is flourishing in this coast. It is said that five vessels have lately left with slaves. The Congo River and its neighborhood have been the headquarters, and American gold is now quite plenty there, having been brought . . . from New York."[7]

McBlair writes that his first destination is Madeira, and that he had read "twenty years as a slaver" (probably Theodore Canot's book) and a book on Central Africa and assigned them to the ship's library. He comments that, "Our little cruiser proves fast . . . we have passed two or three vessels standing same course as ourselves."

By the end of May McBlair had anchored at Funchal, and a week later he wrote that J. W. Livingston, the commanding officer of the *St. Louis*, was now temporary commander of the station since Crabbe departed, and that officer was expected daily from Porto Praya: "It is he to whom I am to report & I must therefore await his arrival."

McBlair remained at Madeira until June 17, by which time the *St.Louis* had arrived and he had reported in. He arrived at Porto Praya on June 26 and wrote: "The small pox has disappeared and all again are healthy here, determined however to run no risks, I have had all the crew inspected and such as required it vaccinated, my self being vacinnated [*sic*] without effect."

McBlair did not leave the Cape Verdes until August 20. In the interim he was, among other things, occupied in watering and provisioning his vessel. This was not a simple evolution, as "this port is very liable to heavy seas & very bad weather, I am consequently anchored so far out as to be ready to put to sea for safety at a moment's warning & compelled to take advantage of every smooth moment to get on board my provisions &

water." He mentions in passing that the kroomen had caught a three hundred–pound sea turtle.

The extended stay at the Cape Verdes was apparently because the interim commander was awaiting the arrival of Captain Conover, and this irritated McBlair, who, on hearing that the *Cumberland* was at Madeira, wrote a bit acidly: "I suppose they are enjoying themselves at Madeira. I hope they will send our letters and orders . . ." He confided that he thought ". . . Livingston has shown great want of judgment in hanging about these islands awaiting the arrival of a commodore three thousand miles off. I believe however, he has acted conscientiously supposing it to be his duty . . . he is 'old maidish.'"

McBlair expected to have sufficient provisions aboard by the middle of August, so that there would be enough "to keep me out of that hateful

Sloop-of-war Dale, *in a post-Civil War photograph.* Dale *was one of a class of 16-gun sloops built in 1838. Others of this class on the squadron were* Decatur, Marion, *and* Yorktown. *Commander William McBlair put the* Dale *to good use during his African cruise: carrying out various nautical ruses to gain unnoticed approach to his quarries. This included disguising his vessel as a whaler and cruising incognito in a British convoy. He captured the slaver* W. G. Lewis *in 1857, as a result of a small-boat expedition up the Congo River.*
Naval Historical Center

port until a more favorable season. We are now all the time on the 'que Vive' expecting a southerly gale during which this port is not safe." Interspersed with provisioning, he took his vessel to sea in the local area to exercise the men, and to Porto Grande to fetch the mail.

On July 30 he wrote that there was again some evidence of smallpox on board, and that Livingston had arrived in *St. Louis* with orders for the *Dale* to proceed to the coast. Apparently McBlair then requested a delay due to the smallpox scare, and Livingston granted it. However, when Conover (finally) arrived, on August 17, McBlair was dressed down: Conover was "disappointed" to find *Dale* still in port, and questioned the "right of a passed assistant surgeon to influence the movements of your vessel."[8]

Three days later McBlair, probably much chagrined at his initial embarrassment with his new commanding officer, was at sea en route to Africa, writing his wife: "We will go immediately south of the line where the climate is said to be delightful and probably will remain there until May." (That part of McBlair's long delay in the islands was due to the dilatory arrival of Conover himself was probably irrelevant as far as his superior was concerned.)

For almost a month *Dale* sailed south, arriving off the Congo in mid-September. During this passage, her commander initiated a series of ruses intended to throw off the slavers by misdirection. *Dale* sailed in company with a convoy of British vessels en route to India, and two smaller vessels going south. He wrote: "Our flag has been lately much used in the slave trade; as none but an American man-of-war can capture it, I am consequently desirous to keep the destination of my ship unknown & to arrive on the coast unexpectedly. . . . The English ships in company daily display their flags to me & I to disguise the character of my ship hoist an English flag & pendant, they salute me by hoisting and lowering their flags . . . If we get so near as to speak which I wish to avoid, I must be Capt. Smith of Her Majesty's ship Rose . . . ."

The weather was dull and unexciting. Three days out he wrote: "Rain, rain, rain but we do not much regret it and are busy catching it to fill up our tanks. We have a long travel before us some two thousand miles before we will reach our cruising ground & we must expect much calm weather in getting across the line . . . My great object is to reach the Congo before it is known that an American man-of-war is on the coast &

to do this I must touch no where." About ten days later they were approaching the line and he reported: "We are still ploughing our way to the Congo a long & unvaried road . . ."

McBlair anchored his ship off the Congo first, and then proceeded to Loango to obtain wood and water. "We have now a most delightful climate," he wrote, and said that he expected to meet the commodore at Loando in the middle of October.

A week later he wrote of sighting French steamers on the coast. After boarding one, he commented: "She proved to be a slaver but a novel kind of one: a French government slaver . . ." getting "apprentices" for the West Indies. Other than these vessels, he had been informed of a suspicious American barque in the vicinity, awaiting a cargo of slaves. He searched "for some days . . . but no doubt their eyes are as good as our own & with the additional aid of signals made by confederates on the coast, I had but little prospect of seeing her."

He then pointed *Dale* southward to Ambriz for provisions, noting that there was some sign of scurvy on board. After this the next destination was St. Paul de Loando, where the British commodore on that station shared a document with him showing "how much our countrymen had been implicated & showing with what success they had been thwarted . . ." This led him to comment: "Our squadron is a farce [,] with a small steamer, I would have ere this been in the Congo & without a doubt have made many prizes, but with sails can do nothing. . . . Sails were never made to contend with currents & calms . . . indeed so soon as my flag was seen off the coast, it was announced by runner far & wide before I reach any place where I may hear of a slaver my departure is announced & my approach anticipated & I find nothing apparently but legal trading."

Shortly after this McBlair sighted an American barque, the *Matthew Thomas*, and had an exchange with her skipper. He inquired as to why she showed no colors and was told that "he had not seen ours." Apparently McBlair was still operating his vessel as much as possible without divulging his nationality.[9]

At Loando, which, in the era of the legal Portuguese slave trade, had been a major nexus, he saw a large stone chair "still standing." This quasi-throne was where "the Bishop used to bless each slave before embarking, this was a perquisite [*sic*] which yielded him a large revenue."

Here McBlair also met with the British commissioner, who gave him "a picture of the prostitution of our flag in the Congo . . ." The up-shot of this meeting was the commander's determination to fit out an expedition in cooperation with the British to examine suspicious vessels.

On October 20 McBlair sailed from Loando, after meeting with Conover on *Cumberland*. He wrote: "I being anxious to get my expedition up the Congo, provided I could have the aid of an English steamer; consequently I kept the land in sight as the probable means of meeting with one and about noon of the 21st was fortunate in doing so . . ." The commander of the British steamer *Myrmidon* proved anxious to assist, and he then towed one of *Dale*'s boats and sixteen men up the Congo.

Two days later, "we were all expectancy [*sic*] & every sailing coming out of the Congo was hailed [as] a prize, sail after sail shot through its mouth wafted swiftly away in the strength of the current, at length one steamer was descried with the Dale's boat in tow . . . it was a death blow to all hope, shortly the arrival of our boat alongside confirmed our suspicions, but two American vessels were in the Congo, the papers of both correct but one very suspicious craft. I perhaps may see more of her . . ." Of course, the steamer in question was the *Myrmidon* itself.

Disappointment set aside for the moment, McBlair sailed for Kabenda and Loango Bay. There, for the second time, he encountered the French contract vessels. The company, he noted, had set up "a regular trading post for the purchase of negroes and that they are brought to it by their owners chained, tied, etc. etc . . ." Each "able bodied hand" was purchased for $16, and 250 were already loaded, with another hundred to come. A second vessel, a steamer, was also in the offing, and it was to load eight hundred.

McBlair's next comment is written as it stands: "I really believe the Negroes themselves & their descendents certainly will be much benefited by this movement of the French government." McBlair believed the conditions in which these blacks were being transported were more humane than those afforded by the illicit slave trader, so he had little objection to this enterprise in this regard. He was also of the opinion that the blacks benefited from being sent away from the uncivilized atmosphere of the "Dark Continent" and brought under the umbrella of white, Christian civilization. He wrote: "I wish honest abolitionists could see the degraded & impoverished condition of the natives . . . when I tell you that fathers sell their children for a bottle of wine, you will have a pretty good idea of their moral [s]." Of course, this was a version of the standard southern slaveholder's rationale for maintaining the slave system on which their economy was borne. As a further rationale for the utility of the slave trade, or at least for slavery itself, McBlair wrote that there was a growing drought in Africa, and he had heard that in earlier droughts the natives had "flocked" to the coast, requesting to be carried "to some other country where they could get something to eat."

Subsequently (November 1), he was back at the Congo. Five days later he sent out another river expedition. This one consisted of a launch with a howitzer and small arms, with orders to penetrate thirty miles up the river in search of slavers. He wrote, with some pessimism: "I do not promise much success, but I shall have done my duty." Two days later, however, the launch and crew reappeared, as well as the slaver *William G. Lewis* under the command of a prize crew—McBlair's lieutenants, Walker and Cummings. McBlair wrote of the capture: "The evidence upon which she was taken may not be sufficient in itself, though enough to justify suspicion. I had at one time decided to let her go when a new idea occurred to me to call for his letter of instruction. This developed the case more fully & pondering over the custom house papers I found important signatures wanting . . ." Two days later, he sent her to Norfolk for adjudication, adding to his wife, ". . . I wish I could stow myself away in her . . ."

Unfortunately, all the work was for nought, as the courts dismissed the libel. In fact, unbeknownst to McBlair, the vessel had been seized earlier in the year at New York and the case had been dropped.[10] McBlair must have had yet more misgivings as he later wrote that "Costa Lima to whom she is consigned & by whom the cargo is owned is a noted slave trader and she was to have shipped a cargo of slaves very speedily. I have therefore wronged no one should a jury even decide to set her free."

There was, however, still work to do. A second expedition was dispatched up the Congo, in search of the suspected slaver *Windward*, which had been seen earlier but which "through want of judgment in my boarding officer" was allowed to pass. One difficulty in navigating the river in these searches was that there were "so many little creeks and hiding places" in which a vessel could be concealed, and in fact the expedition was unsuccessful. The crew of the launch agreed—no doubt with unintended irony—that "exploring the Congo in search of the brig [was] to be very much like hunting for fugitive slaves in the Dismal Swamp." As with that famous area of Virginia, they "were often bewildered and had to depend on Negro guides to conduct them to the broad stream of the river again . . ."

Conning a boat through mangrove swamps did not count as "shore leave," however, and in the same letter McBlair noted a common feeling among sailors long at sea: "My crew want a run on shore. I want one. I have been ashore but three or four times since the 17th June last and then I could take no exercise . . ."

Despite McBlair's obvious desire to be back home and the frustrations of these weeks, after the capture of *William G. Lewis* he seemed to get a second wind as well as a determination to make the best of his situation. A week after the seizure, the *Dale*'s deck log records that the crew was occupied in "blacking ship" inside and out, including guns and gear. With this done, they commenced work in the tophamper. They "sent down mizzen [topgallant] & mizzen topsail & cross jack yard . . ." This was a major effort entailing heavy and dangerous work aloft, and it was in preparation for an elaborate seagoing ruse. As the log records, it was "preparatory to disguising the vessel as a bark."

The next steps included sending down the mizzen topmast and top and fidding [attaching] the fore topgallant mast as a mizzen topmast. Thus, he reduced the rig from a ship—three square-rigged masts—to a barque with two square rigged masts and the mizzen fore and aft rigged. In keeping with merchant and whaling practice, the typical barque also rarely carried sails higher than topgallants, and the barque rig had only a mizzen mast and mizzen topmast; thus the removal of the fore topgallant mast, which was utilized as a mizzen topmast.

Then the other parts of the stratagem rounded out the picture: the guns were run in and secured, and the crew was decked out merchant sailor style— "dressed in many colors," rather than in naval uniformity. Along with this cosmetic change was a deliberate slackening of the naval type of ship handling. Very few men were sent aloft for a given evolution—to accord with the typical small number in a merchant crew—and evolutions were deliberately sloppy—abandoning precision sail handling, Navy style.

With his now motley crew, McBlair sailed to St. Helena, though by an indirect route in order to "examine" the coast again. In the process, on December 1, a Portuguese sloop-of-war was sighted "bearing down toward us . . . [she] fired a shot to bring us to; which we answered with the bow gun: shotted." McBlair then beat to quarters, ran out the guns, and cleared for action. The Portuguese sloop hove to and sent a boat on board with a lieutenant to apologize for "the mistake." The sloop had encountered *Dale* previously on the coast—before the disguise—and had not recognized her in her new, slovenly role. The disguise was obviously convincing, and the sloop dipped her colors three times as she filled away.

The next day *Dale* found a strange sail and began a long chase, though the quarry did not appear to suspect he was a naval cruiser. The chase ended in a calm and McBlair sent a boat with his non-uniformed crew. They found her to be Portuguese and legal. McBlair wrote: ". . . the captain of her was very much surprised to find us a cruiser, supposing from our appearance and manner of working ship that we were manned with but few hands & a whaler."

Dale then continued down the coast, at one point hoisting out one of her cutters with a crew and two days' provisions, with instructions to meet at Benguela. This time the expedition came up empty.

The usefulness of cutter operations on the river gave McBlair another idea: the ship's carpenters began building—or possibly modifying—one of *Dale*'s boats for a faux "English man-of-war launch," complete with spars and sails. The vessel is mentioned in the logs but it is unclear whether the ruse was actually carried out. It is interesting to envision how useful it would be—approaching an unsuspecting American ship with the 'duster' flying. Whether McBlair considered employing fake British uniforms is another intriguing question.

The use of the new launch was to be postponed, however, as McBlair sailed for St. Helena on December 9. On the voyage out, he removed much of the ship's disguise, so as to keep his craftiness a secret as they went into an important port.

Once at the island, he received disappointing news. A British cruiser had captured the *Windward*, the object of his diligent search on the Congo. She was two hundred miles from the coast when she was taken, "with six hundred slaves in her hold . . . one hundred fifty of her slaves died on the passage they were actually packed in each other's laps when taken."

The stay at St. Helena ended two weeks later, when *Dale* sailed back to the coast. In this instance, there was a specific mission: to secure the release of American merchant sailors from the barque *Osceola,* which was being confined at Benguela. He arrived around December 15 and accomplished the mission. Then, turning towards Little Fish Bay, the weather and currents failed to cooperate: "eight days since I left Benguela, and my progress towards Fish bay [*sic*] not more than eighty miles, the whole distance between the two places ought to have been accomplished in twenty-four hours." He then reiterated his feelings about the need for steamers on the station.

The *Dale* continued to skirt the coast in the vicinity of the Congo, Benguela, and Loando until mid-February, when McBlair turned the sloop to the northwest. With stops at Monrovia and Porto Praya, *Dale* reached the Canaries in early June 1858. McBlair returned to Porto Praya on July 1 and resupplied from the storeship *Release*.

At this place his crew was augmented by new kroomen, one of whom was called "John Adams." The man had been a slave in Rio de Janeiro for three years, "but managed to secrete [*sic*] himself aboard the John Adams & has adopted the name." It is interesting that the man assumed that there would be a haven on the American naval ship—or at least transport back to his home.

By late August McBlair was back on the coast, heading east. At Accra he met with the British governor and, either going ashore or returning, the commander "got another dunking, the surf on the coast though not dangerous is very disagreeable."

From Accra, *Dale* continued east past Quitta, Whydah, and Badagry on the way to Princes Island; McBlair wrote to his wife during this time that he did not know yet if there were orders for his return to the States. He probably would not know for certain until January, when he hoped to be back at the squadron rendezvous.

From Princes Island McBlair crossed the line to Loando, arriving in late November. He skirted the coast and mouth of the Congo until mid-December and arrived back at Porto Praya on January 10, 1859. Unfortunately, the orders he received were for a voyage in the opposite direction from home: *Dale* sailed again for the African coast late in January, calling at Sierra Leone, Monrovia, and Goree.

In mid-March *Dale* was, for the last time, heading west for Porto Praya. After a month there, and meeting with the commodore on *Cumberland*, McBlair sailed for home. *Dale* dropped anchor on May 23 at Kittery, New Hampshire. Commander McBlair had been part of the Africa Squadron for just short of two years.

It is instructive to summarize McBlair's experience on the Africa station. In the two years from the time he arrived at Madeira in May 1857 to the day he left Porto Praya in April 1859, the time can be divided into aggregate segments: (1) at Porto Praya, (2) on the western coast of Africa (Sierra Leone and east to Princes Island), (3) on the southern coast of the continent below the equator, (4) at Madeira, St. Helena, and the Canaries, and (5) at sea. (The latter does not include skirting the coast of the continent.)

Of course the most important segment of time to the mission of the squadron was that spent off the continent. McBlair was on site a total of about seven months, eighty days off the western coast and about 130 in the St. Paul de Loando–Congo area. Of secondary importance was the time in the Cape Verdes, which amounted to about 175 days. His stays at St. Helena, Madeira, and the Canaries numbered about fifty days in total. To McBlair's credit, he spent less than two weeks at Madeira, and only three in the Canaries. His longest stay at Porto Praya and vicinity was two months, but his second longest was about five weeks at the start of his tour, and much of that was due to a lack of communication from the flag officer and a smallpox scare on board his vessel.

What is most telling is the number of days McBlair spent at sea, making the usual rounds from Porto Praya to the coast and back, and so forth. This amounted to about 245 days—eight months out of twenty-four on station were spent at sea. It could easily be argued that McBlair was one of the most motivated ship commanders on the station. Certainly his time below the line was substantial, and he eschewed the frivolous times available to him at Madeira and elsewhere. In any event, when a good, conscientious commander spent more than a third of his tour simply traveling to and from his duty station, it is obvious where the wastage and inefficiency existed on the station. Again, we are back to the absence of steam vessels on the station and the inconvenient location of the squadron's depot in the Cape Verdes.

Commander McBlair's letters provide a microcosm of the squadron. In most aspects his experience was typical: long weeks at sea; much frustration in the pursuit of slavers who were generally better informed than he was, and who had faster vessels; poor communication with superiors and others; and the general malaise generated by the climate and confinement on ship.

In other ways, McBlair was atypical. In looking at many deck logs and diaries of the squadron, this author has yet to find another commanding officer who made such efforts to obtain his object. He was nearly unique in applying elaborate nautical ruses, which were usually only seen in wartime, to his mission off Africa. He seems to have done his best to remain on the coast, especially south of the line, as long as possible, and certainly made the best of the time while there. Unfortunately, it is typical of the squadron that little came of it.

The remainder of the sloop-of-war *St. Louis*'s cruise on the Africa station was more typical than McBlair's adventure in *Dale*. Under J. W. Livingston, the sloop had been at Porto Praya when McBlair arrived and remained in that area from April 1857 through most of August. This included a trip to Madeira, arriving at Funchal in mid-June and staying about five weeks.[11] It was during this period that Livingston had been the default squadron commander, while Conover was en route via the Mediterranean.

Livingston was back at Porto Praya at the close of July and stayed through the arrival of Conover to August 28. The sloop made one sortie to the coast, in September, remaining at Cape Palmas for five days. Other than this, Livingston remained in the Cape Verdes until January 8, 1858, when he sailed back to the United States, arriving at Brooklyn Navy Yard on February 9.[12]

The replacement for *St. Louis* was *Marion,* under Thomas Brent. The sloop arrived from Norfolk in early May 1858. After less than six days, Brent sailed to Monrovia, and then stood down the coast in an uneventful cruise to Princes Island, via Cape Coast Castle and other ports. This consumed much of June through mid-July. The next portion of the cruise was below the line, with the occasional boarding. At the end of July, Brent encountered a whaling barque, the *Roanoke*, with severe sickness on board. The captain sent his medical officer over to assist before continuing south. Through August, the *Marion* cruised off the Congo–Kabenda–Ambriz coastline.[13]

Here the cruise became more fruitful. Brent found the British naval steamer *Antelope* amenable to joint operations and arranged to go up the

Congo River. The steamer towed Brent, his lieutenant, and a crew, reaching about thirty-eight miles up the river. There they overhauled and boarded three vessels, two of them the *E. A. Chase* and *E. H. Booth*. All were found to be legal traders.[14]

Back on the coast, on September 8, they sighted a suspicious ketch flying British colors. After a three-hour chase, a shot was put across her bows, and she hauled down the British and raised the American flag. On boarding the vessel, which was found to be the *Brothers* from Charleston via Havana, the papers were found "correct," though they had not stopped at St. Thomas as the documents stated. The crew was composed entirely of foreigners, excepting a naturalized American citizen who was the captain. The vessel's cargo, as one writer said, was "nearly everything needed to buy, confine, and feed a group of Africans. The list is remarkable for its completeness: two tons of rice, a hundred barrels of bread, some preserved fish and dried beef, stacks of empty water casks, enough lumber (thoughfully [*sic*] unmanifested) to build a slave deck, two iron cooking boilers, bricks enough to build furnaces for them, five hundred wooden spoons . . . and $8,416 in hard cash." To top this off, the vessel was owned by James Gage, who also owned the slaver *Lyra*, which was recently seized off Key West. On the strength of this evidence, the ship was seized.[15]

Lieutenant Brent's efforts proved useless however. The federal court in Charleston, South Carolina, parsed the evidence in the most innocent manner possible. Judge Alexander G. Magrath wrote: "I cannot discover what there is in this cargo which of itself leads to a conclusion of a criminal purpose or excludes the fact of such articles having been intended for a lawful purpose." In effect, according to Magrath, circumstantial evidence was not to obtrude on presumed innocence. How much the judge's thought process was influenced by the prevailing mood in Charleston at the time is a matter of speculation. However, the local press was supportive of the recent movement to reopen and legalize the slave trade, and it had taken a strong stance for the innocence of the parties involved with the *Brothers*. The upshot was the dismissal of the charges.[16]

Brent sailed north a few days after dispatching his prize to the United States, returning to Porto Praya on October 1. Late in the month he took *Marion* to Tenerife for two weeks, and then returned to the Cape Verdes. In January 1859 he sailed directly south to Princes Island, the jumping off point for the southern coast. From late February to May 22, *Marion* cruised south of the line, concentrating around the Congo River.[17]

On April 19 Brent arrived off the mouth of the great river and, again, his diligence paid off. There he found the American barque *Orion* of New York, a 450-ton ship built with beams to support a second deck. But *Orion* was not alone: she was anchored under the guns of HBM steamer *Triton*, which had detained the vessel a few days before, first having boarded her to check her papers. Then, on evidence that the vessel was on a slaving voyage, the British cruiser had detained her.[18]

In this instance, the sequence of events recorded in the *Marion*'s deck log is indicative of an unusual situation. First, Thomas Morgan, *Orion*'s first mate, came aboard *Marion* and presumably registered a complaint about the British detention of his ship. Next, Brent called out a boat and visited Capt. R. H. Burton on the *Triton*, no doubt to get both sides of the story. In less than an hour Brent ordered a second boat dispatched, this time with an armed party to take charge of the barque. For unknown reasons, it was two days later before Brent took official possession of the ship on the strength of her cargo, the usual panoply of the trade: lumber, boilers and furnaces, etc. He then put the crew in irons and dispatched her to New York.[19]

It had been an easy capture. Not so the outcome. And, it seems that the question of whether the vessel was in actuality a slaver had little to do with the ultimate result. The first complication occurred on the passage home: the barque's skipper, John E. Hanna, died, and while doing so he confessed to the slaving voyage of the *Orion*, though with the caveat that the mate, Morgan, was not in on the secret. When the ship arrived at New York, the news of Hanna's death aroused the ire of the State Department, which blamed the British for Hanna's death, acting on the crews' allegations against the Royal Navy captain. It was charged that Burton had threatened and attempted to force them to renounce their nationality so he could legally seize the ship. Of course the British commander denied this, only admitting to detaining the vessel until an American cruiser could be contacted.[20]

In any event, at New York, the case against the crew went nowhere. The district attorney did not even take it to the grand jury, and the crew was released. There was, however, still the libel against the vessel, which amounted to something over $17,000. Here an 1847 statute favored the vessel's owner, who was allowed to post bond for the amount and regain possession of the ship and cargo. Amazingly, bonding only required an oath— not an actual cash transaction— so by late 1859 the vessel and cargo were back in the possession of the owners, though technically not "free."[21]

The ship was free enough for its new captain, Thomas Morgan, to return to Africa and complete the original intent of the voyage. Off the coast, *Orion* loaded a cargo of 488 slaves and turned for home, only to be caught red-handed by HMS *Pluto*. Morgan elected not to show the American flag, as the presence of slaves obviated any immunity from prosecution under the American piracy statute. Declared to be without colors or papers, the vessel was confiscated by a British court, forfeited, and dismantled piece by piece. Back in New York, news of the capture reached the circuit court and the $17,000 was declared due. Eventually (July 1861) the bondsman was convicted of perjury—he had no money—and was sentenced to five years in Sing Sing. He was out in two.[22]

Back at the mouth of the Congo, Commander Brent had yet another slaver virtually fall into his lap. In this instance, the commander of Royal Navy steamer *Pluto* came aboard and voiced suspicion about the legality of another American barque, the *Ardennes*, anchored at Point Padrone. Brent sent a cutter to board the ship, and seized the vessel in short order.[23]

It is doubtful that Brent had knowledge of the *Ardennes*'s history. The vessel had been seized five months before by the federal authorities at Jacksonville, Florida. The case had gotten no farther than the circuit judge who quashed it for insufficient evidence. In the vessel's second court appearance, this time before a federal court in New York, the result was the same: the libel was dismissed.[24]

The remainder of *Marion*'s cruise while under Conover's command consisted of a return to Loando and subsequent passages to Porto Praya and Funchal. Brent had kept the vessel on the south coast from late February through May 22, 1859. In two cruises south of the line—thus far— *Marion* had seized three vessels.[25]

The sloop-of-war *Vincennes* was a late arrival to Conover's flotilla, arriving at Porto Praya nearly at the end of December 1857. Her commanding officer, Benjamin J. Totten, had departed from New York in November with orders to await the arrival of Conover at Porto Praya "during the whole month of December."[26] However, Totten had no need to wait; Conover had arrived from Cape Palmas on the last day of November.[27]

Vincennes was one of the oldest vessels to be attached to the squadron, having been commissioned in 1826. Her age did not diminish her hardiness, however. She had been the flagship on Wilkes's exploration team from 1838 to 1842 and had served the same role for Cadwalader Ringgold's 1853 North Pacific expedition. The sloop-of-war had completed at least three circumnavigations of the world and, after her African service, remained active until after the Civil War.

On the Africa station, however, there was little glory or excitement. After two weeks at the Cape Verdes, she sailed for Sierra Leone and Monrovia. She then dropped directly south to Loando and Kabenda, returning to Monrovia in early May. Then, after stays at Porto Praya and Funchal, the vessel returned to the coast in early September.[28]

From Loando, Totten cruised the southern coast and, on October 12, sighted a slaver taking on her cargo off Ambrizette Bay. The slaver, eventually revealed to be the notorious *Wanderer*, cut short her task and headed out to sea. *Vincennes* was initially able to reach only three knots in a light breeze, but Totten had her starboard battery moved inboard to help her trim, and she eventually worked up to seven knots. As Conover reported, the *Vincennes* gave her a "hot chase," but the slaver had the advantage. The *Wanderer* escaped and later landed her cargo on the coast of Georgia. This was the only contact the Navy had with *Wanderer*, and her amazing story is related at the end of this chapter.[29]

After the encounter with *Wanderer*, Totten continued on the coast, stopping at Ambriz and Mayumba before returning to Princes Island. Later, off Cape Coast Castle, Totten seized the barque *Julia Dean* and sent her to the United States, where the courts dismissed the case. Afterwards, Totten sailed to Monrovia, leaving the latter place the first week in February 1859. For three weeks *Vincennes* was at Porto Praya, and then she visited Goree for a week in April. At the end of May 1859 she left the Cape Verdes and the remainder of her African cruise fell under Conover's successor on the station.[30]

The last vessel to be considered was the flagship *Cumberland* itself.

Conover arrived in the Cape Verdes on August 16, 1857, after three weeks at Funchal. After about two and a half weeks he went south, directly to Princes Island. From October 11 through the 26th *Cumberland* was on the coast from Loando to Ambriz and Kabenda. Conover returned to Liberian waters on November 3 and departed for Porto Praya two weeks later.[31]

From the end of November 1857 to August 1858, *Cumberland* was at Porto Praya, Madeira, the Canaries, and again at the Cape Verdes. This included about a month and a half at Funchal and two months at Tenerife.[32]

The second sortie on the south coast began at Loando on September 19, and ended at Ambrizette on November 9, 1858. *Cumberland* then returned to Porto Praya, only visiting the African coast at Goree for sixteen days in February 1859. From the first week in April through August 8, Conover was at Funchal. He wrote on July 2 that he was "awaiting my relief or orders home." [33] He did not return to Porto Praya again before turning the flagship west towards the Navy Yard at Portsmouth, New Hampshire.[34]

Conover's total time on the south coast was about two months, plus nineteen days that were split between Cape Palmas and Goree. This pales when compared to his accumulated time spent in the various watering places among the islands. One recent historian remarked that there was "no excuse for such dereliction."[35] Again, though, Conover may have used the excuse that the crews needed rest and relaxation from the rigors of the African coast; those same crews had spent significantly less time on the coast than many others on his own squadron, as exemplified by the cruises of *Dale* and *Marion* related above.

It is fortunate that Conover's commanding officers were more diligent than he. A total of five slavers were seized in the two-year period, two of them in a single week in 1859.

To wrap up the overall situation at the end of Conover's tour, several things stand out. First, the slave trade was back in full force. A congressional report of 1858 related a substantial list of American vessels suspected or known to be in the trade during the period 1857–1858. A total of forty-one vessels were listed, of which twenty-one had been apprehended. British cruisers had captured nine of these. More than 2,600 slaves were enumerated as having been taken from Africa by these vessels.[36] Second, the movement to reopen the legal slave trade had its first fruits with the yacht *Wanderer*, mentioned above. Though the trade was never legalized, a cabal of prominent Georgians, led by Charles Augustus Lafayette Lamar, determined to openly defy the federal laws. A fast, luxurious yacht—the *Wanderer*—was purchased and fitted out at New York for the expedition. As she made for the open sea, however, the steam Revenue Cutter *Harriet Lane* intercepted and stopped her.[37]

This did not end it, however. The U.S. attorney was invited on board to inspect. Finding nothing askew, and that the ship's captain set a fine table, the vessel was released. After a stop at Charleston, the vessel cleared for Trinidad, a place which she did not visit, showing up rather on the Congo River, where cargo loading was begun and where she was detected by the *Vincennes*, as noted above. Around four hundred blacks were embarked and the yacht easily outran the sloop-of-war. On November 29, the slaves were off-loaded at Jekyll Island, Georgia. None were ever rescued. This was to be the last slave ship to land her cargo on the Atlantic coastline.[38]

The significance of the *Wanderer* was the fact that the effort was a success (though the vessel was eventually forfeited and sold). The extremists had done what they intended and had successfully evaded both the U.S. Navy's Africa Squadron and federal authorities in the United States. The feat was a triumph for the rabid secessionists, and it became another stone in the wall that divided the opposing sections of the country. It may also have resulted in some of the major changes in the squadron that were to be seen under the next squadron commander.

The last significant event of note here occurred off the eastern tip of Cuba, in August 1858. The U.S. brig *Dolphin* seized the brig *Echo* (formerly named *Putnam*) with 318 starving, diseased blacks— all that survived from an original cargo of 455— on board. The conditions were described as "filthy to the last degree" by the naval officers who boarded the vessel. They sent her to Charleston for adjudication. The case should have been open-and-shut, as the evidence was incontrovertible. Instead the judge called the anti–slave trade law of 1820 unconstitutional— echoing the nullification sentiments rampant all over the south—and the crew was acquitted in a jury trial after only ninety minutes of deliberation. Further, the vessel's captain was tried in Key West for piracy and was acquitted on a technicality.[39]

Thus, the end of Conover's tour saw the nation tottering on the edge of dissolution, and sectionalism was now out in the open. Where judicial decisions freeing slavers were previously couched in legal, constitutional terms, now the Southern courts were abandoning the pretexts and joining the growing sentiment against the "Black Republican" North, abolitionism, and what were viewed as restrictions on southern rights.

14

FLAG OFFICER INMAN AND THE GREAT SEA CHANGE, 1859–1861

In looking at the list of slavers captured by the squadron over the course of its existence, one of the most obvious changes was the pronounced upsurge in captures from late 1859 to the end of the squadron's existence in mid-1861. This period saw twenty-two vessels captured at sea between September 1859 and June 1861. The closest approximation to this number was in 1845—47, when thirteen slavers were seized.

These statistics raise two interesting questions. The first is the question of how this marked increase could come about: What changes or factors allowed or precipitated this surge? The second question is why: What motivations were at work in the Navy to instigate a major change in the application of long-standing policies in the war against the slave trade? Aligned with the latter question is the more embarrassing one for the service: Why had the change not occurred before this? Further, can the answers to these questions be related to the impending rebellion of the Southern states? Of these questions, the first is the easiest to answer, and it will be addressed immediately. Afterward, some attempt will be made to address the more penetrating questions.

As has been noted fairly consistently throughout this narrative, there were two extremely sore spots with the officers and leaders of the squadron. One was the need for steam vessels and additional ships on the station; the other was for a supply depot closer to the African coast than Porto Praya. In the year 1859, under the flag of Commodore William Inman, both problems were addressed nearly simultaneously.

The solution to the former problem came about indirectly from a diplomatic incident with the nation of Paraguay. In 1855, a Paraguayan fort fired upon and killed a crewmember of the USS *Water Witch*, which was on a surveying mission up the La Plata River. The Buchanan administration demanded redress and, failing that, began assembling a naval force to fall upon the Paraguayans. It was immediately decided that the proposed force was deficient in the area of small steam vessels suited for river operations. Consequently, the department leased five small steamers, each around five hundred tons and carrying five to eight guns. The vessels were *Wyandotte, Crusader, Sumpter, Mystic*, and *Mohawk*. Then the confrontation with Paraguay was settled peacefully, and thus the rationale for retaining the new ships was gone.

However, the department had been agitating for the construction of small steamers specifically for use in coastal and harbor waters, and a bill had been proposed in Congress in early 1859 to accomplish this. There was sufficient southern opposition—based on the fear that such steamers were in actuality to be used in Southern harbors—to cause the measure to founder in the halls of Congress. In lieu of new construction, the department instead purchased the five vessels leased earlier. Interestingly, the purchases were made in May and June 1859, and as early as July 6, Secretary of the Navy Isaac Toucey wrote the newly appointed Flag Officer

St. Paul de Loando, site of the Navy's supply depot from mid-1859 to 1861.
Loando was over five hundred miles south of the Equator and therefore was a
vast logistical improvement over Porto Praya.
From A. H. Foote's *Africa and the American Flag.*

The sloop-of-war Constellation, *last flagship of the Africa Squadron. Preserved in Baltimore, the vessel was also the last sailing vessel built by the U.S. Navy. Under Capt. William Inman,* Constellation *seized slavers* Delicia, Cora, *and* Triton. Cora *was carrying 705 Africans when captured.*
Naval Historical Center

William Inman that *Sumpter* and *Mystic* were being added to the Africa Squadron.[1]

In all, Inman's squadron would consist of sloops-of-war *Constellation*, *Vincennes*, *Portsmouth*, and *Marion,* and four steamers: *San Jacinto, Mystic, Mohican,* and *Sumpter*. In addition to having steam-powered vessels for the first time, this was nearly double the number of vessels previously on the station. (It has been noted that the Navy had intended to send the steamer *Vixen* to the Africa Squadron in 1853, and the vessel was so noted in the Navy register for the year, but this plan had been dropped.[2])

Further use for the new steamers was found with the Home Squadron, specifically to deal with anti–slave trade operations off Cuba. That squadron received *Mohawk*, *Wyandotte*, and *Crusader,* as well as the older steamer *Water Witch*.[3]

As to the location of the squadron depot, Toucey wrote Inman that a new depot was to be established at St. Paul de Loando. Inman was to ". . . make all necessary arrangements . . . for establishing the principal depot of the African squadron." A storehouse was to be leased for not more than two years "on moderate terms." The first shipload of supplies was already scheduled to be sent out in September,[4] and when September came, Inman was authorized to utilize the storeship *Supply* to transfer stores from the old facility to St. Paul de Loando, completing the transition to the new depot.[5] Thus, in a space of five months, the two key elements that retarded the operations of the Africa Squadron were addressed and rectified.

This begs the related questions: Why?, and why now? One explanation reverts to the British thorn in the American free trade side. Indeed, there had been increasing numbers of American-flagged vessels stopped by British cruisers off Cuba. In May 1858, Secretary of State Lewis Cass suggested to Toucey the "propriety of dispatching one or more armed vessels to Cuba" in response to the "gross outrage" committed against the American vessel *Cortez* by the British steamer *Forward*. The latter had claimed the American vessel was engaged in the slave trade and taken her as a prize.[6] Consequently, as has been seen, the *Dolphin* and *Constel-*

Slave Ship Wanderer. *Prominent Southern pro-slavery extremists openly hired* Wanderer *in an effort to re-open the slave trade. The fast former yacht outdistanced sloop-of-war* Vincennes *and eluded federal authorities in Georgia, landing the last cargo of Africans on the American coast in late 1858. The public and press outcry was such that within three months Buchanan issued directives to enlarge the squadron, assign steamers to it, and, shortly thereafter, move the depot from the Cape Verde Islands to the African coast.*
Naval Historical Center

lation had been dispatched to deal with this situation in 1858; however, it was a year later when the steamers were sent to the Caribbean with specific orders to stop slavers.

The timing of one particular incident and its immediate results seems to have been more likely the spark for Toucey's sudden rousing to action. The yacht *Wanderer*, which had successfully evaded the squadron in Africa, landed her slaves in Georgia on November 29, 1858. By mid-December the Navy's and the government's embarrassment was playing in the nation's major newspapers. There was an immediate response by irate congressmen: a resolution that President Buchanan pass along any information "in relation to the landing of the barque *Wanderer* on the coast of Georgia . . ."[7] On December 19, President Buchanan, in his annual message to Congress responded in part by declaring that "all lawful means were being used to stop the slave trade," and that the *Wanderer* was the only known vessel to have landed slaves in the United States.[8]

Of more concern to Buchanan—a Democrat—was the response of the growing Republican party, which issued a pamphlet declaring that "what is wanted . . . to put down this infamous traffic, is a Republican President . . ."[9] Buchanan now was facing a double threat in the last half of his administration: if Southern extremists continued where Lamar had left off with *Wanderer*, and succeeded, the reverberations would certainly be amplified by the increasingly vocal anti-slavery party of Lincoln. Even more damaging would be more open proof that the administration was unable to enforce the law itself. Indeed, the South was rife with rumors of other slave landings on its shores, from Texas to Florida. Therefore, as one writer said, Buchanan was seeking to "distance himself from proslavery extremism in domestic politics."[10]

With the problem in full view—in the form of the *Wanderer*'s slaves on the streets of the South—Buchanan directed Toucey to take additional measures to strengthen the Africa Squadron. The exact date of this directive is not known, but Secretary Cass wrote Secretary of the Treasury A. J. Dallas on February 23, 1858, that the president had "already" written the directive, and he hoped that "two at least" armed steamers would be added to the Africa Squadron and three to the Cuban detachment. Three months later, negotiations were underway with the British to modify Webster-Ashburton to allow for fewer guns on the station, in light of the assignment of steam vessels in addition to the sailing ships.[11] With the presidential orders in mind, Toucey first went to Congress for funds to build small steamers for the squadron. As has been seen, Southern votes precluded this in March 1859, and the next obvious step was the purchase of the leased steamers. Then the move of the depot was almost inevitable, given the increased need for supplies for the additional vessels and the sudden need for convenient coaling points.

It is unfortunate that these events occurred as late in the game as it proved to be. Indeed the "why now" question may be answered by the fact that strengthening the squadron was one of the few measures Buchanan could take that would throw a bone to the abolitionists and not offend the mainstream southerners—who, for the most part, still abhorred the trade itself. Only the extremists would laugh while dreaming of the slavocracy soon to become reality in Montgomery, Alabama. Indeed, extreme measures were becoming more common as the conflict loomed on the near horizon: late 1859 brought the horrors of extreme abolition to Harpers Ferry, Virginia.

Flag Officer William Inman of New Jersey would be the last commander of the Africa Squadron. Inman was another officer who joined the Navy immediately prior to the War of 1812, which gave him more than forty-five years of service. He was, however, a somewhat doubtful personality. In a recent downsizing, Inman had been twenty-first in the line of those not recommended for continued active service. Two Navy boards agreed on this, and only an appeal to the president gave him a reprieve. He had never commanded a squadron.[12]

Inman reached Funchal in August in the flagship *Constellation*, a nearly new sloop-of-war, built at Norfolk. She was the namesake of the original frigate of the same name, built to a new hull plan.[13] She carried twenty-two guns. The other new steamers on the squadron were *Mohican* and *San Jacinto*. The former was an almost new steam sloop and sister ship to the famed 1861 *Kearsarge*; the latter was a screw steamer commissioned in 1851, with a history of unreliability in her machinery. The steamers were armed as follows: *San Jacinto*, thirteen guns; *Mohican,* six guns; *Mystic*, five guns; and *Sumpter*, five guns. The total number of guns on the squadron was ninety-three.[14]

Secretary of the Navy Isaac Toucey. Under orders from President Buchanan, in 1859 Toucey finally put teeth into the Africa squadron, moving the supply depot to St. Paul de Loando and assigning four steam vessels to the unit. Both moves had been advocated by Africa squadron commanders for over a decade.
Naval Historical Center

The effective use of this force was the subject of an initial letter of instruction to Inman, written by Toucey in July 1859. In fact, the letter was for the most part a copy of the initial instructions passed down from previous commanders, dating back to M. C. Perry. The cruising grounds ran from Madeira to Cape Frio, and from the coast to thirty degrees west longitude. As with the earlier letter, the secretary reiterated that the paramount responsibility was the protection of American commerce, with the suppression of the slave trade a close second. He included hints on what evidence to look for to determine the legitimacy of a vessel, etc. The standard procedure to be followed when approaching a vessel without colors was set forth: First, a blank cartridge could be fired, then a shotted gun, fired so as not to endanger anyone. Once the vessel showed a flag, the commander would decide on the level of suspicion to attach to the vessel. A legitimate American trader was subject to a visit, detention, etc., whereas one flying a foreign flag could only be "visited" and not detained. He also mentioned that one of the stratagems used by the slavers was to fake the U.S. Consular seal on their papers by using an American half-dollar coin.[15] There was little, if anything, new in Inman's document, and much of it could have literally been a copy of the original orders from two decades before.

With his orders from the department in hand, Inman raised his flag at Funchal on August 8 and remained there for nearly a month. He then sailed to Porto Praya to await the other units of the squadron to report. First to arrive was *Portsmouth,* commanded by John Colhoun. She had made a fine, fast passage from Boston: nineteen days, on some of which she ran off more than two hundred miles each. The swiftest day noted on

Flag Officer William Inman. The final commander of the Africa squadron, Inman was ordered to observe new squadron cruising grounds which did not include Madeira, and to establish the squadron depot at Loando. He made detailed itineraries for the steam vessels newly assigned to the station, and oversaw Constellation's *seizure of three slavers.*
Naval Historical Center

the log was June 7, when she logged 232 miles. Colhoun reported in and sailed to the coast July 29. On August 8, she was at Monrovia, from whence Colhoun sailed her to Princes Island, via Cape Coast Castle.[16]

Less than two weeks after leaving Princes Island, while off Loango, Colhoun sent a boarding crew to the barque *Emily*. They found evidence enough to warrant keeping an armed party on her overnight, and she was seized on September 20. There was "abundance of evidence of her intention" of entering the trade. Her hold contained, among other things, fifteen thousand feet of lumber, 103 barrels of water, two boilers and furnaces, two cases of drugs, etc. The barque had cleared New York fully equipped for slaving, but the authorities had allowed her to pass. This was a direct outworking of recent judicial decisions where no cargo of itself was sufficient to warrant confiscation of a vessel.[17] As the vessel had the same cargo when she returned to New York under Colhoun's prize crew, the case against her was dismissed.[18]

Shortly after this Colhoun met the British steamer *Triton*—a familiar sight on that part of the coast. He equipped a cutter and sent it under tow, with the steamer, in search of slavers on the river. Nothing came of this, and another month and a half passed cruising that part of the coast before another suspicious vessel was sighted. In this instance, the encounter was slightly comic, given the customs of the sea. The vessel, under French colors, was hailed and the log records that "the following questions were asked of him, viz.: 'Where are you from?' Answer: 'Very far off.' They were told to heave to and a boat would be sent to board her. He asked 'why'; we said to look at your papers. Answer: his 'commandante did not allow it', and kept on his course." The vessel stood for the land and anchored. Apparently no boarding was attempted by the *Portsmouth*.[19]

The cruise continued until early December, when Colhoun sailed her into Loando where the flagship lay and, in a few days, three other ships of the squadron also converged there. On January 9, 1860, the ship sailed back to the Congo. In February, another boat expedition was mounted, this time in cooperation with the Royal Navy steamer *Viper*, to inspect suspicious vessels. Two days later, the steamer reappeared off Sharks Point, towing the brig *Virginian*. A prize crew was placed on her and she was sailed to Loando, then Norfolk. No slaves were on board, and the disposition of the case is unknown.[20]

Afterward, Colhoun remained cruising the coast until mid-March,

U.S. Steamer Sumpter. *A vessel obtained by the Navy for the Paraguayan Punitive Expedition in 1858, she was one of the first steamers assigned to the Africa squadron.* Sumpter *made the squadron's last seizure: the slaver* Falmouth *in June 1861, three months after the outbreak of the Civil War.*
Naval Historical Center

when *Portsmouth* sailed to Porto Praya and Madeira. The *Portsmouth* was at Funchal for nearly a month, along with the flagship, before returning to the Cape Verdes, then to the south coast. The sloop remained there, ranging as far south as Little Fish Bay and Elephant Bay. Colhoun hovered off around Loando through July 17, 1861. The only break from the routine was a ten-day stay at St. Helena in May. When the squadron dispersed after the beginning of the Civil War, Colhoun sailed the *Portsmouth* to New Hampshire, arriving in late September. [21]

The next vessel to sail for the coast was *San Jacinto.* Inman had awaited her at Madeira, but later learned that the steamer had gone directly to Porto Praya, and he then proceeded there in *Constellation.* He ordered *San Jacinto* to the coast, though her commander, William Armstrong, informed him that the ship's propeller bearings were "cutting more and more" (wearing out)* and were not likely to last much longer. In any event, Inman remained at Porto Praya to greet *Mystic* and *Sumpter.* By the first of October the two small steamers had reported, but Inman did not leave for the coast until four days later.[22]

San Jacinto, however, was at Cape Mount by October 25, and she

---

*   San Jacinto was a wooden-hulled screw steamer, and the wearing out of propeller bearings was common in this era.

was standing down the coast. Inman's orders were to proceed to the Congo and anchor in such a way that, with guns and boats, "you can command the mouth of the river." In mid-November Armstrong made a quite leisurely passage southward, during which there were several calm days. The logs indicate the engines were not run at these times—no doubt due to the predicted destruction of the propeller bearing. Armstrong arrived at the Congo, and remained in that vicinity, including side trips to Loando, until January 11, 1860.[23]

While cruising in the area, there were few notable incidents. Late in November, Armstrong was relieved of command by Inman, on charges he had left his post at the mouth of the Congo and engaged in a chase with the barque *Orion*. It is not clear what these circumstances were, given the earlier history of the vessel, as noted above. A few days after this, the steamer chased a hermaphrodite brig (contemporary term for a half brig and half schooner) up the river, going full speed and using all fore and aft sail. The vessel escaped. Then, shortly before Christmas, a Dutch schooner collided with *San Jacinto*, doing little damage. The warship's carpenters assisted in repairing the schooner. Finally, in the first week in January, a new commander arrived to replace Armstrong. In

Slave ship Falmouth. *Rigged as a schooner,* Falmouth *was captured by Federal authorities in New York using the tug* Only Son *(shown behind* Falmouth*), in 1856. This vessel may have been the same vessel, rigged as a brig, captured by U. S. steamer* Sumpter *in 1861: the last slave ship taken by the Africa Squadron.*
Naval Historical Center

this instance, the replacement was Lt. James F. Armstrong (the earlier commanding officer had been William Armstrong).[24]

In January, *San Jacinto* steamed northward, though the captain again avoided extensive use of her engines. Armstrong had disagreed with his engineers concerning the longevity of his propeller bearing and was authorized by Inman to make for Cadiz, the nearest port where she could be docked and taken out of the water for repairs. After a few days at Monrovia, Lieutenant Armstrong continued on to the Canaries and from there to Spain.[25] The docking and repairs consumed three months, and the steamer was not back at Porto Praya until July 7, 1860.[26] Armstrong made a two-week stop at Madeira also. By this time, Secretary Toucey had realigned the squadron's cruising area, making the northern boundary twenty degrees north latitude—far short of both Madeira and the Canaries—and thus making unauthorized or lengthy stops at those ports unacceptable.[27]

On July 23, 1860, the steamer, now under the command of Thomas L. Dornin, was at Monrovia and on her second sortie down the coast. Off the Congo again in early August, she encountered a hermaphrodite brig and gave chase under steam. A blank cartridge was fired and the vessel was hailed: the answer was "no entiendo," and a boat was sent to board her. The vessel was the *Storm King* and she was carrying "upwards of 600 slaves on board."[28] She was taken in tow by the steamer, sent under a prize crew to the United States, and was confiscated by the courts.[29]

Two months later, still in the vicinity of the Congo, Dornin sighted another brig and gave chase. The logs read: "Ship in chase (going nine knots) fire shot across stern . . . no attention was paid." Then the large pivot gun (probably an eight-inch shell gun) was run out and a series of shots was placed across her stern, causing her to finally heave to after a three-hour chase. The vessel was American in build and rig but showed no colors. She was the 277-ton *Bonito*, which had cleared from New York without papers and carried no less than 750 slaves in her hold.[30]

Dornin sent a mechanic aboard to set up a galley for the blacks and proceeded to take the ship in tow, going, under steam alone, three to five knots. Once the prize crew was on board, the tow was cast off and the brig sailed for Monrovia.[31]

After this, Dornin kept the steamer south of the line through the first week of January 1861, when she steamed for St. Helena. After a two-week sojourn, *San Jacinto* was back on the southern coast, maintaining regular sweeps across the wide mouth of the Congo. In March, the squadron rendezvoused at Kabenda and sortied to sea in company. Inman ordered squadron position-keeping exercises, despite heavy rain. At first, *San Jacinto* lost sight of the other vessels, then, when the weather cleared, she steamed out to meet the flotilla. She came alongside the flagship and maintained her position "with the engines." Once maneuvers were completed, the squadron dispersed again to their duties on coast. There was little of note to report for the next few months. In March, the crew painted the vessel gray; in May, *Constellation* grounded at Loando. To pull her off, a seven-inch hawser was sent from *San Jacinto*, and "made taut with the capstan." After at least six hours of pulling, the flagship was refloated.[32]

After the outbreak of the war, the vessels of the squadron were recalled to the United States, but *San Jacinto*, taken over by Capt. Charles Wilkes, remained on the African coast until mid-September, when she sailed to the West Indies. [33]

The next ship to leave for the African coast in 1859 was the *Marion*, under Thomas Brent, which arrived at Porto Grande from Funchal on October 5—the same day Inman departed in *Constellation*—from Porto Praya.

Brent's cruise was almost uneventful. He first sighted the coast at El Mina, and then put in at Princes Island. At the end of December he was at Kabenda. No slavers were seized in eight months of cruising south of the line— as far south as Loando. The only incidents of interest recorded in the logs were at Ambrizette in February–March 1860. There, an armed party was sent ashore for the protection of American interests and "factories." They had flown the flag "union down" to call for help. A landing party was sent ashore and apparently burned the native settlement to end the confrontation.[34]

On August 13, Brent and his crew received the long anticipated orders for home. Four days later, *Marion* was at sea. After a stop at Monrovia, passage was made to Boston, where she arrived October 3, 1860.[35]

The remainders of Inman's flotilla in 1859 to 1861 were the formerly leased steamers *Mystic* and *Sumpter*. Both vessels had arrived at Porto Praya by October 1 and had proceeded to the coast. As with the other vessels, Inman ordered them directly to Princes Island, from whence they were to go to the Congo. When provisions ran low, they were to resupply at Loando.[36] The exact itineraries of both these vessels is unknown, as their deck logs for this period are not in the National Archives. However, they apparently followed orders and it is known that *Mystic* was off the Congo in November 1859, where her boarding party inspected the infamous *Orion*—which had returned from New York for the second time to finish her business. Again, the American cruiser did not seize her, as the court in New York had released her.[37] Both steamers were busy, however, as Inman reported in January that *Sumpter* had boarded twenty-one vessels and *Mystic* four in the space of a month. [38]

In January 1860, the two ships were conjoined with the newly arrived *Mohican* in Inman's cruising scheme for the south coast. An eight-hundred-mile section of coast was divided into three sections, with a steamer assigned to each. The northernmost vessel was to coal and reprovision at Fernando Po, the southern vessels at Loando. The northern vessel was to pick up— on the 28th—mail from the monthly steamer from England, rendezvous with the "middle" ship, and pass on the mail. The second would hand it off to the third at Loango Bay. The three vessels would exchange positions periodically. Five days were allowed for each vessel to reprovision.[39] The plan was an example of what could be accomplished with ships on a schedule—as opposed to sailing vessels. The schedule, however, was more concerned with the mail and logistics than with catching slavers. Indeed, the adversary could as easily know the schedule as Inman's officers.

In any event, the two steamers snared three slavers between them. *Mystic* took the brig *Thomas Achorn* off Kabenda in June 1860, and the New Orleans brig *Triton* the following month, this time off Loango. The federal courts dismissed the case against the former vessel but confiscated the latter. *Sumpter* had the honor of seizing the squadron's last slaver, on June 14, 1861. The brig *Falmouth*, (possibly the schooner of the same name seized in New York in 1856) was taken off the mouth of the Congo. Again, the court of the district of Southern New York dismissed the case.[40]

Two additional vessels were to join the squadron before it was dissolved in 1861. These were *Mohican* and *Saratoga*. The former was commissioned in late 1859, was in drydock at New York in January 1860, and arrived at Porto Grande on February 7, 1860. The latter would arrive at the end of the year.[41]

Mohican, under Sylvanus Godon, arrived on the coast February 24, 1860. From Monrovia, she steamed to Princes Island and Fernando Po. After coaling, she went south to Kabenda, the Congo, and Loando, where she coaled again. The second week in April she left Loando and proceeded back up to Kabenda, Loango, Mayumba, and arrived at Fernando Po on May 22.[42]

She did not depart from the Princes Island– Fernando Po vicinity until July 3, when she stood along the land for Accra and Cape Coast Castle. From there Godon went to Quitta. The passage was about twenty-three hours; twelve of those were under steam, averaging about four knots. The next stop was Whydah where he inspected three vessels on the morning of July 16. [43]

Mohican returned to Princes Island and Fernando Po and coaled again before returning to the Congo River. On August 8, the ship *Erie* of New York was sighted and a blank cartridge was shot across her bows, which brought her to heel. The vessel was found to be "without papers,

Clipper ship Nightingale, *one of the last slavers captured by the squadron. With 961 Blacks on board, the vessel carried more than the notorious* Pons, *seized in 1845.* Nightingale *had been one of the swiftest American-built clipper ships and was one of the largest vessels used in the slave trade.*
Currier & Ives Lithograph in author's collection

or any person claiming to be captain, and with 893 slaves on board, having a mixed crew of Spaniards, Americans, and Frenchmen."[44] Not a hundred miles away, on the same day, *San Jacinto* stopped and seized *Storm
King*. This was the largest number of Africans freed on a single day off
the coast of Africa. Once the *Erie* was underweigh, *Mohican* steamed
around her and the crew gave three cheers as the vessel made for home.[45]

The outcome of *Erie*'s days in court was unexpected. First, the vessel itself was taken to New York and confiscated, as it should have been.
Second, Nathaniel Gordon, William Warren, and David Hale, officers of
the ship, were tried at New York on charges of piracy. The trial brought
out the "inhumane" manner the slaves had been packed aboard. In fact,
when the naval officers could not "repack" them in the same spaces,
Gordon had shown how to arrange them. Doubts about the nationality of
the vessel clouded the issue, with the defense claiming she had been sold
out of American hands at Havana. Further, after the purported sale, Gordon was ostensibly only a passenger. In any event, the first trial brought a
deadlocked jury. Gordon's second trial and jury, in November 1861, returned a verdict of guilty. Despite an appeal to President Lincoln, Gordon was hanged on February 21, 1862.[46]

Nathaniel Gordon was the only slave trader ever given the death
penalty in the United States. The conviction was obviously a fluke, and
in fact other "piratical" slaver crewmembers in New York City at the
same time were quietly let off with light sentences.[47] And light sentences,
as well as short incarcerations, generally marked the fate of most convicted slave traders throughout the history of the squadron.

The remainder of *Mohican*'s tour on the station was anticlimactic.
With the exception of two weeks at St. Helena, she cruised in pattern
along the coast from Loando northward to Fernando Po and Princes Island. Probably the only relief from constant patrolling was when a naval
battalion made up of parts of the crews of the squadron vessels formed up
and drilled at Loando in June 1861. This was no doubt in response to the
news of war breaking out at home. Godon raised her anchor for the United
States on August 13, 1861, and steamed for Boston.[48]

The last vessel to join the squadron was *Saratoga*, under Alfred
Taylor, which arrived at Monrovia on December 30, 1860. Five days later,
she sailed directly to Loando. Ten days into her first sortie northward, a
suspicious schooner was sighted and a round shot was fired to bring her

to. This vessel was the *Express* and she was seized, "there being conclusive evidence" of her engagement in the slave trade. *Express* was sent to the United States, but the disposition of the case is unknown.[49]

In February 1861 Inman wrote Taylor, directing him to sea south of Loango, "keeping generally out of sight," and to arrive at the mouth of the Congo in three days. He ordered him to check the Kabenda anchorage every day and added a list of American ships that were at the time up the Congo River; among them were *Ardennes*, *Alexina*, *Nancy*, and "Clipper ship Nightingale."[50]

Inman's letter proved accurate. Two months later, off Kabenda, Taylor sighted the American ship *Nightingale*—a famous clipper ship in her early years—lounging off shore in Kabenda Bay. For several days she remained immobile, and Taylor assumed the vessel would quickly take on her cargo as soon as *Saratoga* vacated the area. And it was so: *Saratoga* sailed away, then, that night, Taylor doubled back and sent his boats to board the suspicious ship. They found that 961 slaves had been crowded into her hold since *Saratoga*'s departure. The ship was seized, though her captain, Francis Bowen, and a Portuguese "passenger" escaped while she was moored in the harbor. The *Nightingale*, at something over one thousand tons and about two hundred feet in length, was one of the largest slavers in the trade, and, while in her prime, had been one of the fastest vessels in the merchant marine.[51]

Saratoga spent another four months on the southwest African coast, watching the other vessels of the squadron weight anchor for home. She finally departed and was decommissioned at Philadelphia in August 1861.[52]

The final vessel to be considered is the flagship *Constellation* itself. Again, the pertinent deck logs of this important ship are missing from the National Archives, and her movements are inferred from other sources.

Inman had sailed the sloop from Boston on July 15, 1859, and the change of command with Conover occurred on August 8 at Madeira. Another month went by as Inman awaited the arrival of *San Jacinto*, which had gone directly to Porto Praya. Inman arrived at the Cape Verdes on September 10 but delayed yet more while the two new steamers arrived on station. *Constellation* sailed for Monrovia on October 5. Inman did not arrive at Loando, where he had been directed to look into leasing a warehouse, until November. It is not clear whether Inman remained on board during this interim while setting up the depot at Loando. However, the ship, under her captain, John S. Nicholas, stopped the slaver *Orion*, mentioned above in mid-November off the Congo River. As with the other American boardings of this vessel, *Orion* was released. [53]

In mid-December, Inman wrote his intention to accompany the *Portsmouth* to the Congo, and then cruise "between the latitude of Mayumba . . . to that of this place [Loando]." He would remain some fifty miles from the coast, and the object of this was to "cut, north and south, across the line of slavers . . . bound west."[54]

A week after this letter, on *Constellation,* a suspicious sail was discovered off Kabenda. After a ten-hour chase she was boarded and proved to be the barque *Delicia*. The vessel had no papers and the mate claimed, "no nation, had no flag, no log, no orders." Later, the mate disclosed that the captain and supercargo were ashore with cash, purchasing slaves, and he had been ordered to stand off shore for twenty-five days before approaching land to take on the cargo. It was while he was in the process of coming in that the vessel was stopped. The mate made statements under oath that the vessel "has every preparation" for embarkation of slaves.[55] The vessel was sent to the United States for adjudication, but the authorities abandoned the case.[56]

Subsequently, Inman sailed back to Loando, and remained there until mid-February, presumably involved in setting up the supply depot. He did write of the squadron's boardings, noting that in the previous month there had been forty-four boardings, six of them by *Constellation,* four by *Marion*, and twelve by *Portsmouth*, and the balance by the rest of the squadron. Some days later, Inman set up the elaborate cruising schedule for his three steamers and wrote Toucey commending the commanders of *Mystic* and *Sumpter* for "rendering, the most efficient, and important service ever since they arrived at this station. It may be said that . . . they perform, at greatly less expense, more valuable service than any other vessels in the squadron." [57]

As to the new depot, Inman reported the completion of the warehouse on January 21, and the expenses involved. The squadron provided the labor—both bluejackets and kroomen—and the cost was less than $700 of the $1,000 authorized by the department.[58]

More administrative work followed. Inman set up the stations for watering, coaling, and cruising along the coast. The instructions were specific: "the steamer . . . will positively leave Loango Bay by 1 PM on the

18th of each month . . .," etc. He also directed the skipper of *Sumpter* to not exceed "5 to 6 tons" of coal daily, unless in a chase.[59]

In February 1860 he informed Toucey of his intention to sail to Madeira to give relief for his crew. He reported he had been "mostly at sea" since September 1859. Inman arrived at Madeira sometime in March, and Toucey's reply to the above letter was dated March 21. The secretary wrote: "It is not the wish of the Department that the Constellation should remain at Madeira any length of time. You will therefore return to the coast immediately on the receipt thereof." This preemptory message was followed shortly by Toucey's instructions changing the squadron's cruising grounds to eliminate both Madeira and the Canaries.[60] A few months later, Toucey designated St. Helena as the accepted location for the crews' rest –and relaxation.[61]

Having been taken to task by the secretary, Inman sailed south. The movements of the flagship are uncertain until August, when she was reported at Loando by *Portsmouth*. Fortunately for Inman's credibility with his superiors, August saw the capture of *Storm King* and *Erie*. Then Inman had the good sense to take *Constellation* to sea again, and the good luck to fall upon a suspicious barque, the *Cora* out of New York. What followed was a chase by moonlight, with *Constellation*'s ten-inch rifles carefully aimed to miss the mark. The slaver's crew, frantic to escape, unloaded whatever was loose into the waters to lighten her load, but finally, around 11 PM, gave up the cause. The ship had been arrested at New York, but bond had been paid and she had sailed for the west coast of Africa. On this night she had 705 Africans on her permanent slave deck.[62]

Once the vessel's hatches were opened, one crewman wrote, the blacks "came tumbling out of the hold, yelling and cringing. They ran forward and crouched on the bow. . . . They were nearly starved."[63] The original count by the crew was 694 persons: 175 men, 320 boys, and 199 women, girls and babies.[64]

Once back in the United States under a prize crew, the courts confiscated the ship. Two of the officers escaped but two were convicted. Each received ten months in prison and a fine.[65]

Inman himself remained cruising on the coast, though little excitement occurred for the remainder of his tour. He wrote the department requesting that he be relieved in May 1861, suggesting that his successor meet him at Porto Praya, whither he intended to sail around April 1, 1861.[66]

Toucey answered that the department could not issue such orders so far in advance.[67]

In October, Inman was at Kabenda, then, in December, he was at Loando. The first half of 1861, the flagship was for the most part in and out of Loando, though, Inman seized the brig *Triton* off the Congo in May.[68]

In March 1861, Inman wrote of his accomplishments: "It is but truth to say that since I assumed this command, a check upon the slave trade, by capture of slavers and intended slavers, has been given by this squadron greater in number and effect, than by the whole of the squadrons combined that have preceded me. No less than eleven vessels, and two thousand seven hundred and ninety three (2,793) slaves . . . have been seized . . ." Hoping these positive points would pave the way, Inman then reiterated his request to be relieved.[69]

The secretary did not heed Inman's request, and *Constellation* remained on station for another five months after his latest request for relief. *Constellation* weighed anchor for home on August 13, 1861.[70]

Evaluating Inman's tour as flag officer is, on the surface, relatively easy. Simply in numbers of slavers captured and blacks freed, his squadron was in a category by itself. These numbers, as related in his letter, are impressive in themselves.

The day-to-day study of the squadron reveals a considerably less complimentary story. Inman certainly attempted to avoid commitment on the coast of Africa in the first months there. Had Toucey not chided him, he would have remained uninvolved at Madeira for many more months than he was. He apparently was also a micromanager, which tended to detract from the independence of his ship commanders. Given the fact that the part of the African coast still active with the slave trade had been carved down to the portion south of Princes Island, the area his newly enlarged squadron patrolled was much more manageable than before. It is obvious that more diligence early on in his tour would have reaped considerably greater rewards.

To complete the picture of the Navy's anti-slavery operations in this time period, the activities off Cuba need to be included. The Navy's efforts off the coveted island began in earnest in May 1858. That month, the secretary of the Navy wrote J. N. Maffitt on the brig *Dolphin* that in view of "recent embarrassments" due to British search and detention of American vessels off Cuba, he was being ordered to patrol the north coast of that island. Similar instructions were sent to Commander Bell on *Constellation*. Then, in September 1859, T. A. M. Craven received orders for service on the coast of Cuba on the newly purchased steamer *Mohawk*. In this instance, the vessel had been prepared, wrote the secretary, with "special reference" to service off the island, ". . . the immediate object in view being the suppression of the slave trade between that island and Africa." He was to report to Flag Officer McCauley of the Home Squadron. His coaling station was at Key West and provisions were to be gotten at Pensacola. The steamer *Crusader* received the same instructions and was to alternate with *Mohawk* when provisioning, so as to not leave the patrol area unguarded.[71] Later the steamer *Wyandotte* was added to this flotilla off Cuba.

The upshot of this increase in the naval force off Cuba was nine captures in the period from August 1858 through December 1860. The first has already been mentioned: the *Echo*, which was captured by *Dolphin*. Four of the others were by *Mohawk*: the vessels *Cygnet, Wildfire, Toccoa,* and *Mary J. Kimball*. The latter two were captured on two successive days and were the last ones chronologically in this group. *Crusader* seized three: *Bogota, W. R. Kibby*, and *Joven Antonio*, between May and August 1860. The last of the nine was the barque *William*, taken by the *Wyandotte* in May 1860. Five of the nine were carrying slaves when captured: 570 on the *William,* 530 on *Wildfire*, 411 on *Bogota*, 318 on *Echo*, and three boys on *W. R. Kibby.* The total number of blacks freed was 1,832. [72]

The legal disposition of the vessels was consistent, except for *Joven Antonio*. This ship was found to be a foreign vessel and released. The courts confiscated all the remaining vessels.[73]

It is noteworthy that these captures coincided with the great increase in the size of the Africa Squadron. In fact, all except the *Echo* would have escaped from the African coast after the middle of 1859, precisely when Inman took over as flag officer of the unit. These facts are not complimentary to Inman's leadership, but they point up the continuing ability of the slavers to operate successfully. It should be said here that it is a fact of naval warfare that the blockaders, unless they have a massive preponderance of force, always are in the disadvantageous position, always on the defensive. They must be diligent at all times, whereas the blockade runner needs only to pick his time carefully and make a single, fast, run to be successful.

With the withdrawal of the squadron's ships in the summer of 1861, the Navy's squadron ceased to exist. And, of course, the accession of the Lincoln administration and the coming of the Civil War forever changed the U.S. government's attitude toward the suppression of the slave trade. Indeed, the Lincoln administration soon dropped the longstanding albatross that hindered joint operations with the British: the historical objection to the reciprocal Right of Search. Secretary of State William H. Seward was swift to communicate to the British a willingness to cooperate fully in finally suppressing the trade. On June 7, 1862, a treaty was signed with Great Britain admitting a limited Right of Search—that is, on the high seas and off certain coasts—of American-flagged merchant vessels by British naval vessels. Mixed courts were established at the Cape of Good Hope, Sierra Leone, and New York for the adjudication of offenders. Each of these courts consisted of a judge and an arbitrator for each government, and their decisions were without appeal. Once the offender was condemned, he was subject to the laws of his own nation in respect to this penalty. The Senate approved the treaty on July 11, 1862.[74]

This treaty finally ended the trade from the African—supply—side of the equation. On the other side of the Atlantic, the demand diminished as the Cuban government— pressured by the British—cracked down on the traders. The Cubans finally abolished the last vestige of the system when their "apprentice" system, whereby the "freed" Africans reverted to the state and were hired out to the plantation owners, was ended. This was accomplished in 1869. [75]

CONCLUSION

To this writer, the number of slave-trading vessels seized by the Africa Squadron from its inception to termination is sufficient evidence that the squadron was not a success. There were thirty-six slavers— or suspected slavers—taken by the Africa Squadron from 1844 to 1861. This averages just over two per year. If the vessels taken off Brazil (6) and Cuba (9) are added in, the total is still only fifty-one, raising the average to three per year. And, of course, there were four years when the Africa Squadron captured none: 1848, 1851, 1855, and 1856.

As has been seen, there were extenuating circumstances. However, the squadron was capable of better, and, indeed proved it: In 1845 there were five captures; in 1847, four—and both of these totals were achieved while the squadron depot was at Porto Praya, when there were as yet no steam vessels on the station, and before the trade had been whittled down to operations only on the south coast. Had the squadron even taken five per year, the total number would have been around one hundred captures.

It is also noteworthy than in the two years (mid-1859 to June 1861) *after* the squadron had steamers and the depot was moved to St. Paul de Loando, there were fifteen captures. Of those, only six were by the steamers on the station. The average for the sailing vessels was 4.5 per year in this period.

Two captures per year—one every six months—is, to this writer, inexcusable. The figure is particularly galling in comparison to the same statistics, mentioned elsewhere, for the British African Squadron. Yes, there were years when the trade itself was in abeyance, such as the early 1850s. But, in general, there were always slave traders to be found when some diligence was used. Even in some years when there were no captures by the squadron, slavers were still being seized by federal authorities in various U.S. ports, proving the trade still existed, regardless of whether the Navy was apprehending the offenders. In 1856, for instance, when the squadron found none, there were five seized in the United States: in New York, Rhode Island, Baltimore, and New Orleans.

Given this unhappy conclusion, the question, is, obviously, "Why were there so few captures?" The two consistent answers, when vagaries of individual flag officers and fluctuations in the trade are factored out, are the lack of steam vessels and the inexplicably poor location of the squadron depot. The travel to and from the latter, as has been seen, probably reduced the typical time on station by at least 25 percent for the squadron's ships. It is more difficult to quantify the effect the lack of steamers had on the squadron's efficiency. However, it is painfully obvious that, when on a blockade, having a steady and readily available propulsion system will generally trump an adversary dependent on wind power.

Yes, there were inefficient and even lazy squadron commanders assigned to the squadron, men more interested in avoiding the drudgery of daily cruising on the unattractive and uncomfortable African coast than fulfilling their duty. These men certainly contributed to the dismal squadron record. However, it has also been shown that success in the venture had more to do with the character of the officers on the scene than with the quality of the leadership back at Porto Praya or elsewhere. Commander McBlair is a prime example: his diligence is in sharp contrast to his island-hopping Flag Officer Thomas Conover.

Of course, there have been many who have questioned the diligence of the southern naval officers in the squadron, and pinned the inefficiency of the unit on their sectional, pro-slavery bias. In this regard, it is revealing to look at statistics developed by J. Scott Harmon in his examination of the Navy and the slave trade. He analyzed seventy-one officers, from north, south, and border states, including those on the Brazil and West Indies stations. His conclusions were that 40.7 percent of Southern officers, 25 percent of border state officers, and 46.8 percent of Northern state officers made captures, and that the average of all three was 40.7 percent—the same as that for southern officers alone. Also, in terms of percentage of captures per officer, the Southern officers were more efficient at .85 per officer, as opposed to .75 for Northern officers.[76] Of course, individual records come to mind here: the diligence of William McBlair, from a border state, and John N. Maffitt, from the South, are two examples. Maffitt, stationed in the West Indies on the *Dolphin*, captured five slavers from 1858 to 1861—more than any other naval commander of the era. During the war, Maffitt became the commander of the famous Confederate cruiser *Florida.* [77] McBlair later became commanding officer of a Confederate ironclad. Given these statistics and what I have learned in writing this work, I am reluctant to pin blame across the board on the naval officers commanding the ships on the station, or even on the sometimes-feckless squadron commanders.

Therefore, if the squadron's poor record can be blamed on the tools given it for the work—i.e., sailing ships vis a vis steamers and lack of a convenient squadron depot—then the onus must fall higher up than the squadron commanders. And, in the nineteenth century Navy, the only superior in the Navy Department was the secretary of the Navy himself.

As has been seen, the flag officers and the commanders of the vessels on station had consistently reiterated the need to rectify these two situations. Indeed, the secretaries had often, at least in the first decade of the squadron, promised the addition of steamers, but had never carried through. And, as a matter of fact, the secretaries occasionally wrote of these needs in the annual reports. Generally these were requests for congressional appropriations to build smaller vessels or steamers in general. However, even as early as the Mexican War, there were already steamers available in the service—and they had proven themselves imminently useful even in combat operations. But none were assigned to the Africa Squadron.

In fact, the small steamers were in demand by all the squadrons, for dispatch and utility boats, etc. And the secretary of the Navy was the one who determined the priorities in ship assignments. Obviously, then, the Africa station fell very low on the secretary's list.

In fact, of all the squadrons, the Africa station was the only one founded with a specific, congressionally mandated mission. It was the only squadron that was required to maintain a quasi-blockade on a foreign shore. It was the only unit whose objectives were always in motion—as opposed to the other squadrons whose objectives were the various port cities on their peacetime circuits. In the Mediterranean, a slow passage between Spezia and Leghorn was no great moment, and in fact gave leisure for a bit of sightseeing. Off Africa, the results of unhurried passages could be deadly.

Of course there was always the argument of the high cost of maintaining steamers on foreign stations. However, it is also obvious that the department managed to support steamers in other foreign stations, and none of these units were expected to apprehend lawbreakers. Thus, the problem was not one of adding steamers to the Navy's inventory in order to use them off Africa; the problem was to reassign the available vessels to accomplish the mission assigned it by the ratification of the Webster-Ashburton Treaty, as well as the demands of common humanity.

As to the location of the squadron depot, it is noteworthy that serious discussion of relocating the depot had occurred off and on since the founding of the squadron. Furthermore, after the initial health problems in 1843–44, the unhealthy climate became less and less a factor on the coast of Africa. The British certainly did not let the health issues prevent establishing depot facilities on the coast of the continent. In fact, no mention was made of health issues when the depot was finally moved in 1859. As to the costs involved in setting up a depot, the actual warehouse structure at St. Paul de Loando set the Navy back less than $800, and then it was simply a matter of a leasing fee—which was necessary at Porto Praya in any event— plus the cost of moving the items stored from Porto Praya to Loando.

As to the secretaries of the Navy during this era, it is important to note that of the ten who held the office in this period, seven were from slaveholding states—Virginia, North Carolina, and Maryland—and they controlled the Navy for something like thirteen of the nineteen years the squadron existed. In fact, Isaac Toucey was the only Northerner to hold the office for an entire presidential term. The other two Northerners, Henshaw and Bancroft, were not in office long enough to make a great impression on policy. In fact, in researching Bancroft it is obvious to this writer that he was much more interested in his historical writing than he was in the day-to-day operations of the Navy.

Therefore, I believe that these Southerners were typical examples of this era. They favored slavery and some actually owned slaves, but their attitude towards the slave trade was ambivalent. They professed to hate the trade, and particularly the conditions on board the ships. However, as has been noted earlier, it appears that they would not have objected to the trade at all had it been carried out humanely. After all, from the Southern viewpoint, whether on a slave ship or on the plantation, the slave was an investment not to be mistreated unnecessarily. In fact, there is a sense that the slavery advocates looked on the trade, with its cruelties, as a necessary evil, but it was to be accepted as a means of liberating the blacks from the perceived moral darkness and paganism of the African continent. All of these were simply rationalizations for a great evil, one that was carried out, in fact, because of pervasive racism. North or South, it seems that few men of this era acknowledged that a God-given soul, equal in His sight to every other human's spirit, existed in black people.

In general, the secretaries seemed to merely neglect the Africa Squadron. There was little correspondence to the commanders, and the initial instructions given to the first squadron commander, M. C. Perry, were simply repeated nearly verbatim to the successive flag officers. And, of course, beginning with Upshur, they effectively inverted the mission of the squadron, emphasizing trade and commerce protection over suppression of the slave trade. In fact, some have argued that the squadron was set up in reality to fend the British off American merchantmen. Finally, the secretaries, early on, emphasized patrolling on the northwest African coast, arguably the lesser of the two slave coasts in terms of slave trading operations. Had the ships' commanding officers held strictly to that directive, even less would have been accomplished than was.

Also of some importance in all this were the actions of the various federal courts when presented with seized slave traders on their dockets. With slave trading equated to piracy, the ultimate penalty was available for the crime. That it was only used once, even when the evidence was incontrovertible—that is, when slaves were found on the vessel in question— is indicative of the attitude of the courts, both North and South, toward the trade. Justice was not available for the black people in the holds of the slave ships, much as it was not available to the blacks in the rice or cotton fields, where killing one's slave was regrettable, and a financial loss, but it was not murder. In any event, the actions of the courts, though almost consistently at odds with the opinions of the naval officers who seized the vessels on the high seas, were after the fact. Except for the period when the Navy officers were nearly found liable for false arrest, I do not believe the court decisions were a real deterrence to their work. The naval officers had a job to do and many were very good at it, and there was the possibility of prize money, plus some excitement in the chases and adventure at sea. The court decisions were of little consequence, as long as the commanding officers were not held directly and monetarily responsible for decisions they made as part of their duty.

There may well be lessons to be learned from the study of this sad era in the history of the U.S. Navy. Possibly the most important was the fact that there was a real dichotomy between the expectations of the American public and the squadron's mission as articulated by the Navy Department. The result was an unusual situation where the zeal of individual vessel commanders often exceeded the expectations of the department, which was seemingly content with merely maintaining a presence on the slave coasts and thereby preventing embarrassing actions by the British against American seagoing commerce. In any event, the obvious lesson is that the service should not be required to perform a vital function for the nation, and then not be given the wherewithal to accomplish the mission.

APPENDIX A:
U.S. NAVAL VESSELS

U.S. NAVAL VESSELS: 1842

Name	Guns	Year Built	Status	Location/Assignment
Ships-of-the-line				
Alabama	—		on stocks	Portsmouth NY NH
Columbus	74	1819	Comm.	R/S Boston
Delaware	74	1820	Comm.	Coast of Brazil
Franklin	74	1815	Ord.	NY
New York	—		on stocks	Norfolk
North Carolina	74	1820	Comm.	R/S NY
Ohio	74	1820	Prep.	Boston
Pennsylvania	120	1837	Comm.	R/S Norfolk
Vermont	—		on stocks	Boston
Virginia	—		on stocks	Boston
Washington	74	1816	Ord.	NY
Frigates				
Brandywine	44	1825	Comm.	Mediterranean
Columbia	44	1836	Comm.	Home Sq.
Congress	44	1841	Prep.	Portsmouth, NH
Constellation	36	1797	Comm.	East Indies
Constitution	44	1797	Ord.	Norfolk
Cumberland	—		on stocks	Boston
Hudson	44	1826	Ord.	NY

Independence	54	1814	Comm.	Home
Java	44	1814	Ord.	Norfolk
Macedonian	36	1836	Comm.	West Indies
Potomac	44	1821	Comm.	Coast of Brazil
Raritan	—		on stocks	Philadelphia
Sabine	—		on stocks	NY
Santee	—		on stocks	Portsmouth, NH
Savannah	—		on stocks	NY
St. Lawrence	—		on stocks	Norfolk
United States	44	1797	Comm.	Pacific

Sloops-of-War

Boston	20	1825	Comm.	East Indies
Concord	20	1829	Comm.	Coast of Brazil
Cyane	20	1837	Comm.	Pacific
Dale	16	1839	Comm.	Pacific
Decatur	16	1839	Comm.	Coast of Brazil
Fairfield	20	1828	Comm.	Mediterranean
Falmouth	20	1827	Comm.	Home
John Adams	20	1820	Comm.	Coast of Brazil
Levant	20	1837	Comm.	West Indies
Marion	16	1839	Comm.	Coast of Brazil
Ontario	18	1813	Comm.	R/S New Orleans
Peacock	18	1813	Comm.	Exploring Exped.
Preble	16	1839	Comm.	Mediterranean
St. Louis	20	1828	Comm.	Pacific
Vandalia	20	1828	Comm.	Home
Vincennes	20	1826	Comm.	Exploring Expedition
Yorktown	16	1839	Comm.	Pacific

Brigs

Consort	—		Comm.	R/S Portland ME
Dolphin	10	1836	Comm.	Home
Pioneer	—		Comm.	R/S Baltimore
Porpoise	10	1836	Comm.	Exploring Exped.

Schooners

Boxer	10	1831	Comm.	NY
Enterprise	10	1831	Comm.	Coast of Brazil

Experiment	10	1831	Comm.	R/S Philadelphia
Flirt	—		from War Dept.	Florida
Flying Fish	—	1838	Comm.	Tender to Exploring Exped.
Grampus	10	1821	Comm.	Home
Otsego	—		from War Dept.	Florida
Phoenix	—		from War Dept.	Florida
Shark	10	1821	Comm.	Pacific
Wave	—		from War Dept.	Florida

Steamers

Erie	8	1813	Ready	Boston
Fulton	4	1837		Atlantic Coast
Mississippi	10	1837	Comm.	Home Sq.
Missouri	10	1837	Comm.	Home Sq.
Poinsett	—	1837		Norfolk

Storeships

Lexington	8	1825	Ready	Norfolk
Relief	6	1836	Comm.	Pacific

TERMINOLOGY:

Comm.: in commission; Ord.: in ordinary (laid up); R/S: Receiving Ship

APPENDIX B:

VESSELS SEIZED

AFRICA SQUADRON: 1843–1861

Vessel	Captor	Date	Location
Uncas	*Porpoise*	3/1/44	Gallinas
Spitfire	*Truxtun*	3/24/45	Pongas R.
Patuxent	*Yorktown*	9/27/45	Cape Mount
Merchant	*Jamestown*	12/3/45	Sierra Leone
Pons	*Yorktown*	9/30/45	Kabenda
Panther	*Yorktown*	12/15/45	Kabenda
Robert Wilson	*Jamestown*	1/15/46	Porto Praya
Malaga	*Boxer*	4/13/46	Kabenda
Casket	*Marion*	8/2/46	Kabenda
Chancellor	*Dolphin*	4/10/47	Cape Palmas
Excellent	*John Adams*	4/23/50	Ambriz
Martha	*Perry*	6/6/50	Ambriz
Chatsworth	*Perry*	9/11/50	Ambriz
Advance	*Germantown*	11/3/52	Porto Praya
R.P.Brown	*Germantown*	1/23/53	Porto Praya
H. N. Gambrill	*Constitution*	11/3/53	Congo
Glamorgan	*Perry*	3/10/54	Congo
W. G. Lewis	*Dale*	11/6/57	Congo
Brothers	*Marion*	9/8/58	Mayumba
Julia Dean	*Vincennes*	12/28/58	Cape Coast Castle

Orion	Marion	4/21/59	Congo
Ardennes	Marion	4/27/59	Congo
Emily	Portsmouth	9/21/59	Loango
Delicia	Constellation	12/21/59	Kabenda
Virginian	Portsmouth	2/6/60	Congo
Falmouth	Portsmouth	5/6/60	Porto Praya
Thomas Achorn	Mystic	6/29/60	Kabenda
Triton	Mystic	7/16/60	Loango
Erie	Mohican	8/8/60	Congo
Storm King	San Jacinto	8/8/60	Congo
Cora	Constellation	9/26/60	Congo
Bonito	San Jacinto	10/10/60	Congo
Express	Saratoga	2/25/61	off Loango?
Nightingale	Saratoga	4/21/61	Kabenda
Triton	Constellation	5/20/61	Congo
Falmouth	Sumpter	6/14/61	Congo

Brazil Squadron

Porpoise	Raritan	1/23/45	Rio de Janeiro
Albert	Bainbridge	6/45	Bahia
Laurens	Onkahye	1/23/48	Rio de Janeiro
A.D. Richardson	Perry	12/11/48	Rio de Janeiro
Independence	Perry	12/13/48	Rio de Janeiro
Susan	Perry	2/6/49	Rio de Janeiro

Home Squadron: Off Cuba

Putnam	Dolphin	8/21/58	Cuba
Cygnet	Mohawk	11/18/59	Cuba
Wildfire	Mohawk	4/26/60	Cuba
William	Wyandotte	5/9/60	Cuba
Bogota	Crusader	5/23/60	Cuba
W.R.Kibby	Crusader	7/23/60	Cuba
Joven Antonio	Crusader	8/14/60	Cuba
Toccoa	Mohawk	12/20/60	off Havana
Mary J. Kimball	Mohawk	12/21/60	off Havana

APPENDIX C:

MEDIUM AND SMALL STEAM VESSELS AVAILABLE FOR SERVICE, 1843–1858

Name	'43	'44	'45	'46	'47	'48	'49	'50	'51	'52	'53	'54	'55	'56	'57	'58
Alleghany					A	A	A									
Fulton II										A	A	A	A	A	A	A
Princeton	A	A	A	A	A	A	A				A	A	A			
Saranac							A	A	A		A	A	A	A		A
San Jacinto										A	A	A	A	A	A	A
Spitfire				A	A	A	A									
Vixen				A	A	A	A	A	A	A	A	A	A		A	
Water Witch II					A	A		A	A	A	A	A	A	A	A	A
Totals:	1	1	1	3	5	5	5	3	3	4	6	6	6	4	4	4

Not included:

Fulton II (1837): floating ordnance test vessel

Mississippi, Missouri, Powhatan, and *Susquehanna*: large paddle steamers

Water Witch I: experimental iron vessel

Union: experimental Hunter Wheel vessel

Michigan: iron steamer on Great Lakes

Merrimack, Wabash, Minnesota, Roanoke, Colorado, and *Niagara*: steam frigates

APPENDIX D:

SECRETARIES OF THE NAVY, 1842–1861

- Abel P. Upshur (Virginia) October 1841–July 1843 (President Tyler)

- David Henshaw (Massachusetts) July 1843–February 1844 (Tyler)

- Thomas W. Gilmer (Virginia) February 1844 (Tyler)

- John Young Mason (Virginia) March 1844–March 1845 (Polk)

- George Bancroft (Massachusetts) March 1845–September 1846 (Polk)

- John Young Mason (Virginia) September 1846–March 1849 (Polk)

- William Ballard Preston (Virginia) March 1849–July 1850 (Taylor)

- William Alexander Graham (North Carolina) August 1850–June 1852 (Fillmore)

- John Pendleton Kennedy (Maryland) July 1852–March 1853 (Fillmore)

- James Cochrane Dobbin (North Carolina) March 1853–March 1857 (Pierce)

- Isaac Toucey (Connecticut) March 1857–March 1861 (Buchanan)

- Gideon Welles (Connecticut) March 1861–1869 (Lincoln)

NOTES

CHAPTER 1

1. W. E. B. Du Bois, *The Suppression of the African Slave Trade*, 51.
2. Ibid., 51–52. The constitutional clause reads: "The Migration or Importation of such Persons as any of the States now existing shall think proper to admit, shall not be prohibited by the Congress prior to the Year one thousand eight hundred and eight, but a Tax or duty may be imposed on such Importation, not exceeding ten dollars for each Person."
3. Peter G. Fish, "War on the Slave Trade: Changing Fortunes in AnteBellum U.S. Courts of the Mid-Atlantic Courts." In William S. Dudley and Michael J. Crawford, eds., *The Early Republic and the Sea,* 143–44; Don E. Fehrenbacher, *The Slaveholding Republic* 140.
4. Du Bois, *Suppression*, 84; Fehrenbacher, *Slaveholding*, 140.
5. Horatio Davis Smith, *Early History of the United States Revenue Marine Service* 18–19.
6. Letter, Wolcott to Benjamin Lincoln, June 10, 1799. *Naval Documents: Quasi-War with France*, Vol. 3, 323.
7. Letter, Secretary of the Navy to Secretary of the Treasury, April 18, 1800. *Naval Documents: Quasi-War with France,* Vol. 5, 426; *Dictionary of American Naval Fighting Ships,* Vol. V, 104.
8. Letter, Turell Tufts to Secretary of State, January 1800. *Quasi-War*, Vol. 5, 156–57.
9. *Experiment* Journal Extract, *Quasi-War*, Vol. 6 85–86.
10. Letter, Samuel Hodgson to Pickering, July 10, 1800. *Quasi-War*, Vol. 6, 133–34.
11. Sales account, October 3, 1800. *Quasi-War*, Vol. 7, 429.
12. Mullowny Journal, July 19, 1800 and July 21, 1800, Vol. 7, 163, 164; Letter, Secretary of the Navy to Jared Ingersoll, August 8, 1800. *Quasi-War*, Vol. 7, 232.
13. Letter, Secretary of the Navy to Lt. John Smith, February 2, 1801. *Quasi-War*, Vol. 7, 116.

14. Charles Oscar Paullin, *Commodore John Rodgers* 64–65.
15. Fehrenbacher, *Slaveholding*, 141–43.
16. Du Bois, *Suppression*, 105–8.
17. Fehrenbacher, *Slaveholding*, 144–47; Earl McNeilly, "The United States Navy and the Suppression of the West African Slave Trade, 1819–1862," (PhD dissertation, Case Western Reserve University, 1973), 16; Fehrenbacher, *Slaveholding*, 148.
18. Fish, "War on the Slave Trade . . .," 145–46.
19. Paolo Coletta, "Paul Hamilton," in *American Secretaries of the Navy*, Vol. I, 94.
20. *U.S. Navy Register, 1815* (Appendix to *The Naval Chronicle*).
21. Judd Scott Harmon, "Suppress and Protect: The United States Navy, the African Slave Trade, and Maritime Commerce, 1794–1862," (PhD dissertation, College of William an Mary, 1977), 120–22.
22. Paolo Coletta, "Benjamin W. Crowninshield," in *American Secretaries of the Navy*, Vol. I, 117; *Dictionary of American Naval Fighting Ships*, Vol. VI, 332; *U.S. Coast Guard Record of Movements*, 141.
23. Du Bois, *Suppression*, 114 (Letter from Collector McIntosh to Secretary of the Treasury, March 14, 1818); McNeilly, "The United States Navy . . .," 19.
24. Harmon, "Suppress and Protect . . .," 122–23.
25. McNeilly, "The United States Navy . . .," 20–22; Du Bois, *Suppression*, 117–18; *Dictionary of American Naval Fighting Ships*, Vol. VI, 682–83; Harmon, "Suppress and Protect . . .," 125.
26. Du Bois, *Suppression*, 128–29; John T. Noonan, *The Antelope*, 116–17.
27. Du Bois, *Suppression*, 120–21; Fehrenbacher, *Slaveholding*, 151.
28. Fehrenbacher, *Slaveholding*, 151–52.
29. Harmon, "Suppress and Protect . . .," 89.
30. Harold D. Nelson, ed., *Liberia: a Country Study*, 8-9.
31. Harmon, "Suppress and Protect . . .," 91–92.
32. Fehrenbacher, *Slaveholding*, 154.
33. Samuel Eliot Morison, *"Old Bruin": Commodore Matthew Calbraith Perry*, 62–64.
34. Morison, *"Old Bruin,"* 65–66; McNeilly, "The United States Navy . . .," 46–47; Du Bois, *Suppression*, 126.
35. Morison, *"Old Bruin,"* 67–68; McNeilly, "The United States Navy . . .," 47–48; Harmon, "Suppress and Protect . . .," 103; Logbook, *John Adams,* National Archives, RG80.
36. Nelson, p. 10; Morison, p. 69.
37. Nelson, *Liberia*, 10; Fehrenbacher, *Slaveholding*, 154; Harmon, "Suppress and Protect . . .," 95; Morison, *"Old Bruin,"* 72–73; *Dictionary of American Naval Fighting Ships*, Vol. I, Part A, 208.
38. W. F. Lynch, quoted in Morison, *"Old Bruin,"* 73–75.
39. Fehrenbacher, *Slaveholding*, 155; Peter Duignan and Clarence Clendenen, *The United States and the African Slave Trade, 1619–1862*, 28–29.
40. *Register of the Commissioned and Warrant Officers of the United States Navy, 1842*, 65–66.

CHAPTER 2

1. Howard I. Chapelle, *The History of the American Sailing Navy*, 324–34; Donald L. Canney, *Sailing Warships of the United States Navy*, 177–82.
2. "Condition of the Navy and its Operations," December 3, 1822. *American State Papers, Naval Affairs*, Vol. 1, 804.
3. Quoted in Harmon, "Suppress and Protect . . .," 127.
4. Harmon, "Suppress and Protect . . .," 127–28.
5. Dudley W. Knox, *A History of the United States Navy*, 140–41.
6. Harmon, "Suppress and Protect . . .," 104; McNeilly, "The United States Navy . . .," 81.
7. "Report of the Secretary of the Navy," December 1, 1823. *American State Papers, Naval Affairs*, Vol. 2, 179.
8. Harmon, "Suppress and Protect . . .," 98–99.
9. Harmon, "Suppress and Protect . . .," 99.
10. Harmon, "Suppress and Protect . . .," 104–5; "Condition of the Navy and Marine Corps," 1824. *American State Papers, Naval Affairs*, Vol. 1, 1004.
11. Harmon, "Suppress and Protect . . .," 104; "Report of the Secretary of the Navy," December 1, 1823. *American State Papers, Naval Affairs*, Vol. 2, 179.
12. Harmon, "Suppress and Protect . . .,"Appendix H; McNeilly, "The United States Navy . . .," 81–88.
13. "The Secretary of the Navy to the President," December 1, 1824. *American State Papers, Naval Affairs*, Vol. 2, 180–81.
14. Ibid.
15. Du Bois, *Suppression*, 134–38.
16. Hugh G. Soulsby, *The Right of Search and the Slave Trade in Anglo-American Relations, 1814–1862*, 39.
17. W. F. Ward, *The Royal Navy and the Slavers*, 202–15.
18. Soulsby, *The Right of Search*, 44.
19. Du Bois, *Suppression*, 138–39.
20. Du Bois, *Suppression*, 141–42.
21. Ibid.
22. William Law Matthieson, *Great Britain and the Slave Trade, 1839–1865*, 27.
23. Howard I. Chapelle, *The Search for Speed under Sail, 1700–1855*, 293–99.
24. Ibid., 300.
25. Alan R. Booth, "The United States African Squadron, 1843–1861," in Jeffrey Butler, ed., *Boston University Papers in African History*, Vol. 1, 84.
26. *U.S. Coast Guard Record of Movements*, 74.
27. Fehrenbacher, *Slaveholding*, 153.
28. McNeilly, "The United States Navy . . .," 88–89.
29. Ibid., 81–88; "Annual Report of the Secretary of the Navy . . .," December 5, 1835.
   American State Papers, Naval Affairs, Vol. 4, 30. Harmon, "Suppress and Protect . . .,"Appendix H.

31. McNeilly, "The United States Navy . . .," 88–90; Fehrenbacher, *Slaveholding*, 162–63.
32. Report of Mixed Commission, December 31, 1839, in Papers of William Loney, Royal Navy.
33. Ibid.
34. Report of Mixed Commision, 1839; Warren S. Howard, *American Slavers and the Federal Law, 1837-1867,* 33–35; Fehrenbacher, *Slaveholding*, 164–65.
35. Soulsby, *The Right of Search*, 42, 46.
36. Duignan and Clendenen, *The United States and the African Slave Trade,* 32–33; J. C. Furnas, "Patrolling the Middle Passage," *American Heritage Magazine,* Vol. IX (October 1958), 9; Howard, *American* Slavers, 37–38.
37. Duignan and Clendenen, *The United States and the African Slave Trade,* 31–32.
38. Howard, *American Slavers,* 38.
39. Ibid., 38–39.
40. Fehrenbacher, *Slaveholding*, 165.
41. Ibid.; McNeilly, "The United States Navy . . .," 104.
42. Howard, *American Slavers,* Appendix B, 225.
43. McNeilly, "The United States Navy . . .," 104.
44. Letter, Thomas Botts to Ann Nalle, April 1, 1840. Nalle Family papers.
45. Duignan and Clenenden, *The United States and the African Slave Trade,* 42.

CHAPTER 3
1. Fehrenbacher, *Slaveholding*, 166.
2. Ibid., 166–67.
3. Horatio Bridge, *Journal of an African Cruiser*, 52.
4. Letter, Charles H. Bell to J. K. Paulding, July 28, 1840, in House Document 115, 26th Congress, 2nd session, 58.
5. Fehrenbacher, *Slaveholding*, 168.
6. Ward, *The RoyalNavy*, 144.
7. "The United States and the Slave Trade," *United Service Magazine*, Part II (1842), 171–79.
8. Du Bois, *Suppression*, 147; William Lawrence Beach, *Visitation and Search*, 49; Fehrenbacher, *Slaveholding*, 169.
9. Letter, Louis M. Goldsborough to Upshur, November 16, 1842, in Letters Received from Bureau Chiefs, National Archives, M518.
10. Letter, George C. Read to Mahlon Dickerson, March 17, 1838, in the George C. Read Papers, Historical Society of Pennsylvania.
11. Edward Shippen, *Thirty Years at Sea*, 84.
12. Ward, *The Royal Navy*, 99.
13. Morton Dauwan Zabel, "The Heart of Darkness," in *The Portable Conrad*, 505–6.
14. "The Climate of the Western Coast of Africa," *Nautical Magazine* (1845), 562–71.
15. Sir James Walt, "The Health of Seamen in the Anti-Slavery Squadron," *Mariners' Mirror* (February 2002), 69–78.

16. *Register of the Commissioned and Warrant Officers of the Navy of the United States, 1842*, 64–67.
17. Ibid.; Canney, *The Old Steam Navy*, Vol. I, 1–16.
18. A. H. Foote, *Africa and the American Flag,* 69.
19. Ward, *The Royal Navy*, 146.
20. *Report of the Secretary of the Treasury on Commerce and Navigation*, 1855, 48, 288–89.
21. *Causes of the Reduction of American* Tonnage, 279.
22. Fehrenbacher, Slaveholding, 149.
23. Howard, *American Slavers,* 302–3, note 22.
24. Ibid., 57.
25. Letter, Bell to Paulding, July 28, 1840, House Doc. 115: 26th Cong., 2nd sess., 1841, 58.
26. Ward, *The Royal Navy*, 39–45.
27. John Winton, *An Illustrated History of the British Navy*, 106.
28. Ibid.
29. Howard, *American Slavers,* 5.

CHAPTER 4
1. "Abel Parker Upshur," in Paolo Coletta, ed., *American Secretaries of the Navy*, Vol. 1, 177–93. Claude H. Hall, *Abel Parker Upshur: Conservative Virginian*, 176.
2. Fehrenbacher, *Slaveholding*, 173, 394, note 8.
3. *Register of Officers, 1842*, 65–66.
4. Ibid.
5. *Register of the Commissioned and Warrant Officers of the Navy of the United States, 1847*, 18; *Dictionary of American Naval Fighting Ships,* Vol. III, 117.
6. Letter, Charles W. Goldsborough to Upshur, November 16, 1842, in Letters from Bureau Chiefs, National Archives, M518.
7. *Annual Report of the Secretary of the Navy,* 1842, 2.
8. Hall, *Abel Parker Upshur,* 174–75; Coletta, "Abel Parker Upshur," 186–87.
9. *Annual Report of the Secretary of the Navy,* 1842, 2.
10. Letter, Upshur to Charles Stewart, December 27, 1842, in Secretary of the Navy's Letters to Officers, National Archives, M149.
11. Letter, Upshur to Perry, March 1, 1843, in Letters to Officers, National Archives, M149.
12. Letter, Perry to Goldsborough, March 28, 1843, in Perry Letterbooks, National Archives, M206.
13. Letter, M. C. Perry to Isaac Mayo, March 10, 1843, in Perry Letterbooks, National Archives, M206.
14. Morison, *"Old Bruin,"* 164.
15. Morison, *"Old Bruin,"* 61–64.
16. *Dictionary of American Naval Fighting Ships,* Vol. II, 249, and Vol. V, 291.
17. Letters, Perry to B. Kennon, March 14, 1843, and Perry to A. Upshur, April 7, 1843, in Perry Letterbooks, National Archives, M206.

18. Canney, *The Old Steam Navy*, 25–27.
19. Canney, *Sailing Warships*, 81–84.
20. Ibid., 147–49.
21. Ibid., 144.
22. Ibid., 185.
23. Booth, "The United States African Squadron," 100–101.
24. Letter, Perry to Goldsborough, March 28, 1843, in Perry Letterbooks, National Archives, M206.
25. Robert Erwin Johnson, *Rear Admiral John Rodgers, 1812–1882*, 74–5.
26. Letter, Perry to Secretary of the Navy Henshaw, May 17, 1844, in Perry Letterbooks, National Archives, M206.
27. Morison, *"Old Bruin,"* 168–9; Letter, Perry to Henshaw, May 17, 1844, in Perry Letterbooks, National Archives, M206.
28. Quoted in Morison, *"Old Bruin,"* 64.
29. Ibid., 64–5.
30. Letter, Perry to Mayo, March 10, 1843, in Perry Letterbooks, National Archives, M206.
31. Letter, Perry to Goldsborough, March 11, 1843, in Perry Letterbooks, National Archives, M206.
32. Letters, Perry to Goldsborough, April 6, 1843 and April (?), 1843, in Perry Letterbooks, National Archives, M206.
33. Letter, Perry to W. Barton, April 4, 1843, in Perry Letterbooks, National Archives, M206.
34. Letters, Perry to Kennon, April 11, 1843, and Perry to Upshur, May 11, 1843, in Perry Letterbooks, National Archives, M206.
35. Morison, *"Old Bruin,"* 168.
36. General Order, n.d., in Perry Letterbooks, National Archives, M206.
37. Letters, Perry to Goldsborough, March 28, 1843; to Kennon, April 7, 1843; to Upshur, April 13, 1843, in Perry Letterbooks, National Archives, M206.
38. Letters, Perry to Upshur, May 16, 1843, and to Tatnall, May 20, 1843, in Perry Letterbooks, National Archives, M206.
39. Letters, Perry to K. C. Crane, March 13, 1843, and to I. Mayo, April 15, 1843, in Perry Letterbooks, National Archives, M206.
40. Letters, Perry to Goldsborough, March 20, 1843; to Kennon, April 6, 1843; to Mayo, April 15, 1843; and to A. Lewes, April 17, 1843, in Perry Letterbooks, National Archives, M206; *Dictionary of American Naval Fighting Ships*, Vol. VI, p. 336-7.
41. Soulsby, *The Right of Search*, 129.
42. John H. Schroeder, *Matthew Calbraith Perry*, 100–1.
43. Letter, Upshur to Tatnall, February 15, 1843, in Letters to Officers, National Archives, M149.
44. Morison, *"Old Bruin,"* 167–69.
45. Letter, Upshur to Lewis, January 28, 1843, in Letters to Officers, National Archives, M149.
46. Letter, Perry to W. Lewes, April 17, 1843, in Perry Letterbooks, National Archives, M206; Morison, *"Old Bruin,"* 169.

47. Morison, *"Old Bruin,"* 165; Letter, Perry to Upshur, June 29, 1843, in Letters from Squadron Commanders, National Archives, M89.

48. Letter, Perry to J. Foote, Royal Navy, July 21, 1843, in Perry Letterbooks, National Archives, M206; Letter, Perry to Upshur, July 18, 21, and 22, 1843, in Squadron Letters, National Archives, M89.

49. Morison, *"Old Bruin,"* 165–66.

50. Letter, Perry to Upshur, July 22, 1843, in Squadron Letters, National Archives, M89.

51. Letter, Perry to Kennon, August 4, 1843, in Perry Letterbooks, National Archives, M206.

52. Morison. *"Old Bruin,"* 166, 169; Letter Perry to Upshur, August 3, 1843, in Squadron Letters, National Archives, M89.

53. Letter, Perry to Upshur, August 3, 1843, in Squadron Letters, National Archives, M89.

54. Morison, *"Old Bruin,"* 169.

55. Order, September 14, 1843, in Perry Letterbooks, National Archives, M206.

56. Letter, Perry various . . . October 30, 1843, in Perry Letterbooks, National Archives, M206.

57. Nelson, *Liberia*, 15, 22.

58. Penelope Campbell, *Maryland in Africa*, 141; Morison, *"Old Bruin,"* 171–72.

59. Quoted in Morison, *"Old Bruin,"* 172.

60. Morison, *"Old Bruin,"* 172.

61. Ibid., 172–73.

62. Ibid., 174–75; Foote, *Africa and the American Flag*, 235-8.

63. Morison, 175; Report, April 18, 1844, in Joel Abbott Letterbook, National Archives, RG 45, Entry 395; Ships Logs, RG 24, *Saratoga* and *Macedonian*.

64. Morison, *"Old Bruin,"* 176.

65. Ibid., 177.

66. Deck Log, National Archives, RG 24, *Macedonian*

67. Letters, Abbott to Perry April 18, 1844, and Walker to Perry, January 22, 1844, in Joel Abbott Letter Book, National Archives, RG 45, Entry 395.

68. Abbott Report, April 18, 1844, in Joel Abbott Letter Book, National Archives, RG 45, Entry 395; D. K. Brown, *Paddle Warships*, 46–48.

69. Abbott Report, April 18, 1844, in Joel Abbott Letter Book, National Archives, RG 45, Entry 395.

70. Abbott Report, November 6, 1844, in Joel Abbott Letter Book, National Archives, RG 45, Entry 395.

71. Ward, *The Royal Navy*, 156–57.

72. Letter, Joseph Tatnall to Perry, Senate Document 150, 28th Cong., 2nd sess., February 26, 1845, 110–11; Howard, *American Slavers*, 214.

73. Deck Logs, National Archives, RG 24, USS *Porpoise*, 1843–45.

74. Letter, Perry to Secretary of the Navy Henshaw, May 18, 1844, in Perry Letterbooks, National Archives, M206.75. Letter, Perry to Henshaw, March 21, 1844, in Perry Letterbooks, National Archives, M206.

76. Letters, Perry to Henshaw, March 21 and April 14, 1844, in Perry Letterbooks,

National Archives, M206.77. Letter, Perry to Henshaw, March 2, 1844, in Squadron Letters, National Archives, M89.

78. Morison, *"Old Bruin,"* 176.
79. Booth, "The United States African Squadron," 105; E. DuBarry, Asst. Surgeon, et al, to Perry, November 15, 1844; Kellogg to DuBarry, January 13, 1845; DuBarry to Perry, February 8, 1845, in Squadron Letters, National Archives, M89.
80. Morison, *"Old Bruin,"* 176.
81. Deck Log, National Archives, RG 24, USS *Saratoga*, 1843–44.
82. Morison, *"Old Bruin,"* 176; Letter, Perry to Henshaw, December 9, 1844, in Squadron Letters, National Archives, M89.
83. Morison, *"Old Bruin,"* 178.
84. Deck Logs, National Archives, RG 24, USS *Macedonian*, 1843-45.
85. Letter, Perry to J. J. Roberts, January 27, 1845, in Perry Letterbooks, National Archives, M206.
86. Letter, Alex Bolt to John Y. Mason, September 22, 1844, in J. Y. Mason Collection, UNC.
87. Letter, Perry to Upshur, September 5, 1843, in Squadron Letters, National Archives, M89.
88. Ward, *The Royal Navy*, 193–96; McNeilly, "The United States Navy . . .," 146.

CHAPTER 5
1. Morison, *"Old Bruin,"* 177; *Register of Officers,* 1847, 16.
2. Edward Callahan, ed., *List of Officers of the Navy of the United States and of the Marine Corps, 1775–1900,* 65, 126, 127, 136, 231, 290, 323–24, 358, 453, 500.
3. *Annual Report*, November 25, 1844, 514.
4. Canney, *Sailing Warships*, 152–55, 186.
5. Letter, Freelon to Skinner, April 20, 1845, in Squadron Letters, National Archives, M89; *Dictionary of American Naval Fighting Ships*, Vol. V, 368.
6. Deck Log, National Archives, RG 24, USS *Yorktown*.
7. Letter, Skinner to Mason, March 3, 1845, Squadron Letters, National Archives, M89.
8. Foote, *Africa and the American Flag*, 240–41.
9. Journal of Simon Fraser Blunt, Virginia Historical Society.
10. Ibid.
11. Howard, *American* Slavers, 180–81.
12. Ibid., 181–82.
13. Ibid., 182–83.
14. Ibid., 187–88.
15. Letter, Silas Holms (surgeon) to Bruce, October 3, 1845, in Squadron Letters, National Archives, M89.
16. Letter, Skinner to Bruce, Oct. 10, 1845, and Skinner to Bancroft, Oct. 20, 1845, in Squadron Letters, National Archives, M89.
17. *Dictionary of American Naval Fighting Ships,* Vol. VII, p. 315.

18. Ltr., Skinner to SecNav, June 20, 1845, in Squadron Letters, National Archives, M89.
19. Ibid.
20. Deck Log, National Archives, RG 24, USS *Yorktown*.
21. Howard, *American Slavers*, 215.
22. Deck Log, National Archives, RG 24, USS *Yorktown*
23. Deck Log, National Archives, RG 24, USS *Yorktown*; C. Herbert Gilliland, "Deliverance from this Floating Hell," *Naval History* (December 2003), 49.
24. Gilliland, "Deliverance," 49.
25. Quoted in Gilliland, "Deliverance," 50.
26. Ibid.
27. Foote, *Africa and the American Flag*, 243–44.
28. Ibid., 246.
29. Quoted in letter, William H. Allmand to "My Dear uncle," January 15, 1846, in Allmand Family Papers, Virginia Historical Society.
30. Herbert Gilliland, e-mail message to author, August 20, 2004.
31. Howard, *American Slavers*, 215, 226.
32. Fish, "War on the Slave Trade . . .," 154–55.
33. Ibid., 98–99, 243.
34. Fish, "War on the Slave Trade . . .," 162–63.
35. Deck Log, National Archives, RG 24, *Yorktown*.
36. Letter, Skinner to the Secretary of the Navy, March 4, 1845, in Squadron Letters, National Archives, M89.
37. Letter, Perry to Upshur, April 13, 1843, in Perry Letterbooks, National Archives, M206.; Journal of William Sharp, March 3, 1845, National Archives, RG 45, E392, 68; Deck Log, National Archives, RG 24, *Marion*, December 31, 1846.
38. Deck Logs, National Archives, RG 24, *Truxtun* and *Jamestown*.
39. Letter, Skinner to Bancroft, July 31, 1845; W. Jones (Royal Navy) to Skinner, June 17, 1845 (Enclosure), in Squadron Letters, National Archives, M89.
40. Letter, Lawlin to Skinner, April 23, 1845 (Enclosure), in Squadron Letters, National Archives, M89.
41. Letter, Skinner to Bancroft, November 28, 1845, in Squadron Letters, National Archives, M89.
42. Deck Log, National Archives, RG 24, *Jamestown*.
43. Letter, Skinner to Bancroft, December 5, 1845, in Squadron Letters, National Archives, M89; McNeilly, "The United States Navy . . .," 145.
44. Quoted in Harmon, "Suppress and Protect . . .," 179.
45. Howard, *American Slavers,* 215, 226.
46. Deck Log, National Archives, RG 24, *Jamestown*.
47. Letter, Skinner to Bancroft, January 27, 1846, in Squadron Letters, National Archives, M89.
    : McNeilly, "The United States Navy . . .," 145.
48. Howard, *American Slavers,* 215, 226.
49. Deck Log, National Archives, RG 24, *Jamestown*.
50. Canney, *Sailing Warships*, 183; Letter, W. Nicholson to Board of Navy

Commisioners, February 10, 1840, National Archives, RG 45, E277 (Reports of Sailing Qualities of Vessels).
51. Deck Log, National Archives, RG 24, *Boxer*.
52. Letter, Bispham to G. Read, April 16, 1846, in Squadron Letters, National Archives, M89.
53. Howard, *American Slavers,* 102.
54. Ibid., 102–3.
55. Ibid.
56. Letter, Mason to Bispham, July 12, 1847, in Squadron Letters, National Archives, M89.
57. Ibid., 104; Harmon, "Suppress and Protect . . .," 181; Salary based on USN *Register of Officers, 1847.*
58. Deck Log, National Archives, RG 24, *Marion*.
59. Secretary of the Navy Report, December 5, 1846, Secretary of the Navy Annual Report, 383.
60. Canney, *Old Steam Navy*, 34–39, 168.

CHAPTER 6
1. Howard, *American Slavers,* 215–16.
2. Secretary of the Navy Report, December 6, 1847, in *Register of Officers, 1847*, 1–2;
3. Letter, Bancroft to Read, November 11, 1845, in George Bancroft Papers, Massachusetts Historical Society.
4. *Register of Officers, 1847*, 116–24.
5. Secretary of the Navy Report, December 6, 1847, 2; Paolo Coletta, "John Young Mason," in *American Secretaries of the Navy,* Vol. I, 234.
6. Canney, *Sailing Warships*, 38.
7. Letter, Bancroft to Read, November 11, 1845, and Read to Bancroft, November 12, 1845, in George Bancroft Papers, MHS.
8. Letter, Bancroft to Read, November 14, 1845, in George Bancroft Papers, MHS; Bancroft to Read, January 29, 1846, in Confidential Letters, T0829.
9. Letter, Read to Bancroft, January 31, 1846, in George C. Read Papers, Historical Society of Pennsylvania.
10. Canney, *Sailing Warships,* 38.
11. Letters, Read to Bancroft, June 26, 1846, in George C. Read Papers, HSP.
12. Secretary of the Navy Report, December 5, 1846, 561–63.
13. Johnson, *Rodgers*, 63, 74–76.
14. Letters, Read to G. Welles, July 13, 1846; Read to Bancroft, July 13, 1846, and September 16, 1846, in George C. Read Papers, HSP.
15. Letter, Read to Bancroft, July 13, 1846, in George C. Read Papers, HSP.
16. Ibid.
17. Letter, Read to Bancroft, September 16, 1846, and Read to Charles Morris, January 24, 1827, in George C. Read Papers HSP.
18. Letter, Read to Welles, July 13, 1846, in George C. Read Papers, HSP; Letter, Read to Bancroft, October 19, 1846, in Squadron Letters, National Archives, M89.

19. Letter, Read to Bancroft, September 15, 1846, in Squadron Letters, National Archives, M89.
20. Deck Log, National Archives, RG 24, *Boxer*; Letter, Read to Bancroft, September 15, 1846.
21. Howard, *American Slavers,* 104.
22. Deck Logs, National Archives, RG 24, *Boxer*.
23. Johnson, *Rodgers,* 76.
24. Ibid.; Letter, Lewis Simonds to Read, September 15, 1846, in Squadron Letters, National Archives, M89.
25. Howard, *American Slavers*, 103–5.
26. Letter, Mason to Read, November 16, 1846, National Archives, RG45, E18, Africa Squadron Letters.
27. Letter, Read to Mason, March 10, 1847, in Squadron Letters, National Archives, M89.
28. Deck Log, National Archives, RG 24, *Marion*; Letter, Read to Bancroft, September 16, 1846, in Squadron Letters, National Archives, M89.
29. Deck Log, National Archives, RG 24, *Marion*.
30. Ibid.
31. Coletta, "John Young Mason," 234; Letter, Mason to Read, April 7, 1847, in Confidential Letters, T0829.
32. *Dictionary of American Naval Fighting Ships*, Vol. II, 285; Letters, Read to Bancroft, June 26, 1846, and July 13, 1846; Read to J. Pope, August 14, 1846, in George C. Read Papers, HSP.
33. Deck Log, National Archives, RG 24, *Dolphin*.
34. Captain Theophilus Conneau, *A Slaver's Log Book: or 20 Years' Residence in Africa* 345–48; Ward, *The Royal Navy*, 173; Herbert Gilliland, "Captains of the Slave Coast," Lecture, Naval Historical Center, February 15, 2005.
35. Conneau, *A Slaver's Log Book*, 346–50.
36. Letter, J. J. Roberts to Read, April 20, 1847, in Squadron Letters, National Archives, M89.
37. Letter, Read to Pope, April 7, 1847, in Squadron Letters, National Archives, M89.
38. Howard, *American Slavers*, 162.
39. Howard, *American Slavers*, 98–99.
40. Deck Log, National Archives, RG 24, *Dolphin*.
41. *Dictionary of American Naval Fighting Ships*, Vol. II, 285.
42. Letter, Read to Bancroft, October 5, 1846, in Squadron Letters, National Archives, M89.
43. Letter, Read to Mason, December11, 1846, in Squadron Letters, National Archives, M89.

CHAPTER 7
1. Deck Log, National Archives, RG 24, *Jamestown*.
2. William S. Dudley, ed., *The Naval War of 1812: A Documentary History*, Vol. II , 587.

3. *Dictionary of American Naval Fighting Ships*, Vol. VII, 525.

4. *Register of Officers, 1847*, 16–17; Officer File, Naval Historical Center.

5. Deck Logs, National Archives, RG 24, *Jamestown* and *Boxer*; Letters, Bolton to Mason, October 22, 1847, and to G. Welles, October 27, 1847, in Bolton Letterbooks, National Archives, RG45, E395.

6. Deck Logs, National Archives, RG 24, *Jamestown*; Letters, Bolton to Welles, October 27, 1847, to Mason, October 22, 1847, in Bolton Letterbooks, National Archives, RG45, E395.

7. Letter, Bolton to Mason, December 28, 1847, in Bolton Letterbooks, National Archives, RG45, E395; Deck Log, National Archives, RG 24, *Jamestown*.

8. Deck Logs, *Jamestown* and *Boxer*.

9. Ibid.

10. Frederick Forbes. *Six Months Service in the African Blockade*, 105–6.

11. Canney, *Sailing Warships*, 184.

12. Letter, Bolton to Mason, April 18, 1848, in Bolton Letterbooks, National Archives, RG45, E395.

13. Deck Logs, National Archives, RG 24, *Jamestown*.

14. Letter, Mason to Bolton, October 31, 1848, in Confidential Letters, T0829.

15. Deck Logs, National Archives, RG 24, *Jamestown*.

16. Deck Log, National Archives, RG 24, *Decatur*.

17. Deck Log, National Archives, RG 24, *Bainbridge*.

18. Letter, Bolton to Mason, July 20, 1848, in Bolton Letterbooks, National Archives, RG45, E395.

19. Sands, *From Reefer to Rear-Admiral*, 194–96.

20. Ibid., 196.

21. Ibid., 197–99.

22. Ibid., 199–201.

23. Deck Logs, National Archives, RG 24, *Porpoise*.

24. Ibid., 194. Nine of Sands's sketches are in the Navy collection, and several are reproduced herein.

25. Deck Logs, National Archives, RG 24, *Bainbridge*, *Decatur* and *Porpoise*; Sands, *From Reefer to Rear-Admiral*, 194–201.

26. Harmon, "Suppress and Protect . . .," 183.

27. Letter, Bolton to Secretary of the Navy, April 8, 1848, in Africa Squadron Letters.

28. Officer File, Naval Historical Center.

29. Letter, Mason to Bolton, February 20, 1849, in Confidential Letters, T0829.

30. Officer File, Naval Historical Center.

31. *Navy Register, 1847*, 18–19.

32. William Harwar Parker, *Recollections of a Naval Officer, 1841–65*, 134.

33. Deck Logs, National Archives, RG 24, *Bainbridge*.

34. Deck Logs, National Archives, RG 24, *Decatur*.

35. Ibid.

36. Deck Logs, National Archives, RG 24, *Porpoise*.

37. Letter, Cooper to Mason, December 20, 1848, quoted in Booth, "The United States African Squadron," 100.

38. Booth, "The United States African Squadron," 100.
39. Chapelle, *The History of the American Sailing Navy*, 402.
40. Parker, *Recollections of a Naval Officer,* 129–31.
41. Ibid., 132.
42. Ibid., 132–34.
43. Ibid., 133–34.
44. Ibid., 136–37.
45. Ibid., 136–39.
46. Ibid., 140–43.
47. Deck Logs, National Archives, RG 24, *Portsmouth*.
48. Ward, *The Royal Navy*, 183–85.
49. Letter, Alen Murray, Commander, Royal Navy, to Cooper, February 7, 1849; Letter, Cooper to Mason, May 4, 1849, in Squadron Letters, National Archives, M89.
50. Letter, Cooper to Byrne, July 29, 1849, in Squadron Letters, National Archives, M89.
51. Callahan, *List of Officers*, 129; Secretary of the Navy Report, December 1, 1849, 428.

CHAPTER 8
 1. Canney, *Lincoln's Navy,* 10.
 2. Du Bois, *Suppression*, 159.
 3. Ward, *The Royal Navy*, 133, 163; Fehrenbacher, *Slaveholding*, 177.
 4. Fehrenbacher, *Slaveholding*, 177–78.
 5. Howard, *American Slavers*, 243; Fehrenbacher, Slaveholding, 179.
 6. Letter, Morris to W. Hunter, February 16, 1843, in Squadron Letters, National Archives, M89; quoted in Harmon, "Suppress and Protect . . .," 158.
 7. Furnas, "Patrolling the Middle Passage," 101; Harmon, "Suppress and Protect . . .," 158.
 8. Letter, Turner to Mason, February 17, 1845, in Squadron Letters, National Archives, M89.
 9. Fehrenbacher, *Slaveholding*, 179; Letter, Wise to Caleb Cushing, December 6, 1845, in Wise Family Papers; quoted in Harmon, "Suppress and Protect . . .," 161.
10. Ward, *The Royal Navy*, 164.
11. Letter, Turner to Mason, February 17, 1845, in Squadron Letters, National Archives, M89.
12. Fehrenbacher, *Slaveholding*, 397; Affidavits of William Patterson, 2nd officer of *Kentucky*, no date, and John Williams, of brig *Porpoise*, in Squadron Letters, National Archives, M89; Letter, C. J. Hamilton to Wise, March 4, 1845, in Wise Family Papers.
13. Howard, *American Slavers*, 215, 223; Letter, Lawrence Pennington to Henry Walke, June 27, 1845, in Squadron Letters, National Archives, M89.
14. Letter, Bancroft to Rousseau, October 28, 1845, quoted in Harmon, "Suppress and Protect . . .," 159–60.
15. *Naval Register, 1847,* 110–11.

16. William L. Langer, ed., *An Encyclopedia of World History*, 849.
17. Harmon, "Suppress and Protect . . .," 161–63; Howard, *American Slavers*, 226, 270.
18. McNeilly, "The United States Navy . . .," 151; Harmon, "Suppress and Protect . . .," 163; *Dictionary of American Naval Fighting Ships*, Vol. V, 157.
19. Chapelle, *History of American Sailing Ships*, 304–7; *Dictionary of American Naval Fighting Ships*, Vol. V, 157.
20. Canney, *Sailing Warships*, 186–87.
21. Canney, *The Old Steam Navy*, 28–29; Frank M. Bennett, *The Steam Navy of the United States*, 53–54.
22. Letter, Storer to Mason, January 28, 1848, in Squadron Letters, National Archives, M89.
23. Letter, Storer to Mason, January 28, 1848, in Squadron Letters, National Archives, M89; Harmon, "Suppress and Protect . . .," 163–64; Howard, *American Slavers*, 216, 226, 270.
24. *Dictionary of American Naval Fighting Ships*, Vol. V, 157.
25. Letter, Storer to Mason, June 10, 1848, in Squadron Letters, National Archives, M89; Harmon, "Suppress and Protect . . .," 164–65; Howard, *American Slavers*, 85–86.
26. Howard, *American Slavers*, 87–88; Letter, Storer to Mason, June 10, 1848, in Squadron Letters, National Archives, M89.
27. Howard, *American Slavers*, 89–90; Letter, Hunter to Storer, June 13, 1848, in Squadron Letters, National Archives, M89.
28. Letter, Storer to Secretary of the Navy, October 3, 1848, and Hunter to Storer, October 9, 1848, in Squadron Letters, National Archives, M89.
29. Letter, Storer, to Mason, October 10, 1848, in Squadron Letters, National Archives, M89.
30. Canney, *The Old Steam Navy,* 28–29.
31. Letter, Storer to Mason, December 20, 1848, quoted in Harmon, "Suppress and Protect . . .," 166.
32. Letter, Storer to Davis, December 14, 1848, in Squadron Letters, National Archives, M89.
33. Letter, Storer to Davis, December 11, 1848, in Squadron Letters, National Archives, M89.
34. Letter, Davis to Storer, December 12, 1848, with enclosures, in Squadron Letters, National Archives, M89.
35. Howard, *American Slavers*, 216.
36. Howard, *American Slavers*, 216, 244.
37. Letter, Storer to Mason, January 14, 1849, in Squadron Letters, National Archives, M89; Harmon, "Suppress and Protect . . .," 166–67.
38. Howard, *American Slavers*, 217.
39. Letter, Storer to Mason, December 20, 1848, in Squadron Letters, National Archives, M89.

CHAPTER 9
1. Secretary of the Navy Report, December 1, 1849, 428.

2. *Register of Officers, 1847*, 18–19; Morison, *"Old Bruin,"* 78.
3. Howard, *American Slavers*, 106–7.
4. Harmon, "Suppress and Protect . . .," 183.
5. Deck Log, National Archives, RG 24, *John Adams*.
6. Ibid.; Harmon, "Suppress and Protect . . .," 184.
7. Deck Log, National Archives, RG 24, *John Adams*; Howard, *American Slavers*, 216, 245; Harmon, "Suppress and Protect . . .," 184.
8. Howard, *American Slavers*, 52; Deck Log National Archives, RG 24, *John Adams*.
9. Deck Log, National Archives, RG 24, *John Adams*.
10. Foote, *Africa and the American Flag*, 255–56.
11. Ibid., 256.
12. Letters, Foote to Preston, January 24, 1850, March 3 and March 7, 1850, in A. H. Foote Papers, Library of Congress.
13. Clarence Edward Macartney, *Mr. Lincoln's Admirals*, 78.
14. Foote, *Africa and the American Flag*, 259; Letter, Foote to Preston, March 21, 1850, in A. H. Foote Papers, Library of Congress; Letter, John Lian (?) to Foote, March 26, 1850, in Squadron Letters, National Archives, M89.
15. Letters, Gregory to Foote, May 2 and 6, 1850, in A. H. Foote Papers, Library of Congress.
16. Letter, Gregory to Foote, May 2, 1850, in A. H. Foote Papers, Library of Congress.
17. Letter, Foote to Gregory, June 7, 1850, in Squadron Letters, National Archives, M89 (and in A. H. Foote Papers, Library of Congress); James Mason Hoppin, *Life of Andrew Hull Foote*, 82–83.
18. Ibid., 83.
19. Ibid.; Foote, *Africa and the American Flag*, illustration after p. 286.
20. Foote, *Africa and the American Flag*, 292.
21. Ibid., 290.
22. Ibid., 291.
23. Harmon, "Suppress and Protect . . .," 185; Foote, *Africa and the American Flag*, 301–3; Letter, Gregory to Preston, September 4, 1850, in Squadron Letters, National Archives, M89.
24. Foote, *Africa and the American Flag*, 307–8, 318–19.
25. Ibid., 319–23; Howard, *American Slavers*, 245.
26. Foote, *Africa and the American Flag*, 324–26. Letter, Foote to Collector at St. Paul de Loando, September 17, 1850, National Archives, RG 45, E18, Africa Squadron Letters.
27. Foote, *Africa and the American Flag*, 330–35.
28. Ibid., 336–37.
29. Ibid., 337–38.
30. Ibid., 339–40; W. A. Graham Papers, North Carolina Archives, and Secretary of the Navy Report, November 30, 1850, 195.
31. Foote, *Africa and the American Flag*, 347–50; Deck Log, National Archives, RG 24, *Perry*.
32. Foote, *Africa and the American Flag*, 358–60.

33. Ibid., 377, and Deck Log, National Archives, RG 24, *Perry* ; *Dictionary of American Naval Fighting Ships*, Vol. V. 268. In *Africa and the American Flag*, Foote places his departure from Porto Praya on December 15, 1851, but the *Perry*'s deck log places it on November 15.
34. Parker, *Recollections of a Naval Officer*, 146.
35. Ibid., 145.
36. Ibid., 147.
37. Ibid., 148.
38. Ibid., 150–53.
39. Deck Log, National Archives, RG 24, *Dale*.
40. Ibid.
41. Deck Log, National Archives, RG 24, *Bainbridge*.
42. Ibid.; Deck Log, National Archives, RG 24, *Portsmouth*.
43. Deck Log, National Archives, RG 24, *Porpoise*.
44. Ibid.
45. Ibid.
46. Ibid.
47. John Taylor Wood, "The Capture of a Slaver," *Atlantic Monthly*, Vol. 86 (1900), 451–63.
48. Deck Log , National Archives, RG 24, *Porpoise*.
49. Deck Logs, National Archives, RG 24, *Portsmouth, John Adams, Bainbridge, Perry*.
50. Deck Log, National Archives, RG 24, *Portsmouth*.
51. Ibid.
52. Ibid.
53. In W. A. Graham Papers, North Carolina Archives; Harmon, "Suppress and Protect . . .," 186.
54. W. A.Graham Papers; Harold D. Langley, "William Alexander Graham," in Coletta, 265.
55. Samuel W. Bryant, *The Sea and the States*, 265–66.
56. David MacGregor, *British and American Clippers*, 8–9.
57. Ibid.

CHAPTER 10
1. *Register of Officers, 1847*, 18–19; "Z File," Naval Historical Center.
2. "Z" File, Naval Historical Center.
3. Secretary of the Navy Report, 1851, 3. Chapelle, *American Sailing Navy*, 544.
4. Deck Log, National Archives, RG 24, *Dale*.
5. "Report of Secretary of the Navy: Bureau of Medicine Report," March 12, 1850. (Senate Executive Document 40, 31st Cong., 1st sess.), 2–3.
6. Secretary of the Navy Report, 1851, 402.
7. Deck Logs, National Archives, RG 24, *Portsmouth, Porpoise, Perry, Germantown, John Adams*.
8. Deck Logs, National Archives, RG 24, *Germantown, Porpoise, John Adams*.
9. Letter, 1851, Lavallette Papers, Duke University.

10. Letter, Lavallette to Graham, September 17, 1852, Lavallette Papers, Duke University.

11. Deck Logs, National Archives, RG 24, *Germantown* and *John Adams*.

12. Letter, Lavallette to Graham, Oct. 13, 1851, in Squadron Letters, National Archives, M89.

13. Foote, *Africa and the American Flag*, 369.

14. Ibid., 370–75.

15. Ibid., 375–77; Letter, Foote to Lavallette, October 16, 1851, Lavallette Papers, Duke University.

16. Foote, *Africa and the American Flag*, 377.

17. Deck Logs, National Archives, RG 24, *John Adams, Germantown, Porpoise* and *Dale*.

18. Deck Log, National Archives, RG 24, *Bainbridge*.

19. Deck Log, National Archives, RG 24, *John Adams*; Letter, J. J. Roberts to Lavallette, November 16, 1851, Lavallette Papers, Duke University; Letter, Graham to Lavallette, January 31, 1852, in Confidential Letters, T0829; Letter, Barron to Lavallette, February 7, 1852, in Squadron Letters, National Archives, M89.

20. Deck Logs, National Archives, RG 24, *John Adams* and *Porpoise*.

21. Deck Log, National Archives, RG 24, *Dale*.

22. Deck Log, National Archives, RG 24, *Bainbridge*.

23. In Lavallette Papers, Duke University. Original listing included, "rate of vessel," "name of master," "Nation," and "Number of days out."

24. Deck Logs, National Archives, RG 24, *Germantown, Dale, Bainbridge, John Adams, Perry*.

25. Ibid.

26. Ibid.

27. Ibid.

28. Ibid.

29. Ibid.

30. Deck Logs, National Archives, RG 24, *Bainbridge* and *Germantown*; Howard, *American Slavers*, 51.

31. Letter, Lavallette to Secretary of the Navy Kennedy, November 21, 1852, in Squadron Letters, National Archives, M89.

32. Letter, John Walker to Lavallette, December 30, 1852, Lavallette Papers, Duke University; Howard, *American Slavers*, 216; House Executive Document 7; 36th Cong., 2nd Sess., African Slave Trade, 630.

33. Letter, Lavallette to Manning, November 4, 1852, Lavallette Papers, Duke University.

34. Deck Log, National Archives, RG 24, *Bainbridge*.

35. Deck Log, National Archives, RG 24, *John Adams*.

36. Deck Log, National Archives, RG 24, *Perry*.

37. Deck Log, National Archives, RG 24, *Dale*.

38. Deck Log: National Archives, RG 24, *Germantown*. The incident is entirely from this source.

39. Letter, Lavallette to Kennedy, February 8, 1853, and J. Nicholas to Lavallette, (no date), in Squadron Letters, National Archives, M89.

40. Howard, *American Slavers*, 216.
41. Letter, Lavallette to Graham, November 13, 1851, quoted in Howard, *American Slavers*, 48.
42. Howard, *American Slavers*, 48; Letter, Graham to Lavallette, February 20, 1852, in Confidential Letters, T0829.
43. *New York Daily Times*, October 12, 1852, 3.
44. Annual Report of the Secretary of the Navy, December 4, 1852, 293.
45. *Family Encyclopedia of Amercan History*, 436.

CHAPTER 11
1. *Register of Officers*, 1847, 18–19; Callahan, *List of Officers*, 358.
2. Deck Log, USS *Constitution*, National Archives, Microfilm M1030; Tyrone G. Martin, *A Most Fortunate Ship*, 301.
3. Deck Log, USS *Constitution*, National Archives, Microfilm M1030; Martin, *A Most Fortunate Ship*, 302.
4. Deck Logs, National Archives, RG 24, *Perry, Bainbridge, John Adams, Dale,* and *Germantown*.
5. Canney, *Warships*, 33.
6. W. F. Lynch to J. C. Dobbin, Annual Report of the Secretary of the Navy, 1853, 388–89.
7. Ibid., 298–99.
8. Letters, Kennedy to Mayo, February 28, 1853, and Dobbin to Swartwout, May 27, 1853, in Confidential Letters, T0829.
9. Letter, Dobbin to Mayo, August 30, 1853, in Confidential Letters, T0829.
10. Annual Report of 1853, 348.
11. Deck Logs, National Archives, RG 24, *Marion*.
12. Deck Logs, National Archives, RG 24, *Perry*.
13. Ibid.; Letter, Page to Mayo, July 6, 1853, RG 45, E18, Africa Squadron Letters.
14. Deck Logs, National Archives, RG 24, *Perry*.
15. Deck Log, USS *Constitution*, National Archives, Microfilm M1030.
16. Letter, A. C. Dayton, 4th Auditor of Treasury, to Mayo, January 5, 1854, Africa Sqdrn. Ltrs,
17. Letter, Mayo to Dobbin, August 20, 1853, in Squadron Letters, National Archives, M89.
18. Deck Log, USS *Constitution*, National Archives, Microfilm M1030; Martin, *A Most Fortunate Ship*, 304–5.
19. Deck Log, USS *Constitution*, National Archives, Microfilm M1030; Martin, *A Most Fortunate Ship*, 306.
20. Deck Log, USS *Constitution*, National Archives, Microfilm M1030.
21. Memoranda, C. R. P. Rogers, November 3, 1853, in Squadron Letters, National Archives, M89. (Published in Naval Historical Center Home Page: "Seizing a Slaver, 1853.")
22. Ibid.
23. Ibid.
24. Ibid.

25. Howard, *American Slavers*, 217.
26. Letter, Mayo to Dobbin, November 10, 1853, in Squadron Letters, National Archives, M89.
27. Ibid.
28. Deck Log, USS *Constitution*, National Archives, Microfilm M1030; Martin, *A Most Fortunate Ship*, 306–7.
29. Deck Log, USS *Constitution*, National Archives, Microfilm M1030; Letters, Mayo to Dobbin, April 20 and 21, 1854, "Z" File at Naval Historical Center.
30. Letter, Page to Dobbin, March 11, 1854, in Squadron Letters, National Archives, M89; Deck Logs, National Archives, RG 24, Perry; Howard, *American Slavers*, 71–72.
31. Howard, *American Slavers*, 73–74, 227.
32. Howard, *American Slavers*, 75.
33. Letter, McCrae and Kelly to Page, March 21, 1854, National Archives, RG 45, E18, Africa Squadron Letters; Deck Logs National Archives, RG 24, *Perry*.
34. Letter, Page to Mayo, June 16, 1854, National Archives, RG 45, E18, Africa Squadron Letters.
35. Letter, May to Secretary of the Navy, February 7, 1854, in Squadron Letters, National Archives, M89.
36. Deck Logs, National Archives, RG 24, *Marion*.
37. Ibid.
38. Letter, John D. Skene, Royal Navy, to Mayo, October 24, 1854, in Squadron Letters, National Archives, M89.
39. Letter, Purviance to Mayo, November 30, 1854, and Purviance to Gov. of Angola, December 30, 1854, in Squadron Letters, National Archives, M89.
40. Deck Log, USS *Constitution*, National Archives, Microfilm M1030, and National Archives, RG 24, *Dale*.
41. Deck Logs, National Archives, RG 24, *Dale*.
42. Ibid.
43. Deck Log, USS *Constitution*, National Archives, Microfilm M1030; Martin, *A Most Fortunate Ship*, 308.
44. Martin, *A Most Fortunate Ship*, 308.
45. Deck Log, USS *Constitution*, National Archives, Microfilm M1030.
46. Ibid.; Martin, *A Most Fortunate Ship*, 309.
47. Secretary of the Navy Report, 1856, 730–31. Their report also included statistics for all the squadrons. The squadron with the highest mortality rate was the East Indies (1.30), and that with second lowest was the Brazil station (.26).
48. Deck Log, USS *Constitution*, National Archives, Microfilm M1030; Letter, Mayo to Dobbin, May 16, 1855, in Squadron Letters, National Archives, M89.
49. Letter, Mayo to Purviance, March 26, 1855, in Squadron Letters, National Archives, M89.

CHAPTER 12
1. *Register of Officers, 1847*; Callahan, *List of Officers*, 136.

2. Deck Logs, National Archives, RG 24, *Jamestown*; *Annual Report of the Secretary of the Navy, 1855*, 5.
3. *Annual Report*, 5, 134–35.
4. Ibid.
5. Deck Logs, National Archives, RG 24, *Dale*.
6. Deck Logs, National Archives, RG 24, *Dolphin*
7. Ibid.
8. Ibid.
9. Ibid.
10. Ibid.
11. Ibid.
12. Ibid.
13. Deck Logs, National Archives, RG 24, *St. Louis.*
14. Ibid.
15. Ibid.
16. Letter, Crabbe to Dobbin, August 7, 1855, in Squadron Letters, National Archives, M89.
17. Letter, Crabbe to Dobbin, October 2, 1855, in Squadron Letters, National Archives, M89.
18. Deck Logs, National Archives, RG 24, *Jamestown.*
19. Letter, Crabbe to Dobbin, January 21, 1856, in Squadron Letters, National Archives, M89.
20. Letters, Crabbe to Dobbin, April 18, 1856, and August 26, 1856, in Squadron Letters, National Archives, M89; Deck Logs, National Archives, RG 24, *Jamestown.*
21. Deck Logs, National Archives, RG 24, *Jamestown.*
22. Ibid.; Letters, Crabbe to Dobbin, October 9, 1856, December 1, 1856, February 14, 1857, in Squadron Letters, National Archives, M89.
23. Letter, Crabbe to Dobbin, February 14, 1857, in Squadron Letters, National Archives, M89.
24. Crabbe biography, "Z" File, Naval Historical Center, p. 3.
25. Harmon, "Suppress and Protect . . .," 190–91; Ward, *The Royal Navy*, 202–10.

CHAPTER 13

1. *Register of Officers, 1847*, 20–21; Callahan, *List of Officers*, 127.
2. Canney, *Sailing Warships*, 75; *Secretary of the Navy Report, 1857*, 576.
3. Fehrenbacher, *Slaveholding*, 180; Soulsby, *The Right of Search*, 252–53.
4. Fehrenbacher, *Slaveholding*, 180–81; Harvey Wish, "African Slave Trade Revival in the United States," *Mississippi Valley Historical Review*, Vol XXVII, No.4 (March 1941), 585–86.
5. Phyllis M. Martin, *The External Trade of the Loango Coast, 1576–1870*, 148–49.
6. *Register of Officers, 1847,* 32; William McBlair Papers, Mariners' Museum; *Civil War Naval Chronology,* Vol.VI, 201.
7. Letter, L. Cass to Isaac Toucey, April 20, 1857, McBlair Papers. (The fol-

lowing sequence, until further noted, is from a combination of McBlair's letters and the Deck Logs of *Dale*.)

8. Letter, Conover to McBlair, August 17, 1847, in Squadron Letters, National Archives, M89.
9. Deck Log, National Archives, RG 24, *Dale*.
10. Howard, *American Slavers*, 217.
11. Deck Logs, National Archives, RG 24, *St. Louis*.
12. Ibid.
13. Ibid.
14. Ibid.
15. Ibid.; Howard, *American Slavers*, 96.
16. Howard, *American Slavers*, 94–96, 218.
17. Deck Logs, National Archives, RG 24, *Marion*.
18. Deck Logs, National Archives, RG 24, *Marion*; Howard, *American Slavers*, 170–71.
19. Deck Logs, National Archives, RG 24, *Marion*.
20. Howard, *American Slavers*, 170–71.
21. Howard, *American Slavers*, 174–75.
22. Howard, *American Slavers*, 175–76.
23. Deck Logs, National Archives, RG 24, *Marion*.
24. Howard, *American Slavers*, 218.
25. Deck Logs, National Archives, RG 24, *Marion*.
26. Letter, Toucey to Totten, November 10, 1857, National Archives, Microfilm T829, Secretary of the Navy Confidential Letters.
27. Deck Logs, National Archives, RG 24, *Vincennes* and *Cumberland*.
28. Deck Logs, National Archives, RG 24, *Vincennes*.
29. Howard, *American Slavers*, 145–46; Letter, Conover to Toucey, December 13, 1858, in Squadron Letters, National Archives, M89.
30. Deck Logs, National Archives, RG 24, *Vincennes*; Howard, *American Slavers*, 219.
31. Deck Logs, National Archives, RG 24, *Cumberland*.
32. Ibid.
33. Letter, Conover to Toucey, July 2, 1859, in Squadron Letters, National Archives, M89.
34. Deck Logs, National Archives, RG 24, *Cumberland*.
35. Howard, *American Slavers*, 132–33.
36. House Executive Document 7, 36th Cong., 2nd sess., 200–1.
37. Tom Henderson Wells, *The Slave Ship* Wanderer, 11.
38. Ibid., 15, 22, 27, 31.
39. Howard, *American Slavers*, 144–45; Fish, "War on the Slave Trade . . .," 167.

CHAPTER 14
1. "Isaac Toucey," in Coletta, Vol. I, 312; Letter, Toucey to Inman, July 6, 1859, in Confidential Letters, T0829; *Official Records of the Union and Confederate Navies in the War of the Rebellion,* Ser. II, Vol. 1, 147 and 153.
2. *Register of Officers, 1853*, 129.

3. Letters, Toucey to T. A. M. Craven, September 23, 1859, and J. N. Maffitt, July 26, 1859, and W. J. McCluney, December 2, 1859, in Confidential Letters, T0829.
4. Letter, Toucey to Inman, July 6, 1859, in Confidential Letters, T0829.
5. Letter, Toucey to Inman, September 10, 1859, in Confidential Letters, T0829.
6. Letter, Cass to Toucey, May 3, 1858, M517, Letters from President and Executive Agencies to Secretary Of the Navy.
7. Wells, *The Slave Ship* Wanderer, 37.
8. Henry, J. Buchanan, compiler, *The Messages of President Buchanan*, 102.
9. Howard, *American Slavers*, 147.
10. Fehrenbacher, *Slaveholding*, 187; Howard, *American Slavers*, 143.
11. Letter, Cass to Dallas, February 23, 1859 (extract), and May 14, 1859, M517, Letters from President and Executive Agencies to Secretary Of the Navy.
12. Howard, *American Slavers*, 134.
13. Dana Wegner, Colin Ratliff, and Kevin Lynaugh, *Fouled Anchors: The Constellation Question Answered*, 4–5.
14. *Annual Report, Secretary of the Navy,* 1860, 235–38.
15. Letter, Toucey to Inman, July 6, 1859, in Confidential Letters, T0829.
16. Deck Logs, National Archives, RG 24, *Portsmouth*.
17. Ibid.; Howard, *American Slavers*, 164.
18. Howard, *American Slavers*, 164.
19. Deck Logs, National Archives, RG 24, *Portsmouth*.
20. Ibid.; Howard, *American Slavers*, 220.
21. Deck Logs, National Archives, RG 24, *Portsmouth*.
22. Letter, Armstrong to Inman, September 11, 1859, in Squadron Letters, National Archives, M89; Howard, *American Slavers*, 134–35.
23. Deck Logs, National Archives, RG 24, *San Jacinto*; Letter, Inman to Armstrong, October 24, 1859, in Squadron Letters, National Archives, M89.
24. Deck Logs, National Archives, RG 24, *San Jacinto*.
25. Ibid.; Letter, Armstrong to Inman, September 14, 1859, in Squadron Letters, National Archives, M89; Ltr, Toucey to Inman, October 28, 1859, in Confidential Letters, T0829.
26. Deck Logs, National Archives, RG 24, *San Jacinto*.
27. Letter, Toucey to Inman, March 27, 1860, in Confidential Letters, T0829.
28. Deck Logs, National Archives, RG 24, *San Jacinto*; Howard, *American Slavers*, 138.
29. Deck Logs, National Archives, RG 24, *San Jacinto*; Howard, *American Slavers*, 221.
30. Deck Logs, National Archives, RG 24, *San Jacinto*; Howard, *American Slavers*, 71–72.
31. Deck Logs, National Archives, RG 24, *San Jacinto*.
32. Ibid.
33. Ibid.
34. Ibid.
35. Ibid.
36. Letter, Inman to commanders, September 3, 1859, in Squadron Letters, National Archives, M89.

37. Howard, *American Slavers*, 136.
38. List in Squadron Letters, National Archives, M89.
39. Howard, *American Slavers*, 135–36; Letter, Inman to Toucey, January 14, 1860, in Squadron Letters, National Archives, M89.
40. Howard, *American Slavers*, 221–22.
41. Deck Logs, National Archives, RG 24, *Mohican* and *Marion*.
42. Deck Logs, National Archives, RG 24, *Mohican*.
43. Ibid.
44. Ibid; Howard, *American Slavers*, 138.
45. Deck Logs, National Archives, RG 24, *Mohican*.
46. Howard, *American Slavers*, 200–2.
47. Ibid., 203.
48. Deck Logs, National Archives, RG 24, *Mohican*.
49. Deck Logs, National Archives, RG 24, *Saratoga*; Howard, *American Slavers*, 222.
50. Letter, Inman to Taylor, February 6, 1861, in Squadron Letters, National Archives, M89.
51. Deck Logs, National Archives, RG 24, *Saratoga*; Chapelle, *The Search for Speed*, 350.
52. Deck Logs, National Archives, RG 24, *Saratoga*.
53. Howard, *American Slavers*, 134–35; Letter, Inman to Toucey, December 15, 1859, in Squadron Letters, National Archives, M89.
54. Letter, Inman to Toucey, December 15, 1859, in Squadron Letters, National Archives, M89.
55. Letter, Nicholas to Inman, December 12, 1859, in Squadron Letters, National Archives, M89.
56. Howard, *American Slavers*, 220.
57. Letters, Inman to Toucey, January 14 and January 15, 1860, in Squadron Letters, National Archives, M89.
58. Letter, Inman to Toucey, January 21, 1860, in Squadron Letters, National Archives, M89.
59. Instructions from Inman, February 1, 1860, and Inman to McDonough, January 12, 1860, in Squadron Letters, National Archives, M89.
60. Letter, Toucey to Inmnan, March 21 and March 27, 1860, in Confidential Letters, T0829.
61. Letter, Toucey to Inman, June 16, 1860, in Confidential Letters, T0829.
62. Deck Log, National Archives, RG 24, *Portsmouth*; Howard, *American Slavers*, 138; Glenn F. Williams, USS *Constellation* 21; Letter, Inman to Toucey, September 26, 1860, in Squadron Letters, National Archives, M89.
63. Williams, USS *Constellation,* 21.
64. Letter, Loyall to Inman, September 26, 1860, in Squadron Letters, National Archives, M89.
65. Ibid., 22
66. Letter, Inman to Toucey, September 26, 1860, in Squadron Letters, National Archives, M89.

67. Letter, Toucey to Inman, December 19, 1860, in Confidential Letters, T0829.
68. Deck Logs, National Archives, RG 24, *Saratoga* and *Mohican*.
69. Letter, Inman to Toucey, March 6, 1861, in Squadron Letters, National Archives, M89.
70. Deck Log, National Archives, RG 24, *Mohican*.
71. Letters, Toucey to Maffitt, May 28, 1858, to Bell, June 5, 1858, to T. A. M. Craven September 23, 1859, to Maffitt October 5, 1858, in Confidential Letters, T0829.
72. Howard, *American Slavers*, 219–23; Letter, Thomson to Cass, November 30, 1860, Records . . . Suppression of the African Slave Trade & Negro Colonization, M160.
73. Howard, *American Slavers*, 219-23.
74. Du Bois, *Suppression*, 150, 192.
75. Ward, *The Royal Navy*, 226–27.
76. Harmon, "Suppress and Protect . . .," 213–14
77. Harmon, "Suppress and Protect . . .," 212–13.

BIBLIOGRAPHY

ARCHIVAL SOURCES

Government Documents: Congressional and Naval

American State Papers. Naval Affairs, Vols. 1 & 2. (Annual Reports of the Secretary of the Navy: 1822 and 1823.)

Annual Reports of the Secretary of the Navy: 1824, 1825, 1826, 1827, 1828, 1829, 1830, 1831, 1832, 1833, 1834, 1835, 1836, 1837, 1838, 1839, 1840, 1841, 1842, 1844, 1846, 1847, 1848, 1849, 1850, 1851, 1852, 1853, 1855, 1856, 1857, 1858, 1859, 1860.

Commerce and Navigation: Report of the Secretary of the Treasury, 1855.

House Document 115. 26th Cong., 2nd sess., 1841. Message from the President . . . in Relation to Seizures or Search of American Vessels on the Coast of Africa.

House Executive Document 7: 36th Cong., 2nd sess. African Slave Trade.

Register of the Commissioned and Warrant Officers of the Navy of the United States: 1815 (Appended to *Naval Chronicle)*, 1842, 1847, 1853.

Senate Document 150. 28th Cong., 2nd sess., February 26, 1845. Message from the President . . . Information Relative to the Operations of the United States Squadron on the West Coast of Africa.

Senate Executive Document 40. 31st Cong., 1st sess., March 12, 1850. Bureau of Medicine Report, Annual Deaths, Africa Squadron.

Senate Executive Document 40: 31st Cong., 1st sess., March 12, 1850. Bureau of Medicine Report.

Senate Executive Document 53. 37th Cong., 2nd sess., May 30, 1862. Ltr. from Secretary of the Interior . . . Vessels arrested in S. District of NY.

National Archives

Africa Squadron Letters: Record Group 45, E18.

Deck Logs of U.S. Naval Vessels [*Bainbridge, Boxer, Constitution* (Microfilm 1030), *Cumberland, Dale, Decatur, Dolphin, Germantown, Jamestown, John Adams, Macedonian, Marion, Mohican, Perry, Porpoise, Portsmouth, San Jacinto, Saratoga, St. Louis, Truxtun, Vincennes, Yorktown*]: Record Group 24.
Joel Abbott Letterbook: Record Group 45, E395.
Journal of William Sharp: Record Group 45, E392, 68.
Letters from the President and Executive Agencies to the Secretary of the Navy: M517.
Letters Received by the Secretary of the Navy from Bureau Chiefs: M518.
Letters Received by the Secretary of the Navy from Officers: M149.
Letters to the Secretary of the Navy from Squadron Commanders: M89.
Matthew C. Perry Letterbooks: M206.
Miscellaneous Records of U.S. Naval Records and Library: Confidential Letters, T0829.
Officer's Files ("Z" Files): Naval Historical Center.
Records Relating to Suppression of the African Slave Trade and Negro Colonization: M160.
Reports of Sailing Qualities of Vessels: Record Group 45, E277.
William F. Bolton Letterbooks: Record Group 45, E395, 23.

OTHER DEPOSITORIES
Allmand Family Letters (William Allmand on *Jamestown,* 1846), Virginia Historical Society.
Andrew Hull Foote Papers, Library of Congress.
Elie A. F. Lavallette Papers, Duke University.
George Bancroft Papers, Massachusetts Historical Society.
George C. Read Papers, Historical Society of Pennsylvania.
John Y. Mason Collection, University of North Carolina, Chapel Hill.
Journal of Simon Fraser Hunt, Virginia Historical Society.
Nalle Family Papers (Thomas Botts, USS *Dolphin*), Virginia Historical Society.
William A. Graham Papers, North Carolina State Archives.
William Loney, Royal Navy: Web Site: William Loney, Royal Navy, Victorian Naval Surgeon.
William McBlair Papers, Mariners' Museum.
Wise Family Papers, Virginia Historical Society.

SECONDARY SOURCES: BOOKS, ARTICLES, PUBLISHED AND UNPUBLISHED THESES & DISSERTATIONS
"The African Slave Trade." *New York Daily Times* (Oct. 12, 1852): 3.
Bennett, Frank M. *The Steam Navy of the United States.* Pittsburgh: Warren & Company, 1896.
Booth, Alan R. "The United States African Squadron, 1843–1861." From

Boston University Papers in African History, Vol.1. Boston: Boston University Press, 1964.

Bridge, Horatio. *Journal of an African Cruiser . . . by an Officer of the U.S. Navy*. Edited by Nathaniel Hawthorne. New York: Wiley and Putnam, 1845.

Bryant, Samuel W. *The Sea and the States*. New York: Thomas Y. Crowell, 1967.

Brown, D. K. *Paddle Warships*. London: Conway Maritime Press, 1993.

Callahan, Edward, ed. *List of Officers of the Navy of the United States and of the Marine Corps, 1775–1900*. New York: L. R. Hammersly & Company, n.d.

Campbell, Penelope. *Maryland in Africa: The Maryland State Colonization Society, 1831–1857*. Urbana, IL: University of Illinois Press, 1971.

Canney, Donald L. *The Old Steam Navy, Vol.1, Frigates, Sloops and Gunboats, 1815–1885*. Annapolis: Naval Institute Press, 1990.

Canney, Donald L. *Sailing Warships of the U.S. Navy*. Rochester, Kent, U.K: Chatham Publishing, 2001.

Canney, Donald L. *U.S. Coast Guard and Revenue Cutters, 1790–1935*. Annapolis: Naval Institute Press, 1995.

Causes of the Reduction of American Tonnage and the Decline of Navigation Interests. Washington, D.C: Government Printing Office, 1870.

Chapelle, Howard I. *The History of the American Sailing Navy*. New York: W. W. Norton, 1949.

Chapelle, Howard I. *The Search for Speed Under Sail, 1700–1855*. New York: W. W. Norton, 1967.

"The Climate of the Western Coast of Africa." *Nautical Magazine*, UK, (1845): 562–71.

Coletta, Paolo, ed. *American Secretaries of the Navy*. 2 Vols. Annapolis: Naval Institute Press, 1980.

Conneau, [Canot] Captain Theophilus. *A Slaver's Log Book, or, 20 Years' Residence in Africa*. Englewood Cliffs, N.J.: Prentice-Hall, 1976.

Civil War Naval Chronology, 1861-1865. Washington, D.C.: Naval History Division, Navy Department, 1971.

Dictionary of American Naval Fighting Ships. 9 Vols. Washington, D.C.: Naval Historical Center, 1955–91.

Du Bois, W. E. Burghardt. *The Suppression of the African Slave-Trade to the United States of America, 1638–1870*. Baton Rouge: Louisiana State University Press, 1896.

Dudley, William S., ed. *The Naval War of 1812, A Documentary History*. 2 Vols. Washington, D.C.: Naval Historical Center, 1992.

Duignan, Peter and Clarence Clendenen. "The United States and the African Slave Trade, 1619–1862." Hoover Institution Studies, Stanford University: The Hoover Institution on War, Revolution and Peace, 1963.

Fehrenbacher, Don E. *The Slaveholding Republic*. London: Oxford University Press, 2001.

Fish, Peter G. "War on the Slave Trade: Changing Fortunes in Antebellum U.S. Courts of the Mid-Atlantic South." In Dudley, William S. and Michael J. Crawford. *The Early Republic and the Sea*. Washington, D.C.: Brassey's Inc., 2001.

Foote, Andrew Hull. *Africa and the American Flag*. Folkstone & London: Dawsons of Pall Mall, 1970.

Forbes, Frederick. *Six months' Service in the African Blockade*. London: Dawsons of Pall Mall, 1969. (Reprint of 1849 ed.)

Furnas, J. C. "Patrolling the Middle Passage." *American Heritage Magazine,* IX (Oct. 1958): 4–9, 101–3.

Gilliland, C. Herbert. *Voyage to a Thousand Cares: Master's Mate Lawrence with the Africa Squadron 1844–1846*. Annapolis: Naval Institute Press, 2003.

Gilliland, C. Herbert. "Deliverance from this Floating Hell." *Naval History* (Dec. 2003): 48–51.

Hall, Claude H. *Abel Parker Upshur, Conservative Virginian, 1790–1844*. Madison, WI: The State Historical Society of Wisconsin, 1963.

Harmon, Judd Scott. "Suppress and Protect: The United States Navy, the African Slave Trade, and Maritime Commerce, 1794-1862." Ph.D Dissertation, College of William and Mary, 1977.

Henry, J. Buchanan, compiler. *The Messages of President Buchanan*. New York: 1888.

Hoppin, James Mason. *Life of Andrew Hull Foote, Rear Admiral, U.S. Navy*. New York: Harper & Bros., 1874.

Howard, Warren S. *American Slavers and the Federal Law, 1837–1862*. Berkeley and Los Angeles: University of California Press, 1963.

Johnson, Robert Irwin. *Rear Admiral John Rodgers, 1812–1882*. Annapolis: Naval Institute Press, 1967.

Knox, Dudley W. *A History of the United States Navy*. New York: G. P. Putnam's Sons, 1936.

Langer, William L., ed. *An Encyclopedia of World History*. Boston: Houghton, Mifflin Company, 1972.

Lawrence, William Beach. *Visitation and Search, or an Historical Sketch*. Boston: Little Brown and Company, 1858.

Martin, Phyllis M. *The External Trade of the Loango Coast, 1576–1870*. Oxford: Oxford University Press, 1972.

Martin, Tyrone G. *A Most Fortunate Ship*. (Revised Edition) Annapolis: Naval Institute Press, 1997.

Matthiesen, William Law. *Great Britain and the Slave Trade, 1839–1865*. London: Longmans, Green & Co., 1929.

McCartney, Clarence Edward. *Mr. Lincoln's Admirals*. New York: Funk & Wagnalls Company, 1956.

MacGregor, David. *British & American Clippers*. Annapolis: Naval Institute Press, 1993

McNeilly, Earl. "The United States Navy and the Suppression of the Slave Trade." Ph.D Dissertation, Case Western Reserve University, 1973.

Morison, Samuel Eliot. *"Old Bruin"*: *Commodore Matthew Calbraith Perry*. Boston: Little, Brown and Company, 1967.

Naval Documents Related to the Quasi-War Between the United States and France. 7 Vols. Washington, D.C.: Government Printing Office, 1937.

Nelson, Harold D. *Liberia: A Country Study*. Washington, D.C.: Government Printing Office, 1985.

Noonan, John T. *The Antelope*. Berkeley: University of California Press, 1977.

Official Records of the Union and Confederate Navies in the War of the Rebellion. Series II, Vol. 1. Washington, D.C.; Government Printing Office, 1921.

Parker, William Harwar. *Recollections of a Naval Officer, 1841–1865*. New York: Charles Scribners' Sons, 1883.

Paullin, Charles Oscar. *Commodore John Rodgers*. Cleveland: The Arthur H. Clark Company, 1910.

Sands, Benjamin F. *From Reefer to Rear-Admiral*. New York: Frederick A. Stokes Company, 1899.

Schroeder, John H. *Matthew Calbraith Perry: Antebellum Sailor and Diplomat*. Annapolis: Naval Institute Press, 2001.

Shippen, Edward. *Thirty Years at Sea*. New York: Arno Press, 1979.

Smith, Horatio Davis. *U.S. Revenue Cutter Service, 1789–1849*. Washington, D.C.: U.S. Coast Guard, 1989.

Soulsby, Hugh G. *The Right of Search and the Slave Trade in Anglo-American Relations, 1814–1862*. Baltimore: Johns Hopkins University Press, 1933.

United States Coast Guard Record of Movements. Washington, D.C.: U.S. Coast Guard, 1989.

"[The] United States and the Slave Trade." *United Service Magazine*, Part II (1842): 171–79.

Walt, Sir James. "The Health of Seamen in the Anti-Slavery Squadron." *Mariners' Mirror* (Feb. 1902): 69–78.

Ward, W. E. F. *The Royal Navy and the Slavers*. New York: Pantheon Books, 1969.

Wegner, Dana. *Fouled Anchors: The* Constellation *Question Answered*. Bethesda, MD: David Taylor Research Center, 1991.

Welles, Tom Henderson. *The Slave Ship* Wanderer. Athens, GA: University of Georgia Press, 1967.

Williams, Glenn F. USS *Constellation*. Virginia Beach, VA: Donning Company Publishers, 2000.

Winton, John. *An Illustrated History of the Royal Navy*. San Diego: Thunder Bay Press, 2000.

Wish, Harvey. "The Revival of the African Slave Trade in the United States, 1856–1860." *Mississippi Valley Historical Review,* XXVII (1940–41): 569–88.

Wood, John Taylor "The Capture of a Slaver." *Atlantic Monthly*, Vol. 86 (1900): 451–63.

Zabel, Morton Dauwan, ed. *The Portable Conrad*. New York: Viking Press, 1950.

INDEX

ABOUT THE AUTHOR

DONALD L. CANNEY, a naval historian and an authority on the nineteenth century U.S. Navy, is a prolific author whose books include *Lincoln's Navy: The Ships, Men, and Organization, 1861–1865* and *Sailing Warships of the U. S. Navy*. He lives in Bowie, Maryland.